Sustainable Biomass Practices in China

About the Authors

Darshini Mahadevia is a Professor at Faculty of Planning, CEPT University, Ahmedabad, India. She is Director, Centre for Urban Equity (CUE) at CEPT University. She has held the position of Dean at the Faculty of Planning. She concurrently holds honorary position as Distinguished Professor at the Tianjin University of Finance and Economics (TUFE), Tianjin, China under the Tianjin Recruitment Program of Global Experts (Key Discipline Short-term Project). Prof. Mahadevia holds a Ph.D. from Jawaharlal Nehru University, New Delhi. She has held visiting positions at number of international universities and has collaborated on research with national and international universities and organizations.

Liyan Zhang is Professor and Director of Center for Innovation and Entrepreneurship, Tianjin University of Finance and Economics, Tianjin, China. She has coordinated several international projects, focusing on the innovations by the poor and how the innovations contribute to the inclusive development. She also works on how the university involves in the value addition to the grassroots innovators.

Priyadarshi R. Shukla is a retired Professor at Indian Institute of Management, Ahmedabad, India, where he holds adjunct position now. He has held position as Honorary Distinguished Chair Professor at the Tianjin University of Finance and Economics, a position supported by the Tianjin Education Committee. Currently he is the co-chair of Working Group III (WG III) of the Inter-governmental Panel on Climate Change (IPCC). He holds Ph.D. degree from Stanford University. He has collaborated with numerous research teams on Climate Change modeling, energy modeling and Climate Change and Energy Policy issues and has large number of publications to his credit on these issues.

SUSTAINABLE BIOMASS PRACTICES IN CHINA

Case Studies and Policy Environment

Darshini Mahadevia

Liyan Zhang

P. R. Shukla

CONCEPT PUBLISHING COMPANY PVT. LTD.
NEW DELHI-110059

ISBN-13: 978-93-5125-188-0

First Published 2017

Published and Printed by

Concept
Since 1974

Concept Publishing Company Pvt. Ltd.
Regd. Office:
A/15-16, Commercial Block, Mohan Garden,
New Delhi-110059 (INDIA)
Phones : 25351460, 25351794, *Fax* : 091-11-25357109
Email : publishing@conceptpub.com
Website: www.conceptpub.com

Editorial Office: H-13, Bali Nagar, New Delhi-110 015, India.

Cataloging in Publication Data—DK Courtesy: D.K. Agencies (P) Ltd. <docinfo@dkagencies.com>

Mahadevia, Darshini, author.

Sustainable biomass practices in China : case studies and policy environment / Darshini Mahadevia, Liyan Zhang, P.R. Shukla.
pages cm
Includes bibliographical references and index.
ISBN 9789351251880

1. Biomass energy—China. 2. Renewable energy sources—China. 3. Agricultural innovations—China. 4. Biomass energy—Government policy—China. I. Liyan, Zhang, author. II. Shukla, P. R., author. III. Title.

TP339.M34 2017 DDC 662.880951 23

Preface and Acknowledgements

This book is an outcome of research undertaken when Prof. Darshini Mahadevia held the honorary distinguished professor position under the program 'Tianjin Recruitment Program of Global Experts (Key Discipline Short-term Project), Prof. P.R. Shukla held the honorary distinguished chair professor position supported by the Tianjin Education Committee and got opportunity to collaborate with Prof. Liyan Zhang. Since 2012, Prof. Mahadevia and Prof. Shukla have visited China to study the ongoing rural transformations; some of these are presented in this book as case studies. The gratitude goes to the funding available under the two programs to support these travels and periodic stay in Tianjin of Prof. Mahadevia and Prof. Shukla to collaboratively work with Prof. Zhang.

China's rapid transition to a global economic giant, consequent challenges of climate change, equity and sustainable development faced by the country are now widely discussed and researched. But, addressing these macro level challenges requires local actions, in the rural and the urban areas and by the local governments and by the individual households. This book brings together these individual efforts at innovations to take advantage of national level commitments, policies and programs related to environment and climate change in the area of biomass use.

Young scholars and students working with the Center for Innovation and Entrepreneurship (CIE), Tianjin University of Finance and Economics (TUFE), have assisted immensely in the data collection, case study documentation and translation of materials from Chinese to English. In particular, we are happy to report the important contribution of Xie Weiwei, our key research coordinator and translator for the materials in this book and also the manager of Prof. Mahadevia's and Prof. Shukla's programs at TUFE. This book would have reached nowhere without her smiling face and contribution. Students affiliated with CIE, TUFE, Chu Honghong, Li Kang, Zhang Junyan, Wang Rao, Liu Jia, Guan Shenqi etc. have helped in data compilation from the internet about innovations, data processing, case study documentation and occasional translations of the work. We are grateful to them and hope that research experience will benefit them in their future careers. CIE's staff Niu Lei, Liu Tao, Guo Jing, Wang Jiwen etc. have made Prof. Mahadevia's and Prof Shukla's stay in Tianjin comfortable and productive, overcoming language barriers.

Our gratitude to the grassroots innovators, Gao Dedian, Liu Yongquan, Sue Wenbin, and Liu Haibing for allowing us to peek in their lives and with generosity of their time for case preparation. We are also grateful to all local government officials and key informants for their time in discussing the case studies and issues. This book owes to Sonal Mahadevia for careful language editing and proof reading.

Lastly and importantly, our gratitude to the Tianjin University of Finance and Economics, and in particular the President and Vice President of the University, who have made the program of distinguished Professorship possible. While the book owes a great deal to many who have been named and not named in this acknowledgement, we owe the lacunae of this product.

Contents

List of Tables, Figures, Maps and Photographs

LIST OF TABLES

LIST OF FIGURES

LIST OF MAPS

LIST PHOGRAPHS

1

Rural Development, Biomass Use and Grassroots Innovations in China

The Context

China has made a significant transition from an agriculture-based economy to secondary and tertiary sector economy, while also transiting to an urban economy. In 2010, half of the country's population resided in urban areas (China, National Bureau of Statistics – NBS–2011a), which increased to 55 per cent in 2014 (China, NBS, 2015a)[1]. In spite of urban transition, 45 per cent of the total population still lives in the rural areas, accounting for 618.7 million people, which is quite large in terms of numbers. Further, 227.9 million population (29.5 per cent of the total workers) are dependent on primary sector. Assuming all the agriculture dependent workers to be living in rural areas, it can be argued that 60 per cent of the total rural workers are dependent on primary sector. But, the composition of output of primary sector indicates that 54 per cent of the rural output is from farming while the rest is from livestock, fishing and animal husbandry. Farming in terms of volume is still important for rural China and has significant proportion of rural workers dependent on it. While the dependency of rural population on primary sector is high (60 per cent), the Gross Domestic Product (GDP) from the primary sector has declined to 9.2 per cent of the total in 2014, as compared to 14.7 per cent in 2000. The incidence of rural poverty is at 7.2 per cent in 2014, which has increased from 3.5 per cent in 2000. The rural per capita income (PCI) was RMB 9,892 in 2014, which was quite low in comparison to (34 per cent of) the urban PCI of RMB

29,381. But, the rural PCI has consistently increased; it was RMB 2,253 in 2000.

The economic growth achievement of China is stupendous—a unique case in world history, where a country has maintained two-digit national income growth for three decades in the running. The high economic growth has posed a challenge of reducing Green House Gas (GHG) emissions to meet the climate change commitments on one hand and reducing inequalities on the other. High economic growth rate has resulted in increase in inequalities, as depicted by increase in the Gini coefficient, which is a big development challenge. Another development challenge is that 45 per cent of the country's population is living in the rural area and there has to be continued emphasis on rural development as well increase in agricultural productivity and rural incomes. There is also a challenge of rural to urban transition in China, characterized by what is called rururbanization, i.e. bringing urban living standards to the rural areas. Increase in income causes increase in energy consumption and hence providing energy security to the country as a whole is a challenge but more importantly is to meet the challenge of rural energy demand, part of which is still met by direct combustion of biomass.

The challenge is to deploy biomass for productive use, since only 6 per cent of it is being used currently (data presented later in the chapter ERI, NDRC 2010). Biomass is being wasted or inefficiently used. Traditionally agricultural waste was being burnt, but now, with the new environmental laws and their stringent implementation, burning of such waste is banned. However, biomass waste is still burnt in many rural areas for many reasons. For example, rural households lack access to new technologies for efficient biomass use and its conversion to energy. For example, rural households' access to new devices, that can convert biomass to energy or that reduces local pollution in the process of its combustion, is very limited. The rural households continue to have low incomes and there is a need to improve incomes and living conditions in the rural areas. Lastly, as a country with the largest emission of Green House Gases (GHGs), China also needs to address this new challenge that has come about due to her reaching a middle-income country status with large population. The country faces challenges of both developed countries (with regard to GHG emissions) and that of a developing country (of poverty, inequality and rural development).

The improvement of rural income from RMB 2,253 in 2000 to RMB 9,892 hides the fact that rural areas and rural population still require a push for structural transition and economic growth. The rural poor tend to live in harsh conditions, sometimes in inaccessible areas and with poor infrastructure or supportive services. Hence, in such situations, they tend to initiate Grassroots Innovations (GRIs), which build on local resources, knowledge base, skills, culture and creativity. One important way to improve rural productivity and bring the population out of poverty is to support the farmers' own efforts in GRIs in agricultural technology, production organization and institutional development[2]. GRIs can contribute greatly to inclusive development on one hand and reach out to populations and areas not reached by or ignored by the formal sector on the other.

The GRIs form a large number of total patents applied in China. For example, since 1985, when the Patent Law of People's Republic of China was promulgated, of the total number of patents applied and granted, the 'non-service invention-creations'[3] have made up for over a half of the total patents applied and granted[4]. In other words, more than half the patents have been filed for 'invention-creation' by individuals, which in essence are the grassroots innovations. In Hua County (*see* Zhang and Mahadevia, 2012), only 14 (4.8 per cent) of the total 288 patents granted from 1985 to October 2007, belonged to the service sector[5]. The innovations have been with regard to improving agricultural implements so as to reduce labor, improving rural energy efficiency and reducing pollution in use of biomass.

Biomass Resources in China

Biomass is a very important resource for economic development and energy in rural China. Agricultural production itself is an important economic activity in rural China. Agricultural production leads to generation of agriculture waste, mainly stalk and straw, used traditionally as energy source for domestic and other productive uses by the rural households and small enterprises. Agricultural waste is also used as fodder for livestock and other purposes, such as input for mushroom cultivation. Part of the agricultural waste is put back in the earth for improving soil productivity. With deployment of biogas technologies in rural areas, stalk and straws have also been used as feeder in these plants. The rural households have been directly combusting the straw and stalk for heating and cooking purposes, however, with adverse consequences related to health. The remaining biomass, which could not be disposed of, was burnt—something that the country's environment policy now prohibits. There is a real issue of disposal of the agriculture waste in the rural areas now. Hence, the Government of China has proposed generation of bio-energy as one of the solutions to sustainably use the agricultural waste and other biomass resources of the country.

China has a large stock of biomass. Since 1980, with the increase of crop yield, the total yield of straw also increased rapidly (Cao *et al.*, 2008). There are varying estimates of biomass availability. Their methodologies have varied (Liu & Shen, 2007; Cui *et al.* 2008; Gao *et al.*, 2009; Xie *et al.*, 2010). According to Jiang *et al.*, (2012), methodology of assessing quantum of biomass has been mainly based on agricultural statistical data available at the provincial level. For reuse of biomass, such as for bio-energy (Lin & Juan, 2008), mushroom growing etc., it is necessary to estimate different types of crop residues that are available. Moreover, not all straws are available for biomass use because some of them need be returned to the soil as residue to prevent erosion and enhance soil quality (Shi 2008; Bi *et al.*, 2008). Jiang *et al.*, (2012: 1382) estimate that the agriculture residues were at 806.9 million tons in 2009, and averaged at 716.0 million tons per year over a ten-year period of 2000-2009.Considering conservation requirements, the production of net available crop residues is about 505.5 million ton/year. The bio-energy potential is about 253.7 million tons standard coal/year (7.4 EJ/year), which account for 8.27 per cent of total energy consumption of the country in 2009 (Jiang *et al.*, 2012: 1382). Zhang *et al.*, (2013: 785) estimate that the annual output of crop residues in China is about 728 million tons.

Biomass resources consist of various natural and derived materials such as agriculture residues, wood and wood wastes, animal dung and municipal solid wastes. In theory, every year China produces almost 820 million tons of straw and residues from agricultural production; this includes straws from corn, rice, wheat, cotton and oil-bearing crops. Amongst them, about 690 million tons can be used as available resource (Table 1.1). The largest contribution is from corn stalk (265 million ton), followed by rice straw (205 million ton) and then wheat straw (150 million ton). Every year, 350 million tons of these available resources are used as fertilizer, feedstuff, basic material of edible fungi and papermaking, and about 340 million tons of straws can be used as energy (Twelfth Five Year Plan). In addition, every year, China produces about 120 million tons of the residues from agricultural products, such as rice hull, sugarcane dregs etc., and about 60 million tons of them are available for energy use (Twelfth Five-Year Plan).

Table 1.1: Agricultural Waste Estimates, China

	Crop residues per year (10,000 tons)
Rice	20,500
Wheat	15,000
Corn	26,500
Cotton	2,584
Oil seeds	3,737
Bean stalk	2,726
Potato straw	2,243
Total	82,000

Source: Twelfth Five-Year Plan.

An Example: Application of Cotton Stalk

In May 2014, research team of Tianjin University of Finance and Economics (TUFE), selected 9 counties from among the "top one hundred cotton production counties" and "top one hundred agricultural counties" for interviews on use of agricultural waste, that is straws and stalk after the completion of the agriculture cycle. The relevant departments' staffs, as mentioned in Table 1.2, were interviewed through telephone. As this table depicts, the sample consisted of either agriculture bureau (or committee) or environment protection bureau.

The survey result shows that straw and stalks are mainly being returned back to fields or are being burnt. They are seldom compressed into briquettes or used for energy production. The detailed findings of this quick survey are given in Table 1.2.

Although all nine districts prohibited burning of straw, it was still being burnt. The main reason for burning was that the straw

Table 1.2: The Interviewed Samples

Place	*Department Interviewed*	*Among*
Dafeng City of Hubei Province	Agricultural Committee	Top one hundred cotton production counties
Tianmen City of Hubei Province	Agricultural Bureau	Top one hundred cotton production counties
Qianjiang City of Hubei Province	Agricultural Bureau	Top one hundred cotton production counties
Dengzhou City of Henan Province	Environment Protection Bureau	Top one hundred cotton production counties
Gongyi City of Henan Province	Agricultural Bureau	Top one hundred agricultural counties
Anyang City of Henan Province	Agricultural Bureau	NA
Wuan City of Hebei Province	Agricultural Bureau	Top one hundred agricultural counties
Nanhe County of Hebei Province	Agricultural Bureau	NA
Wendeng City of Shandong Province	Agricultural Bureau	Top one hundred agricultural counties

and stalk do not decompose easily after being returned back to fields. They continue to remain as waste if they lie on the fields for more than a year. They then tend to attract pests and also harbour some insects that would damage crops. Hence, the next season's crop is damaged. In case of wheat, it can also lead to withering and death of wheat seedlings. The farmers, therefore, believe that straw and stalks should be returned back to fields every two years instead.

The second finding was that the farmers do not transport the straw and stalk to their homes for using them as fuel. For domestic fuel use, the straw and stalk have to be dried. Since homesteads do not have sufficient space, the drying has to be carried out on the fields, and as discussed above, if done so, the next season's crop gets damaged. Hence, the farmers are left with no option but to burn this waste than use the same for domestic energy needs. Transportation to homes requires additional effort and costs.

Some farmer-households burnt straw and stalk as fuel, others used it as feed for animals or they just discarded it. Four out of the nine districts compressed straw and stalk into briquettes for fuel. For example, Wuan City of Hebei Province promoted and trained people in the use of briquetting machine. In Tianmen City of Hubei Province, some enterprises produced straw and stalk briquettes.

In contrast, the enterprises of Wendeng City of Shandong Province and Gongyi City of Henan Province, which were producing straw and stalk briquettes, had stopped their production due to the unfavourable market conditions. Among those "top one hundred cotton production counties", only Tianmen city compressed cotton stalks into briquettes. Others all returned cotton stalks back to fields.

Benefits of Comprehensive Use of Biomass

Increase in Farmers' Income

Comprehensive utilization of agricultural wastes is an effective way to increase farmers' income. As per the market situation in 2015, the price of one ton of straw varied from RMB 200 to RMB 250. If the 2012 estimated stock of straw were to experience 10 per cent increase in its utilization, an additional about 70 million tons of straw had potential to increase the farmers' income by RMB 14 billion[6]. According to estimation of National Energy Administration, the annual sales income of biomass industry could reach up to RMB 100 billion and create about 3.6 million jobs by 2015. Thus, biomass use is likely to accrue farmers both economic and social benefits[7].

Take mushroom production as an example. Up to the end of 2013, in Hebei Province, about 3.6 million tons crop straws were used to grow mushrooms. Mushroom's annual production value reached RMB 9 billion and the annual net income was more than RMB 6 billion. It is estimated that by 2015, about 5 million tons of cotton stalks, wheat straws and corn stalks could be recycled throughout Hebei, which could be used to produce 2 million tons of mushrooms every year. The annual production value could be RMB 12 billion and the annual net income RMB 8 billion. Pingquan County is the biggest mushroom production base of Hebei Province. In 2012, the mushroom production value of this county was RMB 3.5 billion. Baoshenmiao Village of Qijiadai Township is one of the first village of Pingquan County to produce *agaricusbisporus*[8]. In the past, straws and excrements of livestock were everywhere, which resulted in heavy local environment pollution. Since villagers began to grow *agaricusbisporus* demand for these wastes increased. Also, the village households' incomes have increased.

Energy Conservation and Emission Reduction

Generally, straw and stalk are used as fuel. One ton of straw and stalk can generate over 3,000 calorie of heat. Although its calorific value is lower than coal, it has the advantages of inflammability, less smoke, sulphur-free and low soot emission. Hence, straw utilization is an effective way to produce rural energy and reduce emission. Taking Hebei Province as an example, which is an agricultural province, the straw output of Hebei is 61.76 million tons. Hebei Province is the biggest energy consuming province of China. The annual coal consumption of its rural households is more than 40 million tons, heavily polluting the environment (Lei and Yang, 2014)[9]. Hence, reduction in consumption of energy in Hebei Province would benefit air quality in Beijing and Tianjin, two national level cities adjacent to Hebei Province. Thus, efficient utilization of straw and stalk benefits not only the farmers directly, as already discussed in the previous section, it also has positive externalities of improving air quality in the surrounding regions.

Biomass energy can replace fossil fuel energy. Its development is good for energy conservation, emission reduction and the proper control of energy consumption. Air pollutants produced by extensive utilization of coal in the rural areas not only pollute rural environment but also create urban air pollution. The pressure of energy conservation and emission reduction is high in China. In order to achieve the energy conservation goal, some places even switch off power and limit power supply.

It is estimated that by 2015, the annual utilization of rural residues would reach 75 million tons. The annual utilization of various energy crops will reach 25 million tons. 560 million tons of excrements of livestock, 64 million tons of urban household garbage, 15 million tons of sludge produced by urban sewage treatment plants, and 0.9 million tons of waste oils would be used by 2015. These wastes could replace about 50 million tons of standard coal, which is equal to the reduction of 95 million tons of CO_2 and 0.65 million tons of SO_2.[10]

In some 'coal-burning free' areas, biomass boilers have been used, for example, in garment factories, chemical industry, food industry, rural breeding and planting industry. Central heating of residential areas, heat and gas supply in factories; all burn biomass briquettes or pellets instead of coal.

National laws framed for reduction of air pollution, energy conservation, environment protection and renewable energy resources also direct the rural households and agricultural production to the comprehensive use of biomass resources. The relevant laws are Air Pollution Prevention and Control Law of the PRC, 2000; Environmental Protection Law of the PRC, 2014; Energy Conservation Law of the PRC, 2008 and Renewable Energy Law of the PRC, 2005. These are discussed at length in Chapter 3.

Complying with Climate Change Goals

There is no need to labor the argument about reduction of Green House Gases (GHG) emissions in China, which is now the largest emitter in the world. Besides, the air quality parameters in the major cities of China are still very poor and one of the contributing factors to the same is biomass burning in the rural areas. Hence, there is, without doubt, an urgent need to reduce air pollution in the cities and indoor air pollution in rural areas. While these issues are being addressed, there is a continued need to ensure economic growth to penetrate down to the rural areas, which are still in the transition phase.

China has committed to peak its CO_2 emissions by 2030 and to make best efforts to peak earlier. It will increase non-fossil energy in its total energy consumption to 20 per cent by 2030, which will require it to install 800 to 1,000 gigawatts (GWs) in non-fossil capacity, equivalent to the entire current US generating capacity. She has also pledged RMB 20 million ($3.1 billion USD) to the South-South Climate Cooperation Fund to help developing countries address climate change. China's other commitments with regard to climate change relate to increase in carbon intensity of the GDP, climate adaptation and forestry. Shift to renewable energy is an important component of achieving Nationally Determined Contribution (NDC). Bio-fuels are part of this effort.

On June 30, 2015, the Chinese government submitted its NDC, detailing its commitment to climate change mitigation and adaptation for the post-2020 period. Highlights of the NDC include specific goals such as[11]:

- To achieve peak carbon dioxide emissions by approximately 2030, or sooner as best efforts allow;

- To lower carbon dioxide emissions per unit of GDP by 60-65 per cent from 2005 levels;
- To increase the share of non-fossil fuels in the primary energy mix to approximately 20 per cent;
- To increase the volume of forest stock by approximately 4.5 billion cubic metres over 2005 levels; and
- To continue to proactively adapt to climate change through: enhanced mechanism and capacity-building; effective management of climate change risks in sectors such as agriculture, forestry, and water resources and in regions including urban, coastal, and ecologically vulnerable areas; improved early warning and emergency response systems and disaster prevention and mitigation mechanisms.

Zhang *et al.* (2014) estimate that rural energy consumption has resulted in tripling of CO_2 emissions from 0.79 billion metric tons (referred to hereinafter as 'tons') in 1979 to 1.98 billion tons in 2008, while indirect emissions have quadrupled from 0.27 billion tons to 0.85 billion tons during the same period (p. 641). These authors also state that the non-commercial energy resources like biomass are not included in the national energy consumption estimates and hence the emissions from these sources are not sufficiently accounted for in the overall national figures. Due to urbanization and lifestyle changes, the rural population is going to transit to commercial energy and hence their current carbon emissions need to be assessed. Besides, usage of biomass also emits other pollutants such as SO_2, NOx and CO_2; in 2000 their estimates were 0.22 Mt, 0.43 Mt and 573.09 Mt respectively (p. 642).

It is incumbent upon China to participate in the promotion of energy conservation and combating global climate change (Zhang, 2010; Zhang *et al.*, 2011a; Zhang *et al.*, 2011b). Use of renewable energy sources is therefore suggested as the possible solution to reducing GHGs (Liu *et al.*, 2010). Biomass is the most important form of renewable energy in China and the government has chosen ambitious targets to make use of biomass energy (Ma *et al.*, 2010; Zhang *et al.*, 2010).

Improvement in Rural Energy Consumption and Life Quality

The development and use of biomass energy would improve the rural domestic energy consumption situation and further the development of the rural areas. During the Twelfth Five-Year Plan, about 10 million rural households' energy consumption situation would have improved, amongst which an estimated 8 million households would use biogas, 0.5 million households would use pipeline gas and 1.5 million households would use biomass briquettes. The utilization of rural biomass energy would accelerate the equalization of urban and rural energy public service[12].

The Twelfth Five-Year Plan (2012-17) states that in terms of energy supply, due to the lagging infrastructure development, about seven million rural residents had no electricity access in China. Hence, they have not been able to reap the benefits of a modern lifestyle. In addition, about 70 per cent of rural energy sources come from crop straws and firewood, which have very low energy efficiency. On the other hand, biomass resources are very abundant in the country areas. Application of these biomass resources can help resolve the problem of electric power supply to the remote rural areas. Full use of the local biomass energy resources with efficient technology has potential to provide rural residents with clean energy and improve their life quality (ERI, NDRC, 2010). Biomass resources and energy generated from it can promote rural industry and small township development. This will help reduce the urban-rural gap in the living standards.

Historically, China has paid attention to rural development all the way since the Chinese Revolution of 1949 and introduced improved stove programs way back in the 1950s and 1960s. After the end of the Cultural Revolution (1976) and with the economic reforms, greater emphasis has been given to rural energy, in particular, biogas and micro-hydro projects (Smith *et al.*, 1993). One important component of the effort was to introduce improved cook-stoves in rural China. Efforts were made to set up nationwide rural energy infrastructure, implement the policies in pilot counties chosen for the purpose where intensive efforts could be put in place. In these selected counties, leading groups were set up, which consisted of all voluntary members, appointed by the county chief and chaired by the vice-chief to coordinate and administer the contracts for improved cook stoves' installation. All these were supported by research and development, setting up of rural energy companies, and funded by the appropriate arm of the government.

"In recent years, a large number of studies have tried to clarify the impacts of household energy use patterns on rural livelihoods (Gupta, 2003). These studies have shown that energy transition can change rural livelihoods in various ways. Conventional burning of biomass with low thermal efficiency usually causes waste of resource (Chen *et al.*, 2006; Chen *et al.*, 2009). It negatively impacts human health through indoor air pollution, and causes huge damages to environment and ecological system such as deforestation, land degradation, biodiversity decrease and soil erosion, accompanied by increase in GHG emission (Fan *et al.*, 2011). On the contrary, adopting modern fuels could bring positive effects on rural livelihoods by improving quality of life and enhancing environmental protection (Gosens *et al.*, 2013). One option for this transition is developing biomass energy from agro-residues, which can (a) provide clean and sustainable energy for rural areas, (b) promote economic development in rural areas, (c) enhance rural incomes, (d) accelerate industrialization of agriculture and small and medium town construction, and (e) reduce risk of environmental pollution (Chen *et al.*, 2009: 2694).

Chen *et al.* (2009) also argue that one important possibility is large-scale production of densified solid biofuels through use of briquetting technology. The briquetting technology can convert loose agricultural residues into high-density solid biofuel, which is easy to ignite, convenient to use, has high burning efficiency and low pollution. Chen *et al.* (2009: 2692) have listed four types of briquetting technologies available, namely piston press, screw press, hydraulic press, and roller press. The briquetting technology has to still reach maturity stage and innovations in this technology are further required. One case study of innovations in this book is about innovation in small briquetting machines.

Biomass Energy Potential

China has a large stock of biomass, which is being used as important source of energy particularly in rural China. However, the biomass energy technologies are varied and its application is imbalanced. Some of these have become mature technologies and have been commercialized. But, many at the grassroots level remain fragmented and non-commercialized. Farmers themselves have been making innovations to their traditional technologies of biomass use, with varied results with respect to their success. Straw and stalks, one of the important energy resources, which comprises a large percentage of the total biomass available, is burnt, either directly or through stoves and gasifiers. The outcome of such deployment of agricultural waste is local air pollution and adverse health impacts if used for cooking and heating purposes in the house. Those at the receiving end of the pollution are mostly women and children, who tend to remain in the house for a longer period than men.

The Government of China has set long-term plans for renewable energy development in 2007 and targets have been set up for 2020. Biomass energy figures prominently in these goals. There is a debate as to whether these targets will be achieved with regard to biomass resources, given that there are many varieties of biomass resources and the development status of technologies utilizing them is varied. In particular, the farmers' access to the new technologies for biomass utilization is limited and they tend to innovate on the ones available with them. But, they are unable to commercialize their innovations and hence, there is lack of widespread diffusion of technologies that the farmers innovate on one hand and also the top-down technologies on the other.

Smith *et al.* (1993) state that rural Chinese households have an energy ladder. At the lowest rung is dung, followed by crop residues, followed by wood, then coal, then petroleum, gas, district heating and electricity (p. 949). There was a natural tendency to move from the lower quality fuels towards the higher levels; the exact composition depending on the local conditions.

This argument of Smith *et al.* (1993) of energy ladder has been challenged since the turn of millennium (Masera *et al.*, 2000). Instead, it has been argued (Liu *et al.*, 2013) that between fuels, households choose to use a combination of fuels and conversion technologies. This process of diversifying their energy sources is referred to as switching to multiple fuels, resulting in what is called 'fuel stacking'. When a modern fuel is adopted, traditional fuels and devices are still (at least temporarily) kept in place or in store; that is households make the shift or transition only gradually and partially (Kowsari and Zerriffi, 2011). Liu *et al.* (2013) study finds that in rural China multiple fuels use was common. The energy sources consisted of straw and firewood, coal, electricity, LPG, biogas, natural gas, solar energy and gasoline, each one of them having different use as well as different appliance use. The appliance use is linked to incomes and hence the energy source used was also linked to income, besides availability of devices and energy sources.

Currently, most biomass fuels are used mainly for home cooking and heating by direct combustion and are not tied to major portions of economic activity. In the production sector, fuelwood is mainly used—(but does not account for a large proportion)—for local traditional production, such as tea and food processing and ceramic firing. Breakup of biomass fuels into three main components show that, in contradiction to other energy consumption, the use of agricultural residues and firewood has experienced fluctuation but there has not been much change in the quantity used over the 1980-2007 period for which the data is available, as shown in Figure 1.1. But, the proportion of energy derived from biomass has decreased constantly, from 71 per cent to 31 per cent (Figure 1.2). The decline in proportion is because of increase in (quantity terms) use of coal, oil and electricity. The biomass energy sources are termed non-commercial energy source (Zhang *et al.*, 2009). Further, since 1996, the proportion of non-commercial energy sources, such as straw, firewood and biogas, all combined together has remained nearly constant at about 32 to 36 per cent. Although accused of low efficiency as fuel for direct combustion (in domestic cooking stoves, for example, the conversion efficiency is only 10–20 per cent), biomass energy is and will remain a significant source of energy for much of China's rural population, especially in poor areas (Zhang *et al.*, 2009: 2816).

Biomass still continues to be an important source of energy in rural China, as discussed above. But, due to low level of awareness among local farmers and limited access to advanced energy technologies, a large portion of the rural population relies on direct combustion of biomass for domestic use. This leads to issues of waste of biomass resources, indoor air pollution, rural environmental deterioration and social inequalities. This is true for provinces with low-income levels.

"China has abundant biomass resources, including agricultural waste, forest products waste, livestock manure and municipal refuse. Current biomass resource amount in China is 540 million TCEs. With the increase of organic wastes and the development of marginal land, the amount will reach 1.4 billion TCEs by 2050. From amongst these resources, 890 million TCEs will be available

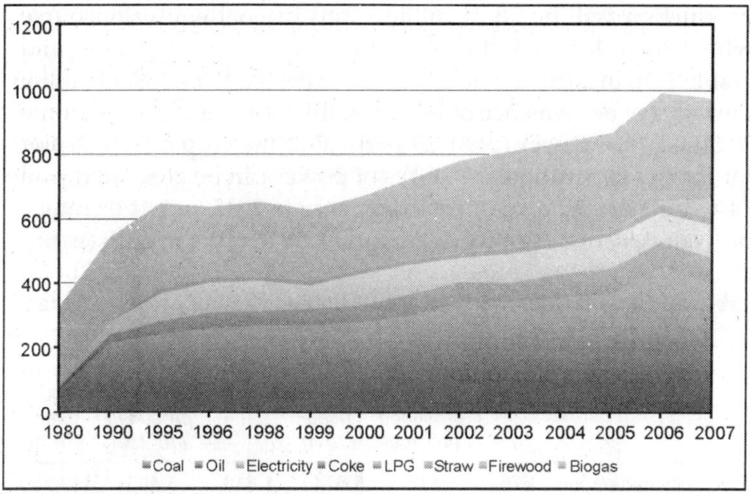

Figure 1.1: Sources of Rural Energy
Source: Data from Appendix given by Zhang *et al.* (2009: 2821-22).

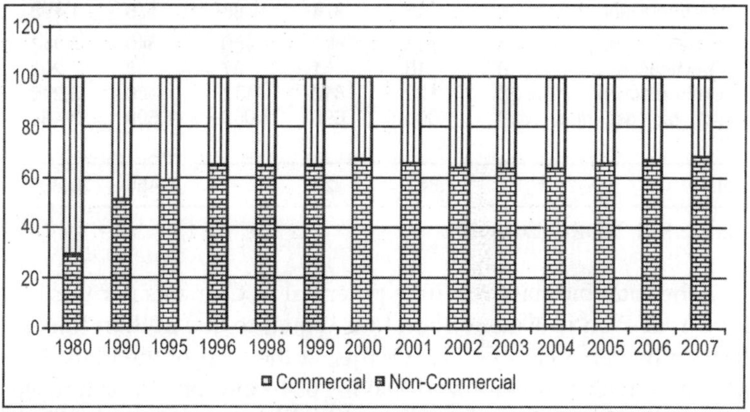

Figure 1.2: Composition of Rural Energy (in %)
Source: Data from Appendix given by Zhang *et al.* (2009: 2821-22).

for clean energy production. In addition to the existing organic wastes (equivalent to 280 million TCEs), various newly-added organic wastes will provide about 270 million TCEs of biomass fuels" (Liu *et al.*, 2014: 145).

Energy Resource Institute (ERI) study (ERI, NDRC, 2010) estimates that by 2015, the total biomass utilized for energy production will be 56.74 million tons of coal equivalence (ce), which includes 14.49 Giga Watts (GWs) of power generation (Table 1.3). In 2020, the numbers are expected to be 139.33 million tons of coal equivalence of biomass utilization and production of 34.50 GWs of power (p. 8). In particular, the crop straws if used for energy generation, 6.75 GWs of power can be generated from 14.45 tons of coal equivalence of energy in 2015 and 34.05 tons of coal equivalence of energy generating 16.18 GWs in 2020 (p. 8).

Table 1.3: Targets for Straw Biomass Technologies and Resource Demand

Technologies	*2015*			*2020*		
	Capacity	*Energy produced (10^4 tce)*	*Resource used (10^4 t)*	*Capacity*	*Energy produced (10^4 tce)*	*Resource used (10^4 t)*
Electricity generation (10^4 kW)	675	1,445	5,674	1,618	3,405	13,995
Co-firing	250	525	1,800	667	1,360	4,800
Direct firing	250	525	2,100	250	510	2,100
Gasification	154	350	1,400	615	1,360	5,600
Carbonization	21	45	374	86	175	1,495
Fuel gas (10^8 m^3)	37	137	861	150	549	3,443
Gasification	9	16	51	37	63	203
Carbonization	28	122	810	113	486	3,240
Pellet biomass fuel (10^4 t)	600	300	690	3,000	1,500	3,450
Total		1,882	7,224		5,454	20,888

Source: ERI, NDRC (2010: 10).

The total biomass resource potential in China as per the 12th Five Year Plan is 696.5 million tons (equal to 460 million tons of coal equivalence) (Table 1.4). Of this, at the start of the Plan only 41.6 million tons were utilized, leaving 654.9 million tons of unused potential. This means that just 6 per cent of the total biomass potential is being used and there is a vast untapped potential of biomass that can be used for energy purposes. The largest biomass potential in China is from organic waste-water (largely from the cities) followed by organic waste (Figure 1.3). Livestock excrement, a resource mainly limited to the rural areas, is also important, followed by straw and other agri-waste and wood-waste from forests. It needs to be stated that deployment of each one of them for energy generation requires different technologies.

Table 1.4: Utilization Potential of Biomass Energy

Source	*Utilization potential*		*Resource used*		*Resource that can be used*	
	Potential quantity (10,000 tons)	*Converted to coal equivalent (10,000 tons)*	*Quantity used (10,000 tons)*	*Converted to coal equivalent (10,000 tons)*	*Quantity of unused resource (10,000 tons)*	*Converted to coal equivalent (10,000 tons)*
Crop straw	34,000	17,000	800	400	33,200	16,600
Processing residue of agricultural products	6,000	3,000	200	100	5,800	2,900
Wood residues of forestry	35,000	20,000	300	170	34,700	19,830
Excrement of live-stock	84,000	2,800	30,000	1,000	54,000	1,800
Municipal solid waste	7,500	1,200	2,800	500	4,700	700
Organic waste water	435,000	1,600	2,700	10	432,300	1,590
Organic waste residue	95,000	400	4,800	20	90,200	380
Total	696,500	46,000	41,600	2,200	654,900	43,800

Source: The Twelfth Five-Year Plan, China.

Note: In this table, biomass energies could also be used in returning back to fields, mushroom production, straw rope production and others. So, the total amount of biomass resource that could be used as energy is less than the utilization potential.

The national government has laid out grand plans to use the agriculture waste as biomass for producing energy. The ERI, NDRC (2010)[13] report states that 38.4 per cent of the non-hydro renewable source of energy was biomass in 2009, and its use as an energy source is expected to rise. In 2009, of the total renewable energy produced, based on ERI, NDRC data, 2.78 per cent of the contribution was from biomass. Its use is much more and is expected to be more than wind power. These estimates do not include direct combustion of biomass within households. China has also embarked on agro-forestry in order to meet the climate change goals as well as reduce soil erosion. It is anticipated that

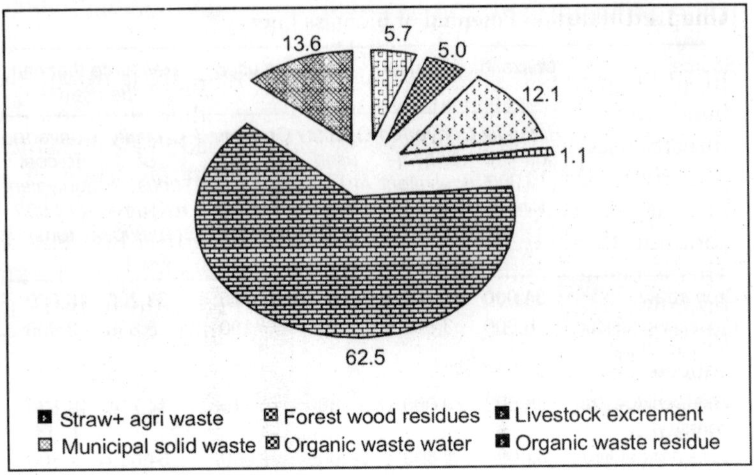

Figure 1.3: Composition of Biomass Potential

Source: Twelfth Five-Year Plan.

there will be an increase in availability of biomass from agro-forestry, which will also support biomass energy production.

"Besides fuelwood forest plantation, Chinese government has insistently prioritized the development and utilization of biomass as an energy resource, such as improved fuel-efficient biomass stoves, biogas, gasification and biomass briquette. Resultantly, China's dissemination of improved biomass stoves (mainly designed for wood or crop residues) is undoubtedly the most successful such program with estimates of over 99 million stoves installed between 1983 and 1988; around 130 million by 1991 and 185 million by the end of 1998"(Zhang *et al.*, 2009: 2819). Zhang *et al.* (2009: 2816) had estimated that there would be 24.87 million family-sized biogas digesters by 2007. However, these would account for 3 per cent of the biomass energy consumption. Chen *et al.* (2009) argue that China has developed four types of briquetting technologies, namely mechanical piston press, screw press, hydraulic press and roller press. But, these technologies still have not matured and much needs to be done with regard to improving them. Thus, the Case of Suo Wenbin, who has innovated small-sized briquetting machine for the poor is important (Chapter 5).

Chapterization

In addition to being an energy resource, biomass is useful and hence reused in rural economy for various other purposes. It is directly used as fuel in the household. It is used in local gasifiers directly or through its conversion into briquettes. This use of biomass for direct energy production at the village level will continue till there is full electrification of all rural households. This is being attempted by the national government under the program of 'New Village Construction', wherein the farmers are relocated to modern housing with electricity and the agri-waste is collected by the local government to be used as feed or co-feed in the power plants. But, that is not feasible in all conditions and all local governments may not be in a position to collect all agri-waste from their respective jurisdictions. In that case, the agri-waste remains with the farmers, who then use the straw and stalk for various other purposes. It is used for mushroom production, as the case of Changde city in Hunan Province illustrates. The straw and stalk are also used for making ropes. In general, if possible, the farmers recycle the agriculture waste.

This book refers to the innovations by the farmers, particularly the use of biomass for productive as well as energy purposes, against the overall context of GRIs in China and the policies related to environmental resources. The farmers left to their own devices innovated and found solutions to improving agricultural productivity, energy security and production of clean energy, disposal of agriculture waste on one hand and their sustainable deployment on the other, and by all means improve their living conditions.

Diffusion of biomass utilizing technologies in such a large country such as China, will require massive decentralized efforts; that of the local government as well as the households. The technologies have to be simple enough for easy diffusion and also need to be well accepted by the rural households. Given that the biomass resource quality varies from one region to another, these technologies have to be flexible enough for local adaptation. The adaptation process will require Grassroots Innovations (GRIs). Chapter 2 in this book shows that the farmers have been continuously innovating—many going ahead to register patents for their innovations related to green technologies such as energy saving devices, use of biomass as renewable energy, and other environmental technologies on one hand and technologies that ease agriculture work and help with seeding, weeding, harvesting and threshing on the other.

This Chapter is based on the data collected by the research team of Center for Innovation and Entrepreneurship, Tianjin University of Finance and Economics (TUFE), through scanning of websites. It gives the overview of GRIs in China by region, type of innovation and profile of innovators; extent of efforts made by the innovators, conditions that facilitate innovations and extent of support received from the government and the private sector. The chapter illuminates as to how widespread the GRIs are in rural China. The chapter also suggests that most GRIs pertain to use of biomass. The policies related to environmental resource use are restrictive on one hand but are also supportive for innovations on the other. Government funds are available for implementation of Science and Technology (S&T) at the grassroots level.

The regulatory as well as facilitative policy framework and their implementation structure are discussed in Chapter 3 of the book. Chapters 4 to 6 pertain to case studies that document the motivation, process, struggles, history of achievements and policy support to an individual innovator. Chapter 4 presents the case of Liu Youngquan who has innovated gasifiers and biomass stoves. Chapter 5 pertains to innovator Suo Wenbin who has innovated on small-sized briquetting machine. Chapter 6 talks about innovator Gao Dedian, who has innovations to his credit, covering the entire cycle of mushroom production. Mushroom production deploys significant proportion of biomass. Chapter 7 brings the findings of the case studies together in the larger policy and development context of China. This chapter presents facts about biomass resources in China, their current use and future potential.

NOTES

1. All the statistics in this paragraph are from China, NBS (2015) except where specific reference is given.
2. There are many political grassroots innovations as well. For example, the major political innovations since late 1970s in rural China were all triggered at the grassroots. *See* Zhang (2012).
3. According to the "Patent law of the People's Republic of China",

'inventions-creations' mean inventions, utility models and designs. The law defines invention-creation as non-service and service. The non-service 'invention-creations' are by individuals and the service 'invention-creations' are by the organizations. The 'invention-creation' by a person in execution of the tasks of the entity to which he/she belongs, or made by him/her by mainly using the material and technical means of the entity/ organization is also called a service invention and the right to apply for a patent in this case belongs to the entity/organization. For a non-service 'invention-creation', the right to apply for a patent is of the inventor/creator.

4. *Source*: http://www.sipo.gov.cn/sipo2008/tjxx/ (accessed on November 21, 2010).
5. *Source*: Hua County Government (2007): "Being a county of lots of GRIs, where shall Hua county go?", *Survey and Communication*, Issue 7 and discussions with Mr. Wang Haoqin, the Vice Director of Science and Technology (S&T) Bureau of the county.
6. Press conference given by National Development and Reform Commission on the 12th Five-Year Plan of Comprehensive Utilization of Straw and Stalk, Implementation Plan on Comprehensive Utilization of Crop Straw and Stalk during the 12th Five-Year Plan, issued by National Development and Reform Commission, Ministry of Agriculture and Ministry of Finance. According to the Energy Channel of chinanews.com, in order to further learn about the implementation plan, journalist interviewed officials of National Development and Reform Commission. January 5, 2012. http://www.chinanews.com/ny/2012/01-05/3582270.shtml
7. The Twelfth Five-Year Plan of Biomass Energy Development, National Energy Administration.
8. *Agaricus bisporus* is an edible mushroom. Its immature white version is called button mushroom. It also has immature brown version.
9. Lei Hanfa and Yang Meiting, "Eco-utilization of Straw and Stalk", *Economic Daily News*, July 8, 2014.
10. The 12th Five Year Plan on the development of Biomass Energy, National Energy Administration.
11. Sha, Fu; Zou Ji, & Liu Linwei (n.d.) *An Analysis of China's NDC, Source*: http://www.chinacarbon.info/wp-content/uploads/2015/07/Comments-on-Chinas-NDC.pdf, accessed on May 3, 2016.
12. The 12th Five Year Plan on the development of Biomass Energy, National Energy Administration.
13. ERI, NDRC (2010), *op. cit.*

2
GRIs in China – Overall Situation, Drivers and Achievements

Farmers and GRIs

Globally, throughout the long history of agriculture, farmers have developed many technologies and built specific knowledge bases for their respective local environments (Reijnties *et al.*, 1992). Such informal research by farmers can be a major source of agricultural innovations (Biggs, 1992; Hippel, 1988). The local people are knowledgeable about their own situations and resources; what works and what does not work, and how one change impacts the other parts of their system (Gupta, 2003; Rajasekaran, 1993; The World Bank, 2005). Therefore, increasingly scientists throughout the world are starting to acknowledge farmers' capacity to experiment and innovate, stressing the importance of participatory approaches for agricultural research and development (For example, *see* Hellin *et al.*, 2008; Hoffmann *et al.*, 2007; Gonsalves *et al.*, 2005; Reece & Sumberg, 2003; Thrupp, 1996). Chambers *et al.* (1989) and Richards (1985) have already, vividly described in the 1980s, that experimentation is part of the farming practices and that partnerships between extension services, formal research and farmers, in improving rural livelihoods, hold far more promise than the conventional top-down approach to Research and Development (R & D). The genuine partnership is possible only when the external factors can appreciate local creativity (Waters-Bayer & Bayer, 2005). Different agro-ecological and market conditions require not only different technologies, but also different providers of technology across the public, private, and civil society sectors (Byerlee & Alex, 1998).

"Because of the changes surrounding and affecting them, the rural areas of the developing world now-a-days resemble a gigantic laboratory, with new initiatives taking place everywhere and across a range of issues and objectives" (Berdegué, 2005). This is the case even in China, where examples abound of farmers' own innovations that have led to local and even national economic development in China. For example, the over-the-winter greenhouses for vegetable production developed by the farmers in Wafangdian, Liaoning Province, have resulted in cultivation of vegetables and hence an increase in the vegetable choices available to the people during winters (Wu & Zhang, 2013). Chen Guangxing has developed new varieties of Chinese onion and garlic, through which there has been increases in local agricultural production (Zhang and Mahadevia, 2014).

This chapter is based on the database of the Grassroots Innovations (GRIs). This database has been created through primary survey and scanning of the websites of local and national newspapers, for an announcement of any new innovation. In all, data has been collected for 422 out of a total of 467 innovations, of which 79 innovations are based on primary survey of 43 innovators. The remaining 343 innovations are of innovators, whose data has been collected from the website. Generally, one innovator has one innovation. The database is of the year 2014 and contains innovations for the period since 1985. The list of variables for which the data is available is given in Annexure 2.1. This is by no means, an exhaustive list of innovations. This database has limitations. It only consists of reported innovations and if an innovation has not been reported in the media, then it has neither been captured in the primary survey nor in the media reports. Another limitation is that all the records do not have entries for all the variables. Hence, the percentages reported in the tables are based on only valid observations of each of the variable.

Overall Situation

The largest reported innovators are from Henan Province (11.6 per cent), followed by Hunan (7.3 per cent) and then followed by Tianjin (6.2 per cent) (Table 2.1). Hebei and Inner Mongolia, have also contributed 5.7 per cent and 5.3 per cent to the total innovations. The least numbers are from Shanghai, Jiangsu, Beijing and Zhejiang, all developed provinces, where rural population would be having access to advanced tools and technology and hence may not have to engage in innovations. There are very few female innovators. They comprise only 2.4 per cent of the total number of innovators.

Table 2.1: Distribution of Innovators by Province and Sex

Province	Male	Female	Total	Distribution by Province
Anhui	18	1	19	4.5
Beijing	5	0	5	1.2
Chongqing	18	1	19	4.5
Guangdong	20	1	21	5.0
Guizhou	11	0	11	2.6
Gunagxi	16	0	16	3.8
Hainan	8	0	8	1.9
Hebei	23	1	24	5.7
Heilongjiang	17	0	17	4.0
Henan	45	4	49	11.6
Hubei	17	0	17	4.0
Hunan	31	0	31	7.3
Inner Mongolia	23	0	23	5.5
Jiangsu	19	0	19	4.5
Jiangxi	14	0	14	3.3
Jilin	10	0	10	2.4
Jiangsu	3	0	3	0.7
Lioning	21	0	21	5.0
Ningxia	11	0	11	2.6
Shanghai	0	1	1	0.2
Shandong	19	1	20	4.7
Sichuan	19	0	19	4.5
Tianjin	26	0	26	6.2
Xinjiang	12	0	12	2.8
Zhejiang	6	0	6	1.4
Total	412	10	422	100.0

Source: Primary data.

The farmers have undertaken a diversity of innovations, in not just areas of their direct interest such as farming, which has 39.4 per cent of the innovators, but also in the areas of green technologies (energy savings, renewables and other environmental technologies) (19.7 per cent) and consumer goods (10 per cent) (Table 2.2). However, the majority of the innovations are directly related to agricultural activities such as planting and weeding (11.2

per cent), harvesting and threshing (7.6 per cent) and then to agriculture-allied activities such as mushroom cultivation (3.6 per cent), and livestock, fisheries and horticulture (3.1 per cent). None of the innovations were found to be area or province specific, nor was there any specific pattern to the innovations. Moreover, the type of innovation made by innovator, had no relationship to his/her level of education (discussed later herein).

Table 2.2: Innovation Types (per cent Distribution)

Innovation Category	*Distribution*
Planting and weeding	11.2
Harvesting and threshing	7.6
Seeding and grafting technologies	3.1
Fertilizers, pesticides and their application	3.6
New varieties of cropping	0.5
Fungus and Mushroom cultivation	3.6
Livestock, fish and horticulture technologies	3.1
Agriculture machinery for all other purposes	3.8
Irrigation	1.2
Greenhouse	1.7
Agriculture, grain and food processing	5.7
Heating and cooling devices	3.1
Alternative energy	7.6
Energy saving devices	5.2
Environmental technologies	6.9
Other mechanical devices	3.8
Health technologies	1.4
Devices/innovations for vehicles	4.5
Consumer goods	8.3
Other Non-farm innovations	10.0
Institutional	1.2
Information not available	3.1
Total	100.0

Source: Primary survey.

The largest proportion of innovators are in the age group of 31-40 years (35 per cent) followed by those in the age group of 41-50 years (24 per cent) (Table 2.3). There are less than 7 per cent innovators in the below 20 years age group. This means that some work experience is required before someone engages in innovation. As we know, and will be seen later in this chapter, the innovator, innovates out of necessity, when he/ she encounters some difficulty in any process. That would be the case, only if one has been

Table 2.3: Distribution of Innovators by Age

Age Group (Years)	*Distribution*
< 21	6.8
21-30	20.6
31-40	34.5
41-50	23.6
51-60	11.1
> 60	3.4
Total	100.0

Source: Primary survey.

working. Further, after innovating, the person thinks about starting a business from the innovation, for which contacts as well as financial wherewithal is required. Hence, the age group of 31 to 50 years is when the most innovations are occurring.

About 56 per cent of the innovations have been carried out after the year 2000 (Table 2.4). This indicates a policy environment to support innovation on one hand and the need from the rural population and farmers to innovate. The Patent Law of People's Republic of China was promulgated in 1985, after which the innovations have increased. Zhang and Mahadevia (2012) state that more than half of the total number of patents applied for and granted are 'non-service invention-creations' (*See* Figure 2.1), with exception of years 1985, 2009 and 2010. The Patent Law defines non-service sector inventions as those made by individuals who are not working for the service sector organizations. Thus, by definition itself, non-service 'invention-creations' are by individuals and the service 'invention-creations' are by the organizations. In other words, more than half the patents have

Table 2.4: Period of Innovation

Period	*Distribution*
Before 1990	13.6
1990-95	11.7
1996-2000	18.0
2001-2005	27.2
2006-2010	25.3
After 2010	4.1
Total	100.0

Source: Primary survey.

been filed for 'invention-creations' by individuals in nearly all the years. Figure 2.1 also shows that the number of patents registered for both, service and non-service sectors, have climbed up from 1998 onwards and from 2003 onwards, have registered a sharp increase in numbers. This explains why more than half the innovations in our database are after 2000.

Majority of the innovators, 85.4 per cent of them, have worked on their own to carry out the innovations. Just 3.1 per cent of them have worked with experts to undertake an innovation. This could be more likely, because the experts do not tend to work with the farmers, in spite of existence of government programs, to support such collaborations, as exemplified through the case of Tianjin farmer Chen Guangxin (Zhang and Mahadevia, 2014). Another 4.6 per cent have worked with friends, 3.1 per cent with relatives and remaining 3.7 per cent with a mix of partners.

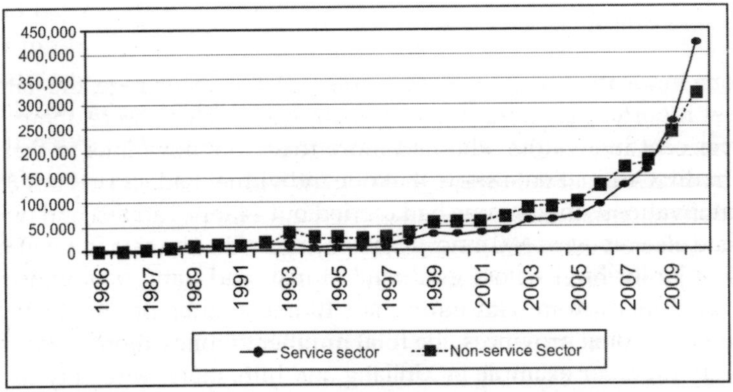

Figure 2.1: Service and Non-Service Sector Patents Registered Over Time, China

Source: Compiled from information in www.sipo.gov.cn[1]

Figure 2.2 shows that 68 per cent of the innovators are either farmers or peasant workers, with farmers dominating (47.2 per cent) the total number of innovators. In other words, the GRIs are carried out by the rural population, but not necessarily all of them are farmers. Some of them are in non-farming activities, for example workshop owners at the local level (16.3 per cent) and local planners (10.9 per cent). Categories of 'others' is diverse.

For 71 innovators, the database did not reveal the number of innovations per innovator. Among the rest, 60 per cent had only

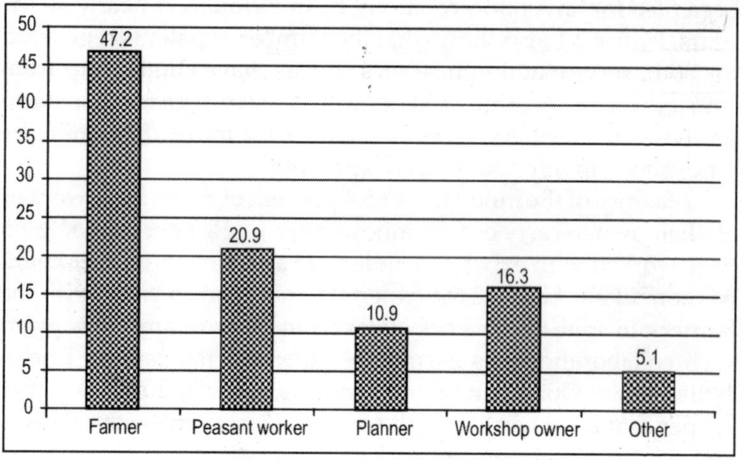

Figure 2.2: Occupation of Innovator (% distribution)

Source: Primary survey.

one innovation to their credit (Table 2.5). On an average, the data set reported, 2.1 innovations per innovator. There were about 5 per cent innovators who had more than 10 innovations to their credit. Original data show that one individual had carried out 30 innovations, another one had carried out 44 innovations, and one had also reported 600 innovations to his credit. The said innovator is a junior high school graduate! Hunan and Jiangsu provinces had 3 innovators with more than 10 innovations per innovator. Also, in some provinces, the total number of innovations was not very high, for example in Xinjiang and Jilin, there were only two innovators with more than 10 innovations. In Beijing, of the total 5 innovators in the database, one had more than 10 innovations. In Henan, which has registered the highest number of innovations (49), 48 per cent had only one innovation each and another 22 per cent had six to ten innovations each. But, Hunan, which had the second largest number of innovations (31), 53 per cent had one innovation each and 18 per cent had more than 10 innovations each. Tianjin with 26 innovations had 35 per cent innovators with six to ten innovations and 42 per cent innovators with one innovation each.

Among those with just one innovation, the largest proportion belongs to the ones working on their own. 90 per cent of those with single innovation worked on their own (Table 2.6). However, 94 per

Table 2.5: Number of Innovations per Innovator

Number of innovations	*Proportion of Innovators (%)*
One	59.3
Two	11.4
Three	8.3
4-5	5.3
6-10	10.4
> 10	5.3
Total	100.0

Source: Primary survey.

Table 2.6: Number of Innovations by Innovation Team

Innovation team	*Number of innovations per innovator*						*Total*
	1	*2*	*3*	*4-5*	*6-10*	*> 10*	
Single person	89.8	80.6	81.0	100.0	65.4	93.8	86.9
With relatives	2.6	11.1	0.0	0.0	3.8	0.0	3.2
With friends	2.0	0.0	19.0	0.0	26.9	0.0	4.8
With experts	2.0	0.0	0.0	0.0	3.8	6.3	1.9
Mixed	3.6	8.3	0.0	0.0	0.0	0.0	3.2
Total	100.0	100.0	100.0	100.0	100.0	100.0	100.0

Source: Primary survey.

cent of those with more than 10 innovations too, worked on their own! A large percentage of innovations are by single innovators, and less than 2 per cent of the innovations are by the experts.

Further, interestingly, if one innovator had more than one innovation to his/ her credit, 59 per cent of them had innovations in unrelated areas. That is, if the innovator had more than one innovation, in 59 per cent cases, these innovations were not related to each other indicating the versatility of the innovator.

Conditions Promoting Innovations

Regular school education is useful for promoting innovation as compared to vocational education. The innovators with a vocational training background are just 7 per cent (Table 2.7), as compared to those with junior high or senior high school backgrounds, who make up nearly two-thirds of the total. Since, number of female innovators is very small, their distribution by

Table 2.7: Education Level at the Time of Innovation

Education Level	*Male*	*Female*	*Total*
Primary	25.3	16.7	25.1
Junior high school	41.2	0.0	40.3
Pre-vocational	3.1	0.0	3.0
Senior high school	24.1	50.0	24.7
Vocational	3.5	33.3	4.2
University and above	2.7	0.0	2.7
Total	100.0	100.0	100.0

education level is not statistically relevant. Nonetheless, half of them have completed their senior high school. China has a policy of compulsory education of 9 years, that is, education till junior high school. Sixty eight per cent of the innovators had an education qualification till junior high school and above.

Education level has impacted the time taken to innovate. For example, those who have taken more than 10 years for carrying out innovation, are educated till primary school, junior high school or pre-vocational level (Table 2.8) and they form three-quarters of the innovators, who have taken more than 10 years before innovating while those with university education and above have taken between 1-5 years (87.7 percent) and less than 1 years (14.3 percent) respectively, for innovation. Seventy per cent of those with senior high school education have taken between 1-5 years to complete an innovation, of which half of them have taken less than a year. While the time taken to innovate is linked to the education level, it is likely that it may also have to do with the type of innovation.

Table 2.8: Education Level and Time Taken to Innovate

Level of Education at Time of Innovation	*Time Taken to Innovate*				*Total*
	< 1 year	*1-5 yrs*	*5-10 yrs*	*> 10 yrs*	
Primary	19.0	27.6	27.6	25.9	100.0
Junior high school	20.8	44.8	13.5	20.8	100.0
Pre-vocational	25.0	37.5	12.5	25.0	100.0
Senior high school	34.5	36.2	13.8	15.5	100.0
Vocational	18.2	45.5	27.3	9.1	100.0
University and above	14.3	85.7	0.0	0.0	100.0
Total	23.5	39.5	17.2	19.7	100.0

The farmer and the peasant worker are the two categories of occupations, which have carried out the largest number of innovations, but education level of a majority of them (72 per cent of farmers and 77 per cent of the peasant workers) is either primary or junior high school (Table 2.9). Those in other occupations (64 per cent of them) have had either vocational education or university education.

Table 2.9: Occupation by Education Level

Occupation	*Initial Education Level*						*Total*
	Primary	*Junior High School*	*Pre-Vocational*	*Senior High School*	*Vocational*	*University and above*	
Farmer	27.3	44.5	1.6	23.4	2.3	0.8	100.0
Peasant worker	19.2	57.7	1.9	21.2	0.0	0.0	100.0
Professional planner	16.0	12.0	8.0	60.0	4.0	0.0	100.0
Agriculture machinery driver	0.0	0.0	0.0	0.0	100.0	0.0	100.0
Workshop owner	39.5	31.6	7.9	15.8	5.3	0.0	100.0
Others	0.0	14.3	0.0	21.4	28.6	35.7	100.0
Total	24.8	40.3	3.1	25.2	4.3	2.3	100.0

Education level did not have any relationship with the number of innovations per person. Those with junior high school education and vocational education have made more than 10 innovations, whereas both, those with just primary education and those with university and higher levels of education, have carried out only one innovation. But, those with higher levels of education, for example, university education, in addition to having a smaller number of innovations to their credit, either one or two (80 per cent of them are in this range) (Table 2.10), have also taken a longer time than the farmers and peasant workers to innovate. Since the data-base does not give details about the process of innovations, it was hard to comment on the appropriateness of the time taken for innovations.

Majority of the innovators (77 per cent of them) stated that they learnt the innovative skills on their own (Table 2.11). Another 17 per cent had an inborn or inbuilt skill necessary for carrying

Table 2.10: Number of Innovations by Education Level

Education Level at Time of Innovation	*Number of Innovations per Innovator*						*Total*
	One	*Two*	*Three*	*4-5*	*6-10*	*> 10*	
Primary	56.9	15.4	12.3	9.2	3.1	3.1	100.0
Junior high school	46.1	4.9	13.7	4.9	15.7	14.7	100.0
Pre vocational	37.5	25.0	12.5	12.5	12.5	0.0	100.0
Senior high school	50.0	6.0	8.0	4.0	28.0	4.0	100.0
Vocational	45.5	27.3	9.1	9.1	0.0	9.1	100.0
University and above	60.0	20.0	0.0	0.0	20.0	0.0	100.0
Total	49.8	10.0	11.6	6.2	14.1	8.3	100.0

Table 2.11: Initial Skills of Innovators

Skill Source	*Distribution*
No skill	3.5
Own skill	17.0
Learnt skill on one's own	76.9
Government training	0.8
Skill acquired through consultation with others	1.8
Total	100.0

Source: Primary survey.

out the innovation. Miniscule proportion (0.8 per cent) stated that they had obtained their innovative skill through government training. However, what emerged as a surprise is that, although there are many government programs for the education and training of farmers, the farmers have not benefited from them (Zhang and Mahadevia, 2014). Hence, possession of skill is an essential factor for carrying out an innovation, although it may not necessarily have been obtained through any formal process.

Majority of the innovators who carried out the innovations, did so, either to solve an immediate problem on hand (reason cited by two-thirds of the innovators) or out of curiosity or as a hobby (cited by one-fifth of the innovators) (Table 2.12). Only 15 per cent of the innovators carried out innovations for economic gains. Furthermore, those for whom economic reason was the motive behind an innovation, would have gone ahead to commercialise their innovation, thus stopping at undertaking only one or two innovations. But, those who had carried out innovations for the purpose of either solving a problem or out of curiosity/hobby have

Table 2.12: Motivation for Innovation *vs.* Environment for Innovation

Motivation for Innovation	*Economic Environment*		*Cultural Environment for Study*		*Cultural Environment for Innovation*		*Total*
	Developed	*Under-developed*	*Yes*	*No*	*Yes*	*No*	
Economic	11.9	18.6	22.22	12.83	19.7	14.0	14.5
Solving problem	68.5	61.9	54.81	70.80	60.6	67.4	65.2
Curiosity/Hobby	18.2	18.6	21.48	15.49	18.1	17.8	19.3
Others	1.4	0.9	1.48	0.88	1.6	0.8	1.0
Total	100.0	100.0	100.00	100.00	100.0	100.0	100.0
Distribution	38.3	61.7	37.60	62.40	35.2	64.8	

Source: Primary survey.

to their credit more than 3 innovations per innovator. This indicates that this latter bunch of innovators were more open to carrying out multiple experiments, as they did not have any pressure or interest in commercialising their findings.

As stated in the theory, that GRIs are an outcome of lack of development, 62 per cent of the innovators are from underdeveloped areas of the country. Amongst those who stated economic reason as motivation behind the innovations (only 15 per cent), 72 per cent belonged to underdeveloped areas. 65 per cent of the innovators were living in the plains, 19 per cent in the high mountainous regions and remaining 16 per cent in hilly areas. In response to whether the cultural environment was supportive of pursuing research for innovations or not, it was found that this was the case with only 63 per cent of the innovators. Further, in those areas having a cultural environment supportive for pursuing innovations, 22 per cent innovators carried them out for economic reasons, whereas on the whole, only 15 per cent innovators have cited this reason. In contrast, in the areas with no cultural environment for taking up study for innovation, need to solve a problem was the reason for innovation by 71 per cent of the innovators. Thus, need to solve a problem, in the situation where they had to rely on their own, led the innovators to study for innovation.

On the whole, only 35 per cent innovators belonged to regions where cultural environment was congenial for innovations. It can also be concluded that the areas that did not have cultural environment for innovations, did not motivate individuals to pursue studies towards innovation. Further, in cultural environments congenial for innovation, 20 per cent, as against 14 per cent, in areas with no cultural environment for innovation, carried out innovations for economic reasons. 67 per cent innovators took up innovations for solving a problem in areas with no congenial cultural environment, while this figure on the whole was 65 per cent.

The developed region has higher chances of having a cultural environment to promote innovation. For example, on the whole, 35.4 per cent innovators stated that there was cultural environment to innovate. Among those living in developed regions, 39.6 per cent reported positive cultural environment for innovation. In contrast, 67.1 per cent of those living in underdeveloped regions, reported lack of cultural environment for innovation as against 64.6 per cent of the total innovators stating the same. However, the difference between the two is very small.

More than three-fourths (77 per cent) of the innovators are located in the areas with convenient transport facilities. This means that the innovators are from areas, which are accessible. Those living in accessibly — poor areas are engaging in innovation (75 per cent of them) to solve a problem, while on the whole, two-thirds had stated this as a reason. This further proves that, if the region is less developed and has accessibility problems, the rural population tends to engage in GRIs to solve their problems. The fact that they are able to innovate is interesting. As in case of other criteria among those with good accessibility, 17 per cent stated that they engaged in innovations for the reason of improving their economic conditions, as against 15 per cent on the whole (Table 2.13).

Little more than half of the innovators (52 per cent) stated that they came from areas that did not have policy environment to support innovations. Of those coming from such deficient regions, 70 per cent cited the reason for innovation as a need to solve the problem, as against 66 per cent on the whole. Further, those innovators located in areas with positive policy environment, 18 per cent engaged in innovation for the purpose of improving their economic conditions as against 15 per cent on the whole.

As high as 70 per cent of the innovators stated that they did not have access to any technical support for innovation. Again,

Table 2.13: Motivation for Innovation *vs.* Support

Motivation for Innovation	*Transport Accessibility*		*Policy Environment for Innovation*		*Technical Support Availability*		*Total*
	Yes	No	Yes	No	Yes	No	
Economic	17.0	11.8	18.1	13.8	17.0	15.4	14.5
Solving problem	61.1	75.3	59.9	69.8	64.3	64.6	65.2
Curiosity/Hobby	20.5	12.9	20.3	15.9	17.9	18.8	19.3
Others	1.4	0.0	1.7	0.5	0.9	1.2	1.0
Total	100.0	100.0	100.0	100.0	100.0	100.0	100.0
Distribution	77.3	22.7	48.5	51.5	30.0	70.0	

Source: Primary survey.

this shows that the GRIs are the initiatives of the innovators themselves to overcome the lack of support of any kind, including the government support.

Innovations were carried out, even though, initially, there was no availability of the necessary equipment. While 26.1 per cent did not require any equipment for carrying out the innovations, another 61.1 per cent did not have the required equipment, initially, for the purpose. Only 12.8 per cent innovators had the necessary equipment for the innovations. Hence, the availability of equipment did not matter and the innovators put in efforts in spite of this initial drawback. Access to the necessary equipment, did not impact the time taken for innovation.

What factors influence the average time taken for innovation? There is no relationship between the initial equipment available and time taken to innovate. For example, while 22.4 per cent of those with access to initial equipment, took less than 1 year to innovate, 18.7 per cent of those without any access to initial equipment, also took the same time. But, while only 18.4 per cent took more than 10 years with requisite equipment, 20.1 per cent took more than 10 years to innovate without the equipment. The difference between the two groups, those with necessary equipment and those without, is very low.

Similarly, the policy environment for innovations did not matter and did not influence time taken for innovation. For example, 23.2 per cent innovators in favourable policy environment took more than 10 years to innovate; this proportion among those in non-favourable policy environment was less, at 16.9 per cent.

Similarly, there was hardly any difference between the proportion of innovators who took less than 1 year to innovate, in context of the policy environment; 24.4 per cent in favourable environment and 24.1 per cent in areas where there was no favourable environment.

Cultural environment for innovation mattered. Those living in areas that had cultural environment to support innovations took less time to innovate than those living in areas with no such cultural environment. 25.6 per cent innovators completed their innovation in less than one year in areas where there was cultural environment to innovate *vis-à-vis* 23.5 per cent achieving the innovation in areas without such cultural environment. 19.2 per cent innovators took more than 10 years to complete innovation in areas without cultural environment whereas this proportion was 18.8 per cent in culturally favourable environment.

Level of economic development of the region, however, did not matter in time taken to accomplish an innovation. For example, only 18 per cent innovators completed their innovation in less than 1 year in the developed region as compared to 27 per cent in the underdeveloped region.

Access to initial funds is important for starting any innovation. In fact 84 per cent stated that they did not have any funds for carrying out their innovation. In other words, the innovators depended on their own resources for the purpose of carrying out innovation. But, 16 per cent did go out to seek funds and they approached multiple sources of funds. 15.8 per cent of those who obtained funds, borrowed from non-financial institutions, 4.3 per cent loaned it from financial institutions, 8.4 per cent obtained government grant, 3.5 per cent obtained funds from the enterprise which could have been interested in the innovation and 24 per cent raised funds through their own personal contacts such as family and friends (Table 2.14). Thus, amongst those who did obtain funds, 40 per cent did so from informal sources. Once again, the innovators have not benefited from any government support for innovations. The government funds available for innovations, seems to be benefiting formal institutions and not the farmer-innovators.

It is somewhat easier to borrow from informal sources as well as from financial institutions in the developed regions as compared to underdeveloped regions. 24 per cent of the innovators in the

Table 2.14: Funds Available for Innovation

Source of Fund*	% Obtaining this Source of Fund
Borrowed from non-financial institutions	15.8
Took institutional loan	4.3
Government grant	8.4
Enterprise	3.5
Raised funds from personal contacts	23.9

* An individual could have accessed multiple sources of funds.
Source: Primary survey.

developed regions were able to borrow funds, either from informal (22 per cent) or financial institutions (2 per cent) for their innovations, while this proportion in the underdeveloped regions was 18.5 per cent (Table 2.15). Although the dependence on government funding was very low on the whole (3 per cent), 4.4 per cent of the innovators depended on this source in the underdeveloped regions as compared to 0.7 per cent in the developed region.

Table 2.15: Source of Funds for Innovation vs. Level of Economic Development (%)

Source of Fund for Innovation	Developed	Under-developed	Total
Borrowed	22.0	18.1	19.6
Loan	2.1	0.4	1.1
Self-contributed	34.0	34.4	34.2
Government support	0.7	4.4	3.0
Enterprise support	1.4	0.4	0.8
Personal contacts	1.4	1.3	1.4
No financial difficulty	38.3	41.0	39.9
Total	100.0	100.0	100.0

Source: Primary survey.

Lastly, derision by the society can discourage individuals from innovating. But, that does not seem to be the case in the sample innovators. 78.9 per cent stated that they were not mocked by the society when they decided to undertake a particular innovation. In other words, the society in general, was supportive of the efforts the innovators were making. But, still in the case of 21 per cent of the innovators, they had to face the scorn of the society! 83.8 per cent stated that their families supported them for undertaking an innovation. Society and family support, therefore, has played an important role for these innovators.

Diffusion of Innovation and Entrepreneurship

Although the innovators stated that they had engaged in innovation to solve their immediate problem (65 per cent) and out of curiosity (19 per cent), just 15 per cent had stated that their innovation was targeted towards entrepreneurship. Nonetheless, all of them were interested in diffusing their innovation. An overwhelming 51 per cent stated that they were successful in diffusing their innovation on a large scale. Another 45 per cent had been able to diffuse their innovation on a small scale. Just 4 per cent stated that they had failed in diffusing their innovation.

Table 2.16: Innovation Diffusion Channels

Innovation Diffusion Channel	*Distribution**
From word of mouth	34.1
Government promotion	18.2
Attending trade fairs	12.5
Media	17.2
Patent transfer	3.1
Self-promotion	32.6
Others	14.8
Total	100.0

* Innovators have used multiple channels for diffusion of their innovation.
Source: Primary survey.

Innovators have used multiple channels to diffuse their innovations. 34 per cent spread their innovation through word of mouth and 33 per cent promoted their innovation on their own (Table 2.16). But, it is interesting to note, that 18 per cent of the innovators' innovations were promoted by the government and 17 per cent of the innovators' innovations were promoted by media. Trade fairs have also played their role and in case of 12.5 per cent innovators, their innovation was diffused through this means. Trade fairs are also organised by the government. Thus, this survey shows that, although the innovators have not benefited from the government support for carrying out their innovations, they have certainly benefited from government support when it came to diffusing their innovation. Just

3 per cent used patent registration as a method of innovation diffusion. A large number of innovators (93 per cent of them) have used two or more channels for diffusion of their innovation.

Table 2.17: Innovation Application

Application of Innovation	*Distribution*
Open access	27.2
Patent transfer	6.1
Start business with others	12.3
Start ones' own business	56.0
Total	100.0

Source: Primary survey.

Overall, out of the total of 467 innovators covered in this study, as many as 208 innovators have clearly stated that they used their innovation for entrepreneurship. This takes the proportion of innovators using their innovation for entrepreneurship to 45 per cent. But, a significant proportion, about one-third of them, did not state what their innovation was used for. Hence, out of the total number of those who gave information regarding application of their innovation, a very large proportion, 68.3 per cent stated that they had either started a business of their own (56.0 per cent) or in partnership with others (12.3 per cent) using their innovation (Table 2.17). Another 27 per cent among them had stated that they had made their innovation freely available to the others for use. Although only 15 per cent of the innovators had stated that their innovation was for economic purpose (Table 2.13), after innovation they were keen to use the same for entrepreneurship, as seen from data in Table 2.17.

Similar to the procurement of funds for innovation, for entrepreneurship also, a large proportion—42 percentage stated that they had put in their own funds for entrepreneurship. But among those who obtained funds from different sources (58 per cent of the total sample), 42 per cent raised the funds from their own personal contacts (self-collected) (Table 2.18). Only 13 per cent stated that they received government support and same proportion stated that they obtained loan from a financial institution. In case of entrepreneurship as in case of innovation, a significant proportion of innovators borrowed from informal

Table 2.18: Funds for Entrepreneurship

Fund Source for Entrepreneurship	*Distribution*	*Distribution**
Borrow	12.4	18.0
Loan	9.0	13.1
Self-collected	28.8	41.9
Government support	9.0	13.1
Enterprise support	6.8	9.9
Support by personal contacts	2.8	4.0
No funds difficulty as they had their own funds	41.8	–
Total	100.0	100.0

* Distribution excludes those who stated 'their own funds'.
Note: Innovators have sourced funds from multiple sources.
Source: Primary survey.

sources (18 per cent) or got support from family and friends (4 per cent). Interestingly, a higher percentage of enterprises supported the innovator for entrepreneurship, in comparision to those that supported the innovation process; about 10 per cent of innovators were financially supported by enterprises in their entrepreneurship whereas just 0.8 per cent of innovators were supported for carrying out innovation by entrepreneurs (Table 2.15). Further, for entrepreneurship, majority (86 per cent) innovators had obtained funding support from single source, whereas 14 per cent had obtained funding support from two or more sources.

According to the statistics in Table 2.19, 58.5 per cent stated that they did not have any difficulty with regards to skills for entrepreneurship; they possessed the skill necessary for entrepreneurship beforehand. But, amongst those who did not possess this skill, 71 per cent obtained the skill through self-study. Only 2.5 per cent of those without skills stated that they used government training for obtaining entrepreneurship skills. There was also some cooperative spirit observed among the innovators and 12 per cent obtained this skill through consultation with individuals and 15 per cent obtained the same through teamwork. Again, government training has not figured into the sources of skill acquisition by the innovators in taking their innovation to the stage of entrepreneurship.

Having started an enterprise based on innovations, skills are required to manage the enterprise. A large proportion of the

Table 2.19: Skills Acquired for Entrepreneurship

Source of Skill Acquisition for Entrepreneurship	*Distribution*	*Distribution**
Learnt through self-study	34.3	70.7
Government training	1.2	2.5
Team research	7.1	14.6
Consultation with individuals	5.9	12.2
No skill difficulty/possessed the skill	58.5	–
Total	100.0	100.0

* Distribution of those who had possessed skill for entrepreneurship and did not require any training.

Note: Innovators have acquired skills for entrepreneurship from multiple sources.

Source: Primary survey.

innovators (56.5 per cent) stated that they themselves learned the management skill to run their enterprise (Table 2.20). Another 14.5 per cent stated that they already had the skill to manage the enterprise. Just 14.5 per cent stated that they had hired a manager to manage the enterprise. 17.7 per cent had problems with regards to managing their enterprise and had not been able to solve this problem.

Table 2.20: Enterprise Management Skills

Enterprise Management Skills Through	*Distribution**
Hiring manager	14.5
Learning skills oneself	56.5
Having management skills	14.5
Unsolved	17.7
Total	100.0

* Multiple options given.

Source: Primary survey.

Out of those who had engaged in entrepreneurship using their innovation, 68.1 per cent stated that they had succeeded. Another 27.2 per cent stated that their success in entrepreneurship was limited to them earning enough to support the family. Remaining 4.7 per cent had failed in their enterprise.

Innovations in Use and Collection of Agriculture Waste

Another database was created, once again searching the internet, to analyse the types of innovations made for the use of agriculture waste, mainly the stalks and straw left over, after the crop has been harvested. As we have discussed in Chapter 1, China has a large potential of biomass, of which only 20 per cent is used as fodder, the rest is all returned back to the field, which is either buried in the earth or burnt. Burying in the earth is done at shallow depths, which causes problems in the next cropping cycle as it is not possible to plough and sow the field. After the amendment of the Environmental Protection Law of the People's Republic of China, 1989, in 2014, the standards of pollution emission and their implementation have been made very strict. In particular, there is now control on the emission of even PM2.5. Thus, farmers have been put in a difficult situation with regard to disposal of their agriculture waste. Some farmers, therefore, have attempted to find local solutions first to efficiently cutting and collecting the stalks and straw that remain in the field after crop is harvested and some other farmers have found innovations to use these waste as they are unable to burn them. The broad use of the biomass found by the farmers is to use it as energy, that is, as a fuel for cooking stoves, largely through gasifiers, water and room heating stoves, again through the technology of gasifiers, or converting the biomass into pellets or briquettes for use in gasifiers; Farmers have attempted to develop and innovate devices that would efficiently give them this energy, without causing indoor air pollution as well as solve the problem of tar as a by-product. Some mushroom producers have begun to use these bio-wastes as raw material for mushroom production. If this biomass waste has to be thus deployed, its collection from the field has to be efficient, for which many devices have been innovated upon. In case, the local farmers are unable to find any use of the biomass waste, the waste has to be disposed of, which is done through burying it in the earth. If it is buried at a greater depth, then the field can be reused in the next cropping season and farmer can take multiple crops in a year. Hence, some farmers have innovated devices to bury the biomass waste deep inside the earth. This burying of the biomass in the earth is called returning waste to the fields. If this is not done, the biomass waste lying around would decay, attracting insects and pests, which would then destroy the standing crops.

The database on use and collection of agricultural waste has 97 records. For data *see* Annexure 2.1. Again, this is not an exhaustive database and there might be many innovations that may have been left out of the database. But, this database, indeed broadly indicates, the types of grassroots innovations that are being taken up by the farmers in rural China. These would continue, as we argue through the book, during this transition phase of China's development.

Energy Related Innovations

Of the 97 innovations listed, 62 (64 per cent) are for devices related to domestic energy use, either for heating or cooking. The farmers in almost all provinces of China have engaged in these innovations. The representation in the sample is from these provinces: Anhui (1), Beijing (10), Gansu (1), Guangdong (1), Guizhou (2), Hebei (10), Heilongjiang (4), Henan (7), Hubei (1), Hunan (6), Inner Mongolia (1), Jiangsu (3), Jiangxi (1), Jilin (4), Liaoning (1), Shaanxi (2), Shandong (8), Sichuan (1), Tianjin (1), Yunnan (2), and Zhejiang (3). The efforts for innovating various technologies for improving the energy technologies for domestic use are ongoing in many different provinces across China, but the agricultural provinces, such as Henan, Hebei and Hunan are leading in these initiatives. The innovations have been captured from the internet after 2003. One innovation was reported to have been completed in 2003. Nine innovations were completed in 2005, 10 in 2006, 3 in 2007, again 10 in 2008, 5 in 2009, 6 in 2010, 5 in 2011, 4 innovations each in 2012 and 2013. Four innovations in the database did not have any date.

The innovations related to energy were: (i) energy saving stoves (13 innovations); (ii) innovation on room heating such as designing a new stove attached with a *kang* and a pipe that sends hot blast to neighbouring rooms of the house; creating a central heating type unit or sending hot blast to other rooms using heat generated during cooking; creating a cellar to keep and burn straw leading to floor heating; (iii) 21 innovations of gasifiers using different biomass waste as fuel, some using both biomass as well as coal; (iv) some multifunctional stoves for cooking, water heating and room heating; (v) some briquette making devices and

(vi) smokeless stoves. Since 62 of the innovations are related to energy, it seems that finding affordable and environmentally sustainable solutions to meeting domestic energy needs is of great importance to the farmer households.

Of these 63 innovations, the innovators had obtained a patent for 32 of the innovations. Some of them had then either sold the patent to a company or partnered with a company to commercially diffuse the innovation. Three of the innovators did not apply for any patent and six of them had applied for the patent at the time of our internet search for the data in 2014. But some of them had not been concerned about patenting and had directly gone into the product's diffusion in the local market as the farmers were happy with the innovation and directly came to purchase the product from the innovator. One innovator, who produced a straw gasifier to reduce smoke, could sell the product nationwide. But, some innovators had also sold their innovations internationally! For example, two farmers belonging to Hunan Province together invented a gasifier that used biomass as well as coal in producing energy and exported the device to Russia, Mongolia, Vietnam and Myanmar. This meant that some of the farmer-innovators had set-up their own production units/company to manufacture their device and sell in the national or local markets. Five of them had setup their own company for diffusion of the innovation. One innovator, having innovated the technique of charcoal-making by using agriculture waste and forest residue, could sell 1,000 tons of charcoal every year and earned a good income. An innovator in Hunan Province sold his patent on energy saving stove with water heating function to a company. Another innovator of Jiangsu Province, innovated a device to be fitted on the stove, so that it will automatically switch-off the stove when the pan was taken-off by the chef and re-ignite it when the pan was put back on the stove. This device saved cooking energy and was purchased by 10 hotels/ restaurants in Changzhou city. These are the efforts made by the individual innovator himself/herself in diffusing his/her innovation.

There were, however, a few instances of government support in the diffusion of innovation. In case of a particular innovator, organizations related to three levels of government, the prefectural city, county and township government, together gave RMB 5,000 as seed capital for starting the production of the innovation.

Similarly, in Henan province, a farmer obtained start-up capital from Jiaozuo City Science and Technology Bureau, for starting the production of the straw gasifier. In another case, the local government gave financial support to market an energy saving stove, innovated by an innovator in Shandong Province.

Devices for Uprooting, Gathering and Efficiently Disposing Straw and Stalk

The use of biomass for domestic energy use in rural areas would work, only if the biomass is collected in efficient ways. If all of agricultural waste is not used, then it needs to be disposed of. The most common traditional method was to burn it, since it could not be returned back to the field; where if buried at shallow depth in the field, it would damage the soil productivity and make the land unsuitable for the next cropping season. If this agriculture waste is allowed to be piled up, along the side of the fields, then it will rot and attract pests and insects, which would damage the standing crops. There was indeed a problem of disposal of this waste. In all, 18 innovators in the database of 97 have worked on innovations that dealt with all these concerns of the farmers. Geographic distribution of these innovations are: Anhui (3 innovations), Hebei (2), Henan (4), Hubei (1), Inner Mongolia (1), Jiangsu (4), and one each in Shandong, Shanxi and Xinjiang Uygur Provinces. In the database, only one innovation was in 1996. All other innovations were after 2000. One innovation each was carried out in 2002, 2003, 2004, 2006, 2007, 2008, and 2013. There were 3 innovations which were completed in 2009, 4 in 2011, and 2 in 2012.

The innovations include: (i) devices to efficiently bury the agriculture waste deep down in the earth and six innovators innovated such devices and (ii) devices to uproot stalk, cut it or pulverize it for use as feed in the gasifiers, some attached to the harvesters and some not. Twelve innovators had engaged with these types of innovations.

Ten of these innovators had applied for patent and obtained them. In fact, one innovator from Jiangsu, who had innovated a device to bury the waste deep in the earth, had applied for five patents on the devices he had innovated. Two innovators had applied for patents at the time this database was created. One innovator of Anhui Province, plans to mass produce his device to bury the agriculture waste deep inside the earth and use the land for replanting another crop during the year. Two farmer innovators, one in Hunan and one in Hubei, decided to help local farmers with their device that assisted in pulverizing the waste. Interestingly, a farmer in Xinjiang Uygur Province set-up his own agricultural machinery plant to manufacture his innovation. While, in majority of the cases, all the efforts of patenting and diffusion by the farmer-innovators has been their own, only one case from amongst the database that we have, had obtained government support. Two farmers who had innovated on a device to bury deep the agriculture waste, obtained financial and policy support from the county agricultural committee, S&T Bureau, Agricultural Machinery Bureau and Huang Cheng town government.

Innovations in Agriculture Machinery

Six farmers have innovated in agriculture machinery. Their innovations are: multi-funcional machines with rotary tillage, fertilizing and sowing functions; multi-functional harvester (2 innovations); a machine to cut rape-seed when it is 70 per cent ripened and harvesting them after drying for five days; a seeding (sowing) machine that is useful after the straw is returned back to the field and other used for planting tomatoes. Two of these innovations each are from Hebei and Anhui Provinces, and one each from Hubei and Shandong Provinces; completed in 2004, 2005, 2010, 2011 and 2013. One innovation did not have information regarding the year of completion of innovation.

Other Uses of Straw

Five farmer innovators found other use of straw such as making straw board with straw waste (2 innovations); making disposable chopsticks with residues of bamboo and timber; wheat straw painting and making of tiles from straw and stalk. All of them were patented. One of the patents is used by more than 10 companies. Two innovators are from Henan, two from Jiangsu and one from Sichuan. One farmer of Henan Province, created biomass pellets as feed for animals, so as to reduce the biomass waste.

Use of Biomass for Mushroom Production

Two innovators, one of whom is Gao Dedian, whose case is discussed at length in this book (Chapter 6), have innovated the technique of using straw as substrate for mushroom production. Gao belongs to Hunan Province and the other farmer belongs to Henan Province. Their innovations were done in 2010 and 2011 respectively. None of them have patented their innovations, but one of them (Mr. Gao Dedian) has obtained a trademark and set up a cooperative to produce mushrooms using straw.

Biogas Plant Innovation

Three farmers have innovated biogas plant. One has improved the technique of biogas production (Hebei in 2007), another has innovated automatic biogas (Shandong in 2010) and the third one has constructed a biogas digester on ground (Inner Mangolia in 2008). Only one of them, the first one, has patented the technique. Other two innovations are widely used locally without the innovator patenting it.

Conclusion

This chapter shows that there have been tremendous local efforts in rural China to innovate, with regards to every technology, related to agricultural production and biomass use. These are largely individual farmer's efforts with very little support in training and financing available from the government. The farmer-innovator has been on his own (these are largely males), who have tirelessly, diligently, pursued their love for innovating or for finding a local solution for the problems that they have encountered. Government's help has come mainly at the time of innovation diffusion. The overall provisioning for public education and a policy of compulsory education up to class 9, along with continuous high economic growth of the country, has resulted in grassroots level creative energies being unleashed for innovating, so as to improve local living conditions in the rural areas. The GRIs have been higher in the less developed regions where new technologies through formal route have lower level of penetration as compared to the developed regions. However, these efforts have to be and can be harnessed and channelized for more sustainable solutions to diffusion of technology at the local level. GRIs will continue to be relevant for some time to come, given that China is undergoing transition from rural to urban economy and less developed regions are experiencing development.

While the process of developmental transition is underway, China has another important challenge of meeting the climate change commitments. This will require that not just industries, but also the households would meet these challenges. Individual households and enterprises will have to meet the climate change goals and for that adapt technologies for the purpose. The adaptation of technologies will also require local level innovations.

Use of biomass as an energy source is one of the goal of China's NDC. But, biomass as a resource is in varied form and with varied quality by different geographic regions. For example, the straw length and thickness can be different for different crops. If bamboo waste is reused then its thickness can vary. Dry regions can have biomass with less moisture content as compared to humid regions and so on. Therefore, biomass using technologies have to be flexible for adaptation at the local level. The adaptation will also require local innovations. Farmers' innovative instincts and initiatives will be useful in the transition to use of biomass as a renewable energy source as well as for economic activities such as mushroom production. Towards this goal, effective and relevant training programs, financing policies and mechanisms will be required along with continued positive environment of publicly funded education and infrastructure development.

NOTES

1. The source of the data is accessed on June 13, 2010 and given by the year in the table below:

Year	*Source:*
2010	http://www.sipo.gov.cn/ghfzs/zltj/gnwszzlsqzknb/shouquannianbiao2010/201101/t20110110_562655.html
2009	http://www.sipo.gov.cn/tjxx/2009.pdf
2008	http://www.sipo.gov.cn/tjxx/2008.pdf
2007	http://www.sipo.gov.cn/ghfzs/zltjjb/jianbao/year2007/b/b4.html
2006	http://www.sipo.gov.cn/ghfzs/zltjjb/jianbao/year2006/b/b4.html
2005	http://www.sipo.gov.cn/ghfzs/zltjjb/jianbao/year2005/b/b4.html
2004	http://www.sipo.gov.cn/ghfzs/zltjjb/jianbao/year2004/b/b4.html

2003	http://www.sipo.gov.cn/ghfzs/zltjjb/jianbao/year2003/b/b4.html
2002	http://www.sipo.gov.cn/ghfzs/zltjjb/jianbao/year2002/b/b4.html
2001	http://www.sipo.gov.cn/ghfzs/zltjjb/jianbao/2001/b/b4.html
2000	http://www.sipo.gov.cn/ghfzs/zltjjb/jianbao/2000/nb/b/b4.html
1999	http://www.sipo.gov.cn/ghfzs/zltjjb/jianbao/1985-1999/99/2.4.htm
1998	http://www.sipo.gov.cn/ghfzs/zltjjb/jianbao/1985-1999/98/2.4.htm
1997	http://www.sipo.gov.cn/ghfzs/zltjjb/jianbao/1985-1999/97/2.4.htm
1996	http://www.sipo.gov.cn/ghfzs/zltjjb/jianbao/1985-1999/96/2.4.htm
1995	http://www.sipo.gov.cn/ghfzs/zltjjb/jianbao/1985-1999/95/2.4.htm
1994	http://www.sipo.gov.cn/ghfzs/zltjjb/jianbao/1985-1999/94/2.4.htm
1993	http://www.sipo.gov.cn/ghfzs/zltjjb/jianbao/1985-1999/93/2.4.htm
1992	http://www.sipo.gov.cn/ghfzs/zltjjb/jianbao/1985-1999/92/2.4.htm
1991	http://www.sipo.gov.cn/ghfzs/zltjjb/jianbao/1985-1999/91/2.4.htm
1990	http://www.sipo.gov.cn/ghfzs/zltjjb/jianbao/1985-1999/90/2.4.htm
1989	http://www.sipo.gov.cn/ghfzs/zltjjb/jianbao/1985-1999/89/2.4.htm
1988	http://www.sipo.gov.cn/ghfzs/zltjjb/jianbao/1985-1999/88/2.4.htm
1987	http://www.sipo.gov.cn/ghfzs/zltjjb/jianbao/1985-1999/87/2.4.htm
1986	http://www.sipo.gov.cn/ghfzs/zltjjb/jianbao/1985-1999/86/2.4.htm
1985	http://www.sipo.gov.cn/ghfzs/zltjjb/jianbao/1985-1999/85/2.4.htm

ANNEXURES

Annexure 2.1

Variables of GRI Database

Background

(i) Name of the innovator
(ii) Age of the innovator
(iii) Sex of the innovator
(iv) Province of stay of the Innovator
(v) Basic education level
(vi) Tertiary/follow-up education level
(vii) Age at the time of first innovation
(viii) Occupation of innovator

Innovation Details

(i) Period during which innovation done (pre-1990, etc. – to link with policies)
(ii) Time taken to innovate
(iii) Innovation team (if any)
(iv) Innovation type/by sector or by product
(v) Number of innovations done by the individual
(vi) Relationship between the innovations of the individual
(vii) Innovation Motivation
(viii) Innovation Trigger

Innovation Environment

(i) Economic environment
(ii) Cultural environment—supporting study, innovation itself, and entrepreneurship for diffusion of innovation
(iii) Geographical environment
(iv) Transportation environment/access
(v) Policy environment—supporting innovation and entrepreneurship for diffusing innovation (how do we measure these?)
(vi) Technical support availability

Initial Conditions

(i) Type of skill
(ii) Availability of equipment(s)
(iii) Access to initial finance

Innovation Process

(i) Access to initial finance
(ii) Access to working capital
(iii) Development of relevant skills
(iv) Method of skill enhancement
(v) Any hardship such as jeers from society
(vi) Family support

Innovation Diffusion

(i) Extent of Diffusion
(ii) Channels of Diffusion
(iii) Application of Innovation
(iv) Trigger for commercial application of innovation (entrepreneurship using innovation)

Process of Entrepreneurship

(i) Finance for entrepreneurship
(ii) Skills for entrepreneurship
(iii) Equipment for entrepreneurship
(iv) Management skill
(v) Outcome of entrepreneurship

Annexure 2.2

Innovations to Use Agriculture Waste

Sl. No.	*Province/ Autonomous Region*	*Year of success*	*Reason for innovation as stated by innovator*	*Application of innovation*	*Innovation*
1.	Zhejiang	2003	A bulb which is lit, produces light and heat both, but heat is wasted. This innovation puts to use bulb's heat	Granted patent	Bulb stove which have bulbs fitted inside
2.	Guizhou	2005	Coal stove used had low efficiency	Granted patent	Energy saving stove using coal and biomass
3.	Henan	2005	Waste of straw and stalks that polluted environment	Granted patent, started a company, and product registered huge sale	Straw gasifier
4.	Henan	2005	On burning wheat straws, yellow smoke, which came out could be ignited. He realized that wheat straw has high energy content	City, county and township government together gave RMB 5,000 to the innovator as seed capital	Gasifier using wheat straw
5.	Henan	2005	Straw burning caused smoke, which is harmful to health	Products sold nationwide	Straw gasifier
6.	Henan	2005	Biomass burning had low heat and high pollution	Patented but no diffusion	Gasifier

(Contd.)

Sl. No.	Province/ Autonomous Region	Year of success	Reason for innovation as stated by innovator	Application of innovation	Innovation
7.	Hunan	2005	The furnace using kerosene and diesel, produced pollution and quick corrosion of the pipes inside.	NA	Electric furnace for steaming seafood
8.	Shandong	2005	Burning biomass wasted resources and damaged environment	Patented and used in the village	Big sized gasifier
9.	Shandong	2005	Traditional charcoal-making method destroyed vegetation; while agricultural and forestry residues were thrown away and wasted.	The innovator's factory could produce over 1,000 tons of charcoal annually.	Using straw and stalk to make charcoal
10.	Yunnan	2005	Using wood for cooking would damage environment	Local government gave financial support to sell the products	Energy saving stove
11.	Hebei	2006			Straw pellet heating stove
12.	Hebei	2006	Straws thrown away in fields after harvesting damaged fields and crops	Had applied for patent	Straw pellet heating stove
13.	Hebei	2006	Hobby	Granted patent, products are exported abroad	Bio-charcoal from straw
14.	Heilongjiang	2006		Currently applying for patent	Straw gas appliance
15.	Heilongjiang	2006	Biomass wasted and polluted	Not applied for patent	Gasifier that used animal waste, rotten leaves, feed and rice hull as feed

(Contd.)

Sl. No.	*Province/ Autonomous Region*	*Year of success*	*Reason for innovation as stated by innovator*	*Application of innovation*	*Innovation*
16.	Henan	2006	NA	Jiaozuo City Science and Technology Bureau encouraged him and supported him with start-up capital	Straw gasifier
17.	Hunan	2006	Heavy smoke caused by coal burning	Granted patent, product exported to Russia, Mongolia, Vietnam, and Myanmar	Gasifer which used both biomass and coal as fuel
18.	Jiangsu	2006	Tar is a big problem produced in straw gasification	Granted patent	Reducing tar using a chemical catalyst
19.	Liaoning	2006	The price of coal increased.	Granted patent in 2007, granted trademark and built a factory	Biomass boiler which could be used for heating and boiling water for bathing
20.	Zhejiang	2006	NA	NA	Gasifier using biomass feed
21.	Hunan	2007	The coal briquettes (called honeycomb coal) after burning have to be manually changed frequently, which can cause burns to the person changing them.	Granted patent and over 100 enterprises would like to cooperate with him	Automatic coal removal from multifunctional coal stove
22.	Shandong	2007	Traditional boiler which provide heating lacked multi-functionality	Granted patent for utility models	Multifunctional household boiler

(Contd.)

Sl. No.	Province/ Autonomous Region	Year of success	Reason for innovation as stated by innovator	Application of innovation	Innovation
23.	Shandong	2007	Straw burning not only polluted environment but also wasted resources	Granted patent	Cooking and heating stove using straw feed
24.	Beijing	2008	Traditionally people burnt coal in winter, heavy smoke; large coal consumption but not warm enough	Granted patent and started a factory	Stoves with functions of cooking, heating room and bed
25.	Gansu	2008	Traditionally people burned coal in winter, heavy smoke; large coal consumption but did not warm enough	Currently applying five patents	Semi-gasifier which burns coal and could be used for both cooking and heating
26.	Hebei	2008	NA	Granted patent, widely accepted by the public	Biomass water heater
27.	Hebei	2008	Straw and stalk burning pollute environment and waste resources.	In 2009, granted trademark.	Environmental protection and energy-saving stove for cooking and heating
28.	Hebei	2008	Biomass wasted; coal price increase requiring search for alternative	Applied for patent but unsuccessful	Gasifier
29.	Hebei	2008	The prices of coal and natural gas increased. Traditional stoves produced heavy smoke.		Energy saving stove
30.	Inner Mongolia	2008	Interest generated from watching television program	Applied for patent	Gasifier using briquettes and animal manure

(Contd.)

Sl. No.	*Province/ Autonomous Region*	*Year of success*	*Reason for innovation as stated by innovator*	*Application of innovation*	*Innovation*
31.	Shandong	2008	Smoke from stove	Patented	Smoke-less stove
32.	Shandong	2008	Interest generated by reading information on briquettes from internet	NA	Honey comb coal (briquettes) of straw and stalk
33.	Tianjin	2008	The stoves are not energy saving	Has applied for patent	Gasifier
34.	Guizhou	2009	NA	Mass produced and sold on the market	Energy-saving stove
35.	Hebei	2009	Biomass were wasted in the village	Set up a small workshop and products sold locally	Stove
36.	Jilin	2009	Heavy smoke while cooking	Set up a company	Smokeless stove
37.	Shaanxi	2009	The mud-stove used traditionally was difficult to make and use	Granted patent of utility model. He set up a small workshop, produced and sold to the local farmers	Energy saving stove connecting with bed
38.	Sichuan	2009	Straw and stalk burning produced combustible gas	Granted patent	Straw gasifier
39.	Anhui	2010	Straws and stalks were wasted, which also polluted environment	Granted patent	Biomass gasifier
40.	Hubei	2010	Traditional gasifier produced heavy smoke; pipe would be blocked	Granted patent and built a factory in 2010	Filter in gasifier so that the pipe is not blocked

(*Contd.*)

Sl. No.	Province/ Autonomous Region	Year of success	Reason for innovation as stated by innovator	Application of innovation	Innovation
41.	Hunan	2010	NA	Applied for patent	Multifunctional water heater
42.	Jilin	2010	Heavy smoke from old stoves	Granted patent	Energy saving stove
43.	Jilin	2010	Smoke from traditional stoves	Granted patent	Energy saving stove
44.	Shandong	2010	To develop biomass energy as encouraged by the government	Mass produced for market	Biomass gasified heating stove
45.	Shandong	2010	Got the news of briquettes from newspaper	More than 70 per cent village households used this innovation	Straw briquetting machine
46.	Hebei	2011	No place to keep straw in the room for heating purpose in winter	Used by local people	Cellar created to keep and burn straw leading to floor heating
47.	Henan	2011	Heavy smoke caused by straw-burning	Granted patent	Making charcoal with straw and stalk
48.	Hunan	2011	Low heating efficiency of the farmer used stoves and heavy smoke.	Granted patent	High efficiency, energy saving stove
49.	Hunan	2011	Wood and biomass burning wasted resources and polluted environment	Granted patent and sold the patent to a company	Energy saving stove with water heating function
50.	Jiangsu	2011	Energy wasted while cooking when chef takes off the pan from stove for adding materials in pan	Granted patent, over 10 hotels and restaurants in Changzhou used this	A device on stove that will automatically switch off stove when the pan

(Contd.)

Sl. No.	Province/ Autonomous Region	Year of success	Reason for innovation as stated by innovator	Application of innovation	Innovation
				innovation	taken-off by the chef and re-ignites when pan put on stove.
51.	Jiangxi	2012	Smoke, low cooking efficiency, and used coal that was too expensive	Adopted by the local people	Bio-fuel saving stove
52.	Yunnan	2012	Traditionally used wood as cooking fuel, which had to be collected from mountains, cutting trees caused deforestation, inefficient use of wood and heavy smoke in house	Set up a company	Energy saving stove for cooking
53.	Yunnan	2012	Low heating efficiency of the farmer used stoves, heavy smoke	Granted patent, cooperated with local company for production	Environment friendly stove
54.	Zhejiang	2012	Extended duration of inhaling smoke from the gasifier damaged individual health	Granted patent, helped others modify stoves	Commercial infrared energy-saving stove with high firing
55.	Guangdong	2013	NA	Granted patent, promoted in whole China	Stove using liquid fuel
56.	Hebei	2013	NA		Wall-hanging straw gasifier stove
57.	Heilongjiang	2013	Heating all the rooms by using heating units was expensive, because of high	Welcomed by the local people	Hot blast stove

(*Contd.*)

Sl. No.	Province/ Autonomous Region	Year of success	Reason for innovation as stated by innovator	Application of innovation	Innovation
			cost of such stoves and use of coal that had become expensive		
58.	Heilongjiang	2013	It is difficult in villages with one floor accommodation to achieve sufficient heating in winter	Granted patent for utility models	A new stove attached with a kang and a pipe that sends hot blast to neighbouring rooms, creating a central heating type unit
59.	Henan	NA	Inspired by the formation principle of coal	NA	Using straw and stalk to make coal
60.	Jiangsu	NA	Low heating efficiency of stove	Granted patented	Energy saving stove
61.	Jilin `	NA	Increasing prices of coal and gas, burning wood damaged environment	Not applied for patent	Gasifier
62.	Shaanxi	NA	Hoped to burn biomass gas just like burning coal gas	Granted patent	Biomass gasifier
63.	Anhui	2010	NA	The innovator plans to mass produce his innovation	Machine to return straw back to the field and then sow
64.	Anhui	2011	Straw waste is generally burnt but it creates pollution. If left on field it affects multi-cropping. Straw waste has to be disposed of	Granted patent	Straw uprooting and crushing machine

(Contd.)

Sl. No.	*Province/ Autonomous Region*	*Year of success*	*Reason for innovation as stated by innovator*	*Application of innovation*	*Innovation*
65.	Anhui	2011	The available pulverizer could not pulverize stalk immediately and return waste to field. Another machine to pull stubble was also required, which was expensive	Granted patent	Two machines invented: (i) warhead type straw uprooting machine and (ii) pulverizer
66.	Hebei	2012	Traditionally, straw is cut and then put in the earth (called returning back to field). Machines could not do that thoroughly and some stalks would remain standing and had to be uprooted manually	it could be used in breeding, mushroom production and straw power generation	Machine can collect stalk and straw totally for use as silage (moist fodder for cattle) or mushroom production
67.	Hebei	2008	Pulverized straw and stalk had to be transported manually	Granted patent	Straw pulverizer that can automatically collect straw, cut it and transport
68.	Henan	2009	All wheat straws were left in fields after harvesting. Manual collection wasted time and energy	Granted patent	Wheat and rice harvester with straw bundling function
69.	Henan	2003	Biomass which was burnt and discarded everywhere polluted environment. He wanted to change the situation	Granted patent as utility model	Small sized straw returning machine
70.	Henan	2004	NA	Granted patent	High efficient straw pulverizer

(Contd.)

Sl. No.	Province/ Autonomous Region	Year of success	Reason for innovation as stated by innovator	Application of innovation	Innovation
71.	Henan	2006	Not easy for the farmers to take biomass to other places for crushing	Welcomed by the farmers	Crushing function added to harvester
72.	Hubei	2013	Farmers were troubled with manual corn threshing and corn stalk harvesting in the past	Helped farmers to harvest stalks and corn for free	Mechanical corn thresher with corn-husking function, straw and stalk harvester
73.	Inner Mongolia	2007	Farmers need to return straws back to fields and at the same time improve soil fertility	Applied for patent	Machine to bury straw deep in the field efficiently
74.	Jiangsu	2012	Straw waste is generally burnt but it creates pollution. If left on field it affects multi-cropping. Straw waste has to be disposed of	Applied for patent	Machine to bury straw and stalk into the earth
75.	Jiangsu	2011	Farmers need to return straws back to fields and at the same time improve soil fertility	Got financial and policy support from the county agricultural committee, S & T Bureau, Agricultural Machinery Bureau and Huang Cheng town government	Machine to bury straw deep in the field efficiently
76.	Jiangsu	2009	Traditional machines used old technology and difficult to operate for returning straw to fields	Granted five patents	Two machines to bury straw deep in the field; one in dryland and one in wet paddy fields

(Contd.)

Sl. No.	Province/ Autonomous Region	Year of success	Reason for innovation as stated by innovator	Application of innovation	Innovation
77.	Jiangsu	2009	Problem of cleaning fields of stalks, as burning them prohibited by local government	NA	Added pulverizer to a harvester
78.	Shandong	2011	Not easy for the farmers to collect cotton stalks	Granted patent	Cotton stalk harvester with crusher function
79.	Shanxi	2002	Difficult to collect wheat stubbles through traditional machines. Required manual removal. Burning being prohibited, these stalks could not be burnt. If wheat stubbles remained, multi-cropping is not possible	Granted patent and innovation used in Ruicheng Feng Wang Company	Self-propelled small wheat straw collecting machine
80.	Xinjiang Uygur	1996	Existing crusher had low efficiency and crushing quality was bad	Granted patent. Set up an agricultural machinery plant	Straw pulverizer
81.	Anhui	2004	In the past, agricultural machinery were of one single size and function and different machines had to be used for different functions	Granted patent, set up a factory	Multifuncional machine with rotary tillage, fertilizing and sowing functions
82.	Hebei	2010	Harvester without crusher resulting in low efficiency	Granted patent, sold widely in China	Multifunction harvester
83.	Hebei	2011	Harvester without crusher resulting in low efficiency	Granted patent and cooperated with a company for production	Multifunction harvester

(*Contd.*)

Sl. No.	Province/ Autonomous Region	Year of success	Reason for innovation as stated by innovator	Application of innovation	Innovation
84.	Hubei	2005	To make money	This technology has been promoted and applied in Jingzhou City, which is the main producing area of rape-seed for oil	Cutting rape-seed when it is 70 per cent ripened and harvesting them after drying for five days
85.	Anhui	NA	After straw returned to the field, the seeding machines were often blocked while sowing	Supported by the local government to install this device in the sowing machines of local farmers	Sowing machine which is suitable for seeding after straw returning to the field
86.	Shandong	2013	Traditional straw reactor technology wasted time and energy	NA	Planting tomatoes with straw reactor (using micro-organism to transform straws into high purity CO_2, heat, disease-resistant micro-organism spores and organic nutrient, which would strengthen photosynthesis and promote the growing of tomatoes)
87.	Henan	NA	In the past, straws and stalks were burned directly or thrown away, which polluted environment. Famers had to	NA	Multifunctional biomass pellet feed of wheat straw, cotton stalk,

(*Contd.*)

Sl. No.	Province/ Autonomous Region	Year of success	Reason for innovation as stated by innovator	Application of innovation	Innovation
			spend more money to buy feed for pig and cattle-raising.		broomcorn stalk, and other crop stalks for animals
88.	Henan	2006	Straws and stalks were thrown away, which not only polluted environment but also wasted resources	Has been used by over 60 real estate companies in Zhengzhou and Xuchang City	Straw board making with straw waste
89.	Henan	NA	Straw and stalk were thrown away, which polluted environment and wasted resources	Granted patent	Production method and machine for making disposable chopsticks using residues of bamboo and timber
90.	Jiangsu	2005	The innovator learned that wheat straw painting was a long-lost palace handicraft of Sui and Tang Dynasty. He wanted to revive it	Granted patent	Wheat straw painting
91.	Jiangsu	2009	In the past, people made tiles out of earth, which damaged earth	Granted patents	A new tile made from straw and stalk
92.	Sichuan	1994	Biomass burned and damaged the air—in rural China 0.6 billion tons of straw produced but only 20 per cent utilised as fodder, rest wasted or burnt	Patented, widely used by more than 10 companies	Straw and stalk board

(Contd.)

Sl. No.	Province/ Autonomous Region	Year of success	Reason for innovation as stated by innovator	Application of innovation	Innovation
93.	Henan	2010	To make money	Got trademark and set up cooperative	Mushroom production with straw
94.	Hunan	2011	High price of cotton shell increased the cost of mushroom production		Using smashed cotton stalks as substrate for mushroom production
95.	Hebei	2007	Biogas digester was small, produced less gas, high cost, not easy to add and take out materials	Patented, more than 300 famer households used	Improved technique for biogas production
96.	Inner Mongolia	2008	Traditional biogas digesters are under-ground and difficult to operate	Local people widely used	This biogas digester can be installed on land surface
97.	Shandong	2010	Traditional biogas plants had manual feeding, mixing and discharging	Over 200 biogas tanks have been built in nearby villages	Automatic biogas plant

3
Biomass Utilization Policy and Implementation Mechanism

Biomass is an important economic resource in rural China. In particular, it is an important renewable energy source due to its continued use in rural households for heating and cooking (See Chapter 2). Biomass is, therefore, not only useful in improving rural living conditions but also in saving consumption of non-renewable energy sources. It is directly used as an energy source or indirectly as input for renewable energy. Biomass sale also enhances incomes of rural households. It has also been used as raw materials for production activities such as mushroom cultivation (Chapter 6). Its use will lead to reducing local environmental pollution as the biomass exists as waste from agriculture, plantations and forests, in the form of dung of animals and lastly of human wastes. However, utilization of biomass for various purposes require appropriate technology application, which is the key to rural transformation. In all, biomass utilization contributes towards equitable and sustainable development of national economy. Therefore, since 1980s, the Chinese government has been paying attention to new technology development and diffusion of biomass utilization, introducing a series of laws, regulations, policies and programs and carrying out a number of biomass utilization projects.

Besides, the Chinese government also has to fulfil the NDC commitments for climate change and also reduce the local air pollution. Chinese cities in particular are one of the most polluted cities in the world, with four of her cities figuring in the top 20 most polluted cities in the world in PM2.5. Incidentally, all four are located in Hebei Province which encircles Beijing city! Amongst the top most polluted cities in PM2.5, there are seven Chinese cities, and all of them are in Hebei Province.[1] Hence, pollution control measures, energy saving measures and environment regeneration measures have become incumbent in China, not just in the urban areas but also in the rural areas. Burning of biomass in the rural areas can also induce air pollution in the cities. This chapter presents the environmental legislation as a macro context within which the case studies in the subsequent chapters are placed.

Relevant Laws

There are four categories of laws that govern wide-ranging biomass utilization in China. These relate to (i) environmental protection and control, (ii) air pollution prevention, (iii) energy saving and (iv) promoting renewable energy (Table 3.1). Generally, relevant laws are first passed by the Standing Committee of the National People's Congress and then decreed by the President of the People's Republic of China (PRC).

The first law—the Air Pollution Prevention and Control Law of the PRC, which was first enacted in 1987 and revised in 2000 and 2015, aims at improving air quality. In 1989, The Environment Protection Law of the PRC was enacted for the purpose of protecting and improving living and ecological conditions, preventing and controlling pollution and protecting people's health. It was revised in 2014. The third important law that followed was the Energy Saving Law of the PRC, enacted in 1997 and then revised in 2008, for promoting energy saving in the society at large, increasing efficiency of energy use and protecting the environment. Since saving energy *per se* does not suffice, there is also a need to promote Renewable Energy, for which the national government enacted The Renewable Energy Law in 2005.

Both, the Air Pollution Prevention and Control Law and the Environment Protection Law highlight the regulatory responsibility of all levels of governments, emphasize information disclosure by the enterprises and organizations, public participation, total quantity control of pollutants, inter-district pollution prevention, pollution monitoring and early warning systems. In addition, these laws also encourage science and technology enhancement and knowledge dissemination related to environment protection among the general masses.

Table 3.1: Laws related to Biomass Utilization

Year	*Title*	*Purpose*	*Relevant content*	*Notes*
1987	Air Pollution Prevention and Control Law of the PRC	To prevent and control air pollution, protect and improve living and ecological environment, safeguard public health and promote sustainable development.	It prohibits burning of agricultural straw in densely inhabited areas. The state encourages and supports adoption of advanced or applicable technologies to make a comprehensive use of crop straws, fallen leaves and weeds, and develop and use biomass energies like methane.	Revised in 1995, 2000 and 2015
1989	Environmental Protection Law of the PRC	To protect and improve living and ecological environment, prevent and control pollution and other public nuisances, safeguard public health, promote socialist modernization construction.	Strengthen scientific and technological research and development for environmental protection; develop national environmental quality standards; supervise and administer environmental protection work. The revised version strengthens prevention and control of rural pollution and increases penalty to enterprises which violate laws and regulations and discharge pollutants.	Revised in 2014
1997	Energy Conservation Law of the PRC	To promote energy conservation in the whole society, enhance energy utilization efficiency, protect and improve environment, guarantee national economic and social development, and meet the need of people's living.	The State encourages and supports development and utilization of new energy resources and renewable energy resources. The revised version lays emphasis on vigorous development of marsh gas, and popularization of biomass, solar power, wind power and other renewable energy in rural areas.'	Revised in 2008
2005	Renewable Energy Law of the PRC.	To promote the development and utilization of renewable energy, increase the supply of energy, improve the structure of energy, safeguard the safety of energy, protect environment and realize a sustainable economic and social development.	It encourages development and utilization of renewable energy in rural areas[2].	Revised in 2009

Source: Compiled by authors.

Air Pollution Prevention and Control

This law was the first to be enacted amongst the four relevant laws. The law was revised in the year 2000 and it emphasized the emission control of sulfur dioxide, which was important for reducing coal-smoke pollution.

The law was further revised in the year 2015 and focused on improving air quality, reducing pollution from the sources, intensifying government's role in pollution prevention and control, capping pollution emissions and highlighting the new technology development for and application in reducing haze. In the recent years, haze pollution has increased nationwide, resulting in the regionalization of air pollution. It has, therefore, become necessary that a mechanism for inter-regional pollution prevention and control were set up in the country. For example, burning of biomass in rural areas can create haze in the cities and hence, the air pollution has to be controlled at source, both in the rural and the urban areas.

The newly revised law clearly indicates the tasks to be undertaken for air pollution control in the key areas, such as taking specific measures on reducing step-by-step the usage of coal and setting up cooperative controlling of pollutants. It also prescribed that China should put into practice target-oriented responsibility and evaluation system of air pollution control.

Environment Protection Law

This law was first enacted in 1989 and was revised for the first time in 2014. The revised law is considered the most rigorous environment protection law in the history of the country. This revised law, has made the degree of punishment for illegal environmental activities very stringent. The company owners can be detained for 15 days if they refuse to complete the environmental impact assessment or ignore warnings to stop persistent pollution[3]. The law has specific stipulations for eliminating and controlling air pollution, especially haze, which is now found in most cities in China.

This amended law has, firstly, endowed the environmental protection departments with law enforcement power and increasing punishment on damaging the environment. The previously enacted environmental laws were not stringent enough with regard to penalties, i.e. penalties were low for violation, while the costs of compliance were high, resulting in the violators preferring to pay the penalty than abide by the law. Hence, in spite of environmental protection laws and regulations, the environmental quality worsened across the country. The new amendments have made the punishment more stringent. It is expected that the law will help in environment protection.

The amended environment protection law lays supervision responsibility on the government organizations. Similar to the air pollution prevention and control law, the environmental protection law, sets rules for local government's responsibility for the local environmental quality. It also puts into practice target-oriented responsibility and evaluation system of environmental protection. It also states that if the competent authority fails to implement the law there will be administrative punishment of the concerned official(s) from the higher level of government. The promotion or demotion of the administrative staff of the competent authority is linked to their performance on environmental supervision responsibilities. The negligence in performance of duties could also result in the officer being forced to resign from office. The definition of negligence is very wide; it includes any cover-up activities, failure to take decision on suspension of production or closure of the polluting activity in pursuant of law, granting of false permits to firms to start production, tempering with the data, and misappropriation of the environmental fines. The onus of monitoring environmental pollution has been strongly passed on to the local government officials of the concerned department.

Moreover, the amended law provides for public service and protection of rural environment. The law encourages the application of new environment protection technologies for agricultural environment protection; strengthening the monitoring and early warning system of agricultural pollution sources; coordinating relevant departments to take measures to prevent the occurrence and deterioration of soil pollution, desertification, salinization, impoverishment, and ground subsidence; preventing and controlling vegetation damage, soil erosion, water eutrophication, water depletion, species extinction and other ecological imbalances, and promote integrated plant pest management in rural China. The law also states that the county and township governments should provide better public services for comprehensive improvement in rural environment.

Since air pollution is a major component in environment, the laws of environment protection and air pollution prevention and control share many similarities such as intensifying cross-regional pollution control and specifying the role of government in environment protection.

Energy Saving Law

This law was first enacted in 1997 and was revised in 2008. Energy saving is a basic national policy of China. It is important for energy security and now more important for meeting the NDC. The State highly promotes efficient utilization of energy for the sustainable development and climate change related reduction. Biomass is an important energy source. The State popularizes energy saving heating and cooking stoves in rural areas and plantation of energy crops and fuel wood in non-farmland.

Rural energy saving is an important priority in China. The law reinforces to increase financial inputs in developing and applying new technologies in energy saving in agricultural production and rural living. The governments from county level and above are expected to act according to local conditions, put into use the integrated energy development methods and focus on comprehensive utilization of energy.

Renewable Energy Law

This law was promulgated in 2005, implemented in 2006 and in four years time, in 2009, amended keeping in view the need to upscale renewable technology use in the country. The law was enacted to promote use of renewable energy sources to increase energy supply, improve the energy supply structure and reduce dependence on non-renewables such as coal so as to protect environment, meet NDC commitments for climate change goals and continue with economic growth but in a sustainable way. The Chinese government now encourages and supports vigorous development of renewable energy, such as marsh gas, biomass, geothermal, ocean, solar and wind energy and various other renewable energy sources. The law states that the State should encourage clean and efficient development and utilization of the biofuels. It also stresses that the State should encourage development and cultivation of energy crops. It also emphasizes that if the gas and heat produced using biomass resources comply with network technology and standards, enterprises could supply biomass energy to the networks. However, the law does not consider low-efficiency stoves which use straw, firewood and animal waste as fuel, as renewable energy sources. Although hydro-power is a renewable energy, setting up a unit requires special approval from the State Council, on account of it having larger ecological and social consequences. The 2009 Amendment has established the Renewable Energy Development Fund to support the costs of renewable energy production.

Important aspect under the law is to facilitate expansion of markets for renewable energy. The responsibility of the State is to encourage setting up of economic entities of various ownerships to exploit renewable energy sources. The energy departments of the local governments are given power to exploit available renewable energy resources in their jurisdiction, draw plans for the same, get these plans approved from the relevant level of the government and make plans public for wider participation by the people and firms.

The law envisages that the State should set up a fund for promoting renewable energy, with an aim at technology research, standard setting and new technology and product demonstration. The fund supports daily use energy projects in rural or pastoral areas, resource exploration, setting up and evaluation of information system and localization of equipment production for renewable energy utilization. Of importance for the rural areas is the State support for exploitation of bio-fuel and development of energy crops. It also supports exploitation of renewable energy in the rural areas.

For promoting development and utilization of renewable energy, the State encourages the application of renewable energy technologies and products in rural areas; requires local government to provide financial support for the projects of bio-gas, household solar, small-scale wind energy etc.

Relevant Policies and their Evolution

Corresponding to the national laws, policies related to the utilization of biomass also fall within the purview of the four areas of air pollution control, environmental protection, energy saving and renewable energy development. These four areas of policies supplement each other, jointly facilitate the technology research and development and its application. More specifically, policies are related to new countryside energy construction, resource conservation and comprehensive utilization activities, sustainable energy development, sustainable development, science and technology application, new rural construction, biomass industry development, comprehensive utilization of crop straw and stalk etc. Policy-making departments include the State Council, National Development and Reform Committee and its predecessor State Planning Commission, State Economic and Trade Commission, Ministry of Science and Technology etc.

After economic reforms in late-1970s, the fast economic development led to high-energy consumption in the production process. Thus, in 1980s, the State realized the strategic importance of energy saving production processes and included lower consumption of resource and energy and clean production as an integral part of China's industrial policy. However, at that time, the technologies of biomass power generation and biomass fuel ethanol production had not been developed. Thus, energy production was mainly for the purpose of guaranteeing rural energy supply and improving ecological environment. The State promoted the development and application of simple and useful technologies, such as biogas and firewood saving stoves.

The importance of energy saving in the process of manufacturing and economic growth in China was also supported by the State Economic and Trade Commission way back in 1994, when it mandated that the economic units transit from extensive to intensive production processes to save energy and increase efficiency. This led to increase in demand for development of renewable energy sources.

Accordingly, in 1999, the State Planning Commission and the Ministry of Science and Technology (MOST), gave notice to accelerate the localization process of renewable energy power generation, such as biomass energy generation. The projects were supported by the State fiscal construction funding and the program of national S&T key projects.

Towards the end of the century, there was awareness about the seriousness of air pollution caused by biomass burning for rural energy needs. There were also some serious accidents of fire due to biomass burning. For the purpose of protecting ecological environment, preventing burning of straws and to maintain public security, in 1999, the State Environmental Protection Administration (SEPA) introduced the policy 'Management Approaches of Biomass Burning Prohibition and Comprehensive Utilization', which was based on the law of environment protection and the law of air pollution prevention and control. This policy mandated that the straw burning in certain areas, such as places near airport, main lines of communication, and high-tension transmission line would not be allowed. Instead, the State popularized the technologies of straw returning into field, straw feed, straw gasification etc. In Chapter 2, where overall situation with regard to biomass related innovations has been discussed, we have listed number of innovations in machines to return straw to the field. Prohibition of straw burning and biomass's comprehensive utilization became important work of environmental protection by governments at all levels. The impacts of the policy were strictly assessed and measured in government target-oriented responsibility system. The policy provided for laying penalty of RMB 20 for those who burned straw in prohibited areas. The policy document "Management Approaches of Biomass Burning Prohibition and Comprehensive Utilization" stated that the straw burning would be strictly controlled. But, in practice, in its actual implementation, the measures suggested for violation of the policy were very weak; the penalty stated was just RMB 20, which was very little. The policy, therefore, did not have teeth, that is the policy was very weak and had no effective impact on the violators. Also, the SEPA did not have law enforcement power.

The Chinese government started paying equal attention to new energy development and energy conservation with regard to energy utilization. Renewable energy is green, environmental friendly and sustainable. There was a need for renewable energy development. This required that the State supported science and technology projects for the development of the renewable energy. In 1999, the State Planning Commission and the Ministry of Science and Technology (MOST), proposed to financially support Science and Technology (S&T) research projects for renewable energy power generation. In 2002, in its Sustainable Development Science and Technology Outline, MOST reiterated research and application of renewable energy technologies and emphasized the relationship of renewable energy development with global warming. Since then, many grassroots innovators who worked on biomass utilization research, received government financial support. These projects were supported by the government organizations of S&T bureaus, agricultural bureaus, environmental protection bureaus, etc. The farmers' research related to better and increased mushroom production, gasifiers, etc.; some of which have been discussed in the chapters in this book.

Earlier in this century, the State pursued the policy of New Village Construction, which took biomass utilization as a useful measure for beautifying the village. The new village construction movement in China laid thrust on not considering biomass as waste, but as a useful input for New Village Construction. New village construction refers to the rural people living in a neat and clean environment. Straws and stalk lying scattered across the village not only caused environmental pollution but was also a fire hazard, while contributing to wastage of useful raw materials. Since straw burning was not permitted due to air pollution laws, the New Village Construction program had to find solution to reuse biomass waste, in particular the straw and stalk wastes from agriculture. This led to the emergence of new energy technologies development and diffusion as a part of this program. The new, energy technologies which emerged were mainly related to biogas and biomass briquettes. As discussed in the first chapter, development and use of smokeless stoves in the rural areas had started way back in 1980s. This policy promoted farmer innovators to work on innovations on gasifiers, semi-gasifiers, biomass stoves, briquetting machines and so on. Farmer Liu Yongquan's innovations on gasifier and semi-gasifier, discussed hereinafter in the book have been supported by local government due to this policy.

Later on, under the national policy 'Action of Science and Technology Accelerating New Village Construction', MOST specified the priority areas for using biomass as raw materials for sustainable (circular) economy and stated to set up demonstration units. The action plan emphasized rural energy saving and research and application of ecological technologies. Gao Dedian's mushroom innovation activities discussed in the book received government support many times. These grants were a result of this policy.

The National Plan for Medium and Long Term Renewable Energy Development (2007-2020) was announced in 2007. The goals it set for 2020 were to produce and consume: (i) 50 million tons of biomass briquettes, (ii) 44 billion cubic metre of biogas and (iii) 10 million tons of biomass fuel ethanol. In its Guidance List of Industrial Restructuring, the National Development and Reform Commission (NDRC), reaffirmed that biomass briquettes fuel and biomass fuel ethanol were encouraged and supported by the State.

In 2008, straw burning was fairly common in rural China, causing air pollution, resultant traffic accidents, and wastage of resources. The State Council issued a document 'Opinions on Expediting Biomass Comprehensive Utilization'. The background for issuing this document was that a series of technologies of biomass utilization had matured, which provided a sound base for propelling biomass's comprehensive utilization. The technologies covered five areas of biomass use; as fertilizer, feed, raw material, fuel, and base stock. The logic of introducing this official document was to promote the application of the technologies to reach the goal of utilizing 80 per cent of the stalks and straws by 2015.

According to an important policy decision in 2008, for facilitating biomass application, the Ministry of Finance issued a document 'Interim Procedures of Fiscal Subsidy for Biomass Energy Utilization', subsidizing the companies producing biomass fuel briquettes, straw gasification, straw carbonization etc. This document is as per the basic framework of China's 'Biomass Energy Development Policy'[4]. The Biomass Energy Development Policy's legal basis is the Renewable Energy Law of the PRC. The Biomass Energy Development Policy provides for low-interest loans and tax relief. The tax relief pertains to refunding a certain proportion of Value Added Tax (VAT)—100 per cent in 2009 and 80 per cent in 2010—for products that comprehensively utilize (i) residues of logging and agriculture processing, (ii) small firewood, (iii) crop straw and (iv) bagasse[5].

The Biomass Energy Development Policy provides for number of front-end incentives: (i) feedstock based subsidy, (ii) straw subsidy for enterprises with a registered capital of more than 10 million RMB and whose straw energy utilization complies with the local straw comprehensive utilization planning and the amount of annual consumption of straw exceeds 10,000 tons; and (iii) fuel ethanol subsidy. The policy also provides for back-end incentives: (i) quota system in the fields of biomass power generation and bio-liquid fuel requiring power companies and oil companies to derive a certain portion of the energy from the biomass energy for the supply of electricity and fuel, thereby promoting market mechanism instead of complete dependence on the government and (ii) pricing mechanism for power and bio-ethanol.

The policy supports both, centralized system of biomass energy production such as biomass briquette boiler heating system as well as decentralized system such as rural household biogas project. Funds are made available for both under the policy. Taking a cue from this policy issued by the Central government, many provinces and cities issued similar policies.

In reality, due to the difficulties in collecting straws and consequent high transportation costs, many biomass utilization companies that were small-sized could not meet the standards laid out for financial support. Therefore, many companies provided fake invoices, false accounts and carried out fake sales to meet the government standards for financial support. Also, many farmers' cooperatives of straw utilization that were set up for the purposes of obtaining the policy support were in difficult situation. One important reason for their failure was that they could not get enough raw materials for production. The cooperatives that could survive were mainly because they were getting government grants for many other projects than for setting up straw cooperative. For example, more than 10 farmers' straw utilization cooperatives were set up in Changzhi city, Shanxi Province. Only Liu Haibin's Li Min (Chapter 5) cooperative survived due to the government financial support for such a demonstration cooperative and other science and technology projects.

Observing the problems mentioned above, the Biomass Energy Development Policy was suspended by the National Ministry of Finance. However, the provincial governments did not stop their financial support to the companies producing straw briquettes although at the national level the policy was discontinued. For instance, Hebei Province, neighbour to Beijing and Tianjin, facing huge pressure from the two cities to reduce CO_2 emission to their benefit, continued the policy of financial support to the cooperatives and rural households. Hebei Province provided support of RMB 150 for one ton briquette, even if the straw using enterprises were unable to meet the requirement of "registered capital of more than 10 million RMB and annual consumption of straw is more than 10,000 tons", as mentioned above as point (ii) in the policy.

In 2012, the State intensively introduced individual plans for energy, renewable energy, biomass energy and straw utilization as a part of the Twelfth Five Year Plan. For instance, the Twelfth Five Year Plan on Energy Development prioritized renewable energy development such as wind energy, solar power and biomass utilization. It set the target of setting up 200 green energy demonstrative counties and 1000 solar power pilot villages by 2015.

In January 2013, haze continuously and widely appeared in Beijing-Tianjin-Hebei region and around, which badly affected people's health and normal life. In order to effectively improve air quality, the State Council introduced Action Plan for Air Pollution Prevention and Control in September 2013. This Plan includes the most dramatic, comprehensive measures in history. It had thorough supporting measures and strict evaluation on performance. The action plan, for the first time, added a criterion of monitoring of the PM2.5 in the system of government officials' performance evaluation. In other words, instead of stating that the implementation of the Environmental Protection Law would be considered for the evaluation of the government officials, a specific criterion of monitoring the particulate matters in the ambient air was suggested. The action plan set the target and claimed that the air quality in China would certainly improve after five years' efforts. That is, by 2017, the concentration of PM10 would decrease by 10 per cent; that of PM2.5 concentration in Beijing-Tianjin-Hebei region would decrease by 25 per cent, in Yangtze River Delta by 20 per cent and in Pearl River Delta by 15 per cent.

China has been under pressure to reduce greenhouse gas emissions, reduce local pollution of air and water and to also meet energy security demand through addressing the energy resource constraint. Thus, in 2014, the State Council made Strategy Action Plan of Energy Development (2014-2020), accelerating revolution in energy production and consumption. Through this Action Plan, the State propelled construction of green energy county, town and village; develop renewable energy in rural areas according to local conditions; encouraged clean and efficient utilization of non-commercial energy and reinforce rural energy saving. The policies related to crop straw utilization have been given in Annexure 3.1.

Biomass Energy in the Twelfth Five Year Plan

The Twelfth Five-Year Plan states that by 2015, commercialization and large-scale utilization of biomass energy in electricity, heating and rural household energy consumption will be realized; the use of biomass energy instead of oil in transportation will be increased; and biomass utilization technology and major technical equipment capability will be enhanced. It states that some large biomass energy enterprises with strong technological innovation capabilities will emerge. The Plan also states that a relatively integral biomass energy industrial system will form.

Table 3.2: Key Indicators of Biomass Energy Development During 12th Five-Year Plan

Indicator	*Utilization*		*Annual Production Capacity*		*Standard Coal Equivalent (10,000 tons per year)*
	Number	*Unit*	*Number*	*Unit*	
Biomass power	1,300	GW	780	TWh	2,430
Biogas supply			220	100 million m^3	1,750
Biomass briquette	1,000	10,000 tons			500
Biomass liquid fuel					500
Total					5,180

Source: Twelfth Five Year Plan.

By 2015, the annual renewable energy consumption will reach 50 million tons of standard coal equivalents (TCE) (Table 3.2). The installed renewable energy capacity will reach 13 million KW. The annual electricity production will reach 78 billion KWh, annual biogas will reach 22 billion m^3, biomass briquette 10 million tons, and biomass liquid fuel 5 million tons of coal equivalence. A group of new industries having technologies that comprehensively use the biomass energy will be set up as demonstration projects.

Climate Action Plan

China has committed to peak its CO_2 emissions by 2030 and to make best efforts to peak earlier. It will increase non-fossil energy to 20 per cent of its energy consumption by 2030, which will require it to install 800 to 1,000 gigawatts (GW) in non-fossil capacity, equivalent to the entire current US generating capacity. She has also pledged RMB 20 million ($3.1 billion USD) to the South-South Climate Cooperation Fund to help developing countries address climate change. Other China climate commitments relate to carbon intensity, adaptation and forestry. Shift to renewable energy is an important component of achieving NDC. Bio-fuels are part of this effort.

On 30 June, 2015, the Chinese government submitted its Intended Nationally Determined Contribution (INDC), detailing its commitment to climate change mitigation and adaptation for the post-2020 period. Highlights of the INDC include specific goals such as[6]:

- To achieve peak carbon dioxide emissions by approximately 2030, or sooner as best efforts allow;
- To lower carbon dioxide emissions per unit of GDP by 60 per cent to 65 per cent from 2005 levels;
- To increase the share of non-fossil fuels in the primary energy mix to approximately 20 per cent;
- To increase the volume of forest stock by approximately 4.5 billion cubic metres over 2005 levels; and
- Continue to proactively adapt to climate change through: enhanced mechanism- and capacity-building; the effective management of climate change risks in sectors such as agriculture, forestry, and water resources and in regions including urban, coastal, and ecologically vulnerable areas; improved early warning and emergency response systems and disaster prevention and mitigation mechanisms.

Programs for Biomass Utilization and Energy

Program and its Implementation—Two Cases

The policy implementation is mainly through projects. A number of projects have been carried out to ease the shortage of rural energy since late 1970s. For example, the Ministry of Agriculture has set out and implemented the projects, such as "Promoting firewood saving stoves" and "Promoting household biogas". The Ministry of Water and Power took responsibility of the development of rural small hydropower and rural electrification pilots and demonstration projects in the counties. The Ministry of Forestry conducted the pilot project of "Planting Firewood". The former State Planning Commission, the State Agriculture Commission and the State Economy Commission carried out utilization of solar energy project (solar water heater, solar cookers, solar house etc.) in more than ten provinces and many other new energy demonstration projects were also put into practice, such as the use of wind power, geothermal utilization. Subsequently, in the course of the development of rural energy, the National Development and Reform Commission and the Ministry of Agriculture put up the projects of power supply and biogas supply for the farmers and fishermen in poverty-stricken areas. Later, these single-technology projects evolved into county-wide rural comprehensive energy construction projects, integrating different energy projects together.

Entering 21st century, China implemented several nation-wide projects, such as the "West Development" project and "New Village Construction" project. The National Energy Bureau, the Ministry of Finance and the Ministry of Agriculture jointly launched the project of "Green Energy Demonstration County" in 2011, supporting biomass gasification, and construction of rural energy service system etc. In this section, two programs of "Firewood-saving Stove Promotion" and "Pilot County Construction of Rural Energy Comprehensive Utilization" have been presented to explain how a program was designed and implemented.

Case 1: *Firewood-saving Stove Promotion Program*

Background

In the early 1980s, the rural energy in China was in short supply and at the same time, terribly wasted. The daily rural energy consumption was 250 million tons of biomass, 100 million tons of firewood (which could have even been used for purposes other than burning) and 50 million tons of raw coal. But, there were perennial fuel shortages for 2 to 3 months in each year in most of rural China and in some other areas, the fuel shortage lasted for even half a year. On the other hand, the biomass wastage was also huge. Old types of cook stoves were in use upto early 1980s in rural China. These stoves had just 10 per cent efficiency and wasted fuel equal to 100 million TCE[7]. Compare this amount with the total power generation in whole of China of 99 million TCE in 1981[8].The wastage of thermal energy sources too was humongous. Annual waste of thermal energy was equivalent to more than 100 million tons of standard coal equivalence. Energy shortage led to farmers making attempts to find any source of energy, which led them to cut trees, pull off the tree barks and dig roots causing serious environmental damage.[9]

The challenge to design energy saving cookstoves was taken up by the technical and scientific experts in partnership with the farmer-experts identified based on the cookstoves these farmers were using. More than one hundred types of firewood saving stoves were designed. These stoves were not only suitable for local conditions but had higher thermal efficiency rate (of 20 per cent) as compared to traditional stoves. Compared with traditional stoves, the new stoves could save about one-third to one-half of the firewood. Thus, the State Planning Commission and the Ministry of Agriculture decided to promote firewood saving stoves in China.

From 1983 to 1990, the firewood saving stoves were distributed for use in 7,368,200 households across 786 counties in China[10] through the Ministry of Agriculture's initiative. In addition, many provinces, municipalities and autonomous regions also had their own programs whose implementation process in the pilot counties was simplified. As a result, the total number of households using energy saving firewood saving stoves reached 129 million households accounting for 58.1 per cent of the total rural household of 222 million in China[11]. The large-scale of national promotion plan of firewood saving stoves was completed in 1990. After that, the project of promoting firewood saving stoves was integrated into the project of "County-wide rural energy comprehensive construction"of the Ministry of Agriculture.

Energy efficient cookstoves not only increased thermal efficiency of the stoves, but they saved firewood, reduced indoor air pollution and improved overall health of the household. In addition, it also saved the labor cost of collecting firewood and cooking time. After using firewood saving stoves, the phenomenon such as stealing coals and cutting down trees was decreased year by year.

Project Implementation

The project of "promoting firewood saving stoves" in China was initiated in 1982 by the State Planning Commission.[12] The Environment and Energy Department of Ministry of Agriculture coordinated the project implementation. The promotion of firewood saving stoves at the provincial level was coordinated by its rural energy office. In each pilot county, a rural energy leadership team was set up to promote the new stove application. Figure 3.1 shows the organization structure for the project implementation.

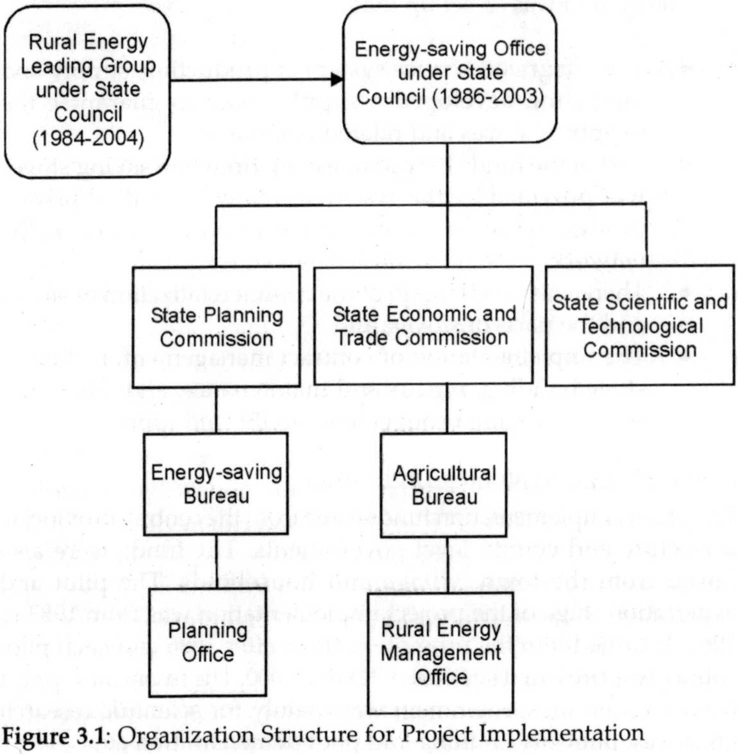

Figure 3.1: Organization Structure for Project Implementation

Nationwide project implementation of promoting firewood saving stoves needed a well-developed system that first dealt with manufacturing of technologically sound stoves, distribution of the stoves through sales networks, marketing the stoves, helping farmers to install stoves in their houses, giving demonstration of stove's functioning and then ensuring that the stoves worked in the household condition and were used.An elaborate system was set up which had three levels—county level, town level networks and installing teams. The county-level service system coordinated the project implementation in each pilot county. Town level service system bridged county level system and installing teams. Installing teams were responsible for installing stoves at the household level. The service networks at the county and town levels played the roles of providing service supports. The system contributed greatly to the project implementation and allowed thousands of rural households in China to use firewood saving stoves.

The system was so set up that:

- The integrated service system of production, supply and marketing developed a supply chain to guarantee the supply of stoves and related materials;
- Part of the funds for popularizing firewood saving stoves was provided by the system as many individual private producers, sellers, and service providers were in the network;
- There was acceleration of the commercialization of stoves and the parts of stoves; and
- The implementation of contract management, including stove building, repairs and maintenance, and other paid service provided convenience to the end users.

Financial Support and Its Application

The project implementation funds came from the central, provincial, prefecture and county level governments. The funds were also raised from the town, village and households. The pilot and exploration stage of the project implementation was from 1983 to 1985. It turned into the promotion stage after 1986 and each pilot county was provided support of RMB 25,000. The financial support from the Central Government was mainly for scientific research on stoves, publicity, training and pilot demonstration etc.

During the 1983-1990 period, the national government financially supported 786 pilot counties (Table 3.3), reaching out to 58.91 million rural households. The national government support came to RMB 37,000 per county and to RMB 0.49 per household. The central support was comparatively quite small and hence there would have been much more dependence on the local governments' support and the household contribution.

Table 3.3: National Financial Support to Energy Efficient Stoves, Over Time

Year	*Number of Pilot Counties*	*Number of Households Installing New Stoves (million households)*	*National Financial Support*		
			Total (RMB Million)	*Support to Each County (RMB 10,000)*	*Support to Each Household (RMB)*
1983	90	2.62	8.20	9.1	3.14
1984	200	11.03	8.29	4.1	0.75
1985	100	8.37	2.50	2.5	0.30
1986	97	9.90	2.40	2.5	0.24
1987	101	8.92	2.58	2.5	0.29
1988	96	10.01	2.40	2.5	0.24
1989	51	4.50	1.28	2.5	0.13
1990	51	3.56	1.28	2.5	0.36
Total	786	58.91	28.92	3.7	0.49

Source: Promoting Rural energy projects, http://max.book118.com/html/2015/1112/29302785.shtm, access on 20 June, 2016.

***Case 2:** Development of Rural Energy Comprehensive Utilization for Pilot County*

Project Introduction

From 1978 to 1983, in order to alleviate the shortage of energy in rural areas and the consequences of damaging the ecological environment, the Chinese government implemented several projects of promoting single energy technology in rural China. Such individual promotion projects of energy technologies were piecemeal type and were usually implemented at the household, village or town level. However, the related organizations lacked coordination and cooperation during project implementation. Therefore, improving rural energy supply sometimes could not go hand in hand with improving local ecological environment and economic situation. For example, if a small, rural hydropower plant was set up when the water availability was abundant. There was no organization to ensure that the water availability should not decline. Water availability can decline if there is deforestation in the upstream areas. But, since the forest department was not involved in the implementation of the small hydropower plant, it did not know about such a plant. Decline in water availability upstream would influence the actual functioning of the small hydropower station.

Therefore, from 1983 to 1986, the State Economic and Trade Commission worked together with the Ministry of Agriculture, Ministry of Forestry and Ministry of Water Resources to implement the pilot project of rural energy comprehensive development. A county was selected as a unit of project implementation. Three counties were selected as pilot counties. The comprehensive energy development project integrated many projects together, such as the project of overall agriculture development, rural electrification, small hydropower station construction project, minor drainage basin management, afforestation, township enterprises energy saving project and technology for poverty alleviation. Under the leadership of the county project leading-group, the project implementation was systematically planned to meet the objectives of economic and social development of the county.

During the 1986-1990 period, this project became MOST's key project, being implemented in twelve counties, each one having different components. A total of 12 different methods of rural energy comprehensive development were identified and modified. Besides, more than 80 matching technologies were developed. The new technologies and products development were aimed towards upgrading rural energy technologies, promoting these technologies through economies of scale and ultimately improving economic conditions and social well-being of the rural households.

From pilot stage, this project entered the stage of large-scale demonstration from 1991 onwards and lasted for 5 years, during which 138 counties (6 per cent of the total counties of China) were involved, covering about 8 billion population. The investment for the project mainly came from the local government and farmers. The State provided advanced technologies and training programs. By 2000, there had been 358 counties implementing comprehensive rural energy projects. The project not only explored the experience of energy development and utilization in China's rural areas, but also made great effects in promoting the local socio-economic development and improving the ecological environment (Wang, 2001: 1; Dai and Li, 2001).

Project Implementation

The core of the comprehensive construction of rural energy was to take energy, economy and ecology as an integrated system, that is, to strive towards sustainable development and not just focus on socio-economic developmentin rural areas. To successfully carry out the project, the following steps were necessary:

- Firstly, preparing a development plan that matched the objectives of local economic and sustainable development;
- Secondly, according to the plan, developing new energy technologies and promoting the application of energy-saving technologies with a focus on single technology or a set of integrated technologies;
- Thirdly, through experiments, demonstration and other means, to implement on large-scale technologies that were reliable and economically feasible; and
- Finally, the implementation of the project was evaluated and analyzed.

The detailed roadmap for the implementation of the project is given in Figure 3.2. It lays out the possibility of developing all different sources of energy.

For the purpose of project implementation, leading groups of rural energy comprehensive construction at Central Government, provincial and county levels were set up. They took the responsibility of project leadership, coordination and implementation respectively. The project management offices under the leading groups were responsible for the specific organization and implementation of the work. For example, energy office at the county Agriculture Bureau searched for appropriate technologies that were suitable to local conditions.

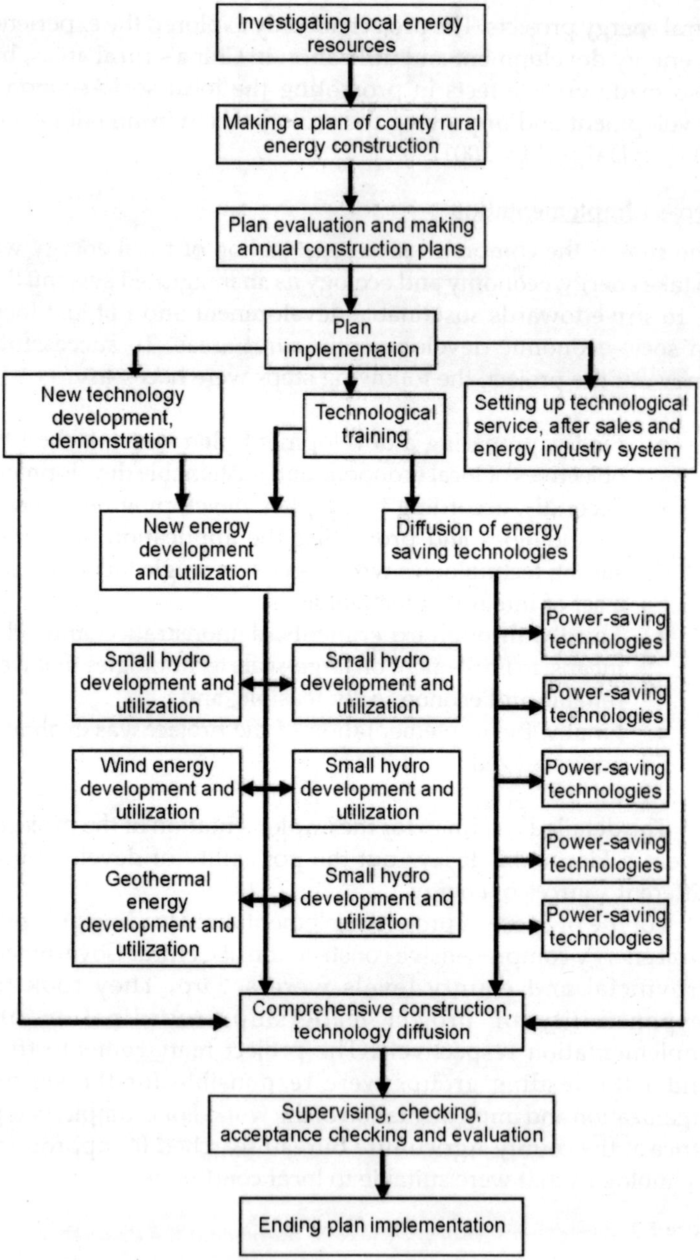

Figure 3.2: Road Map of Project Implementation[13]

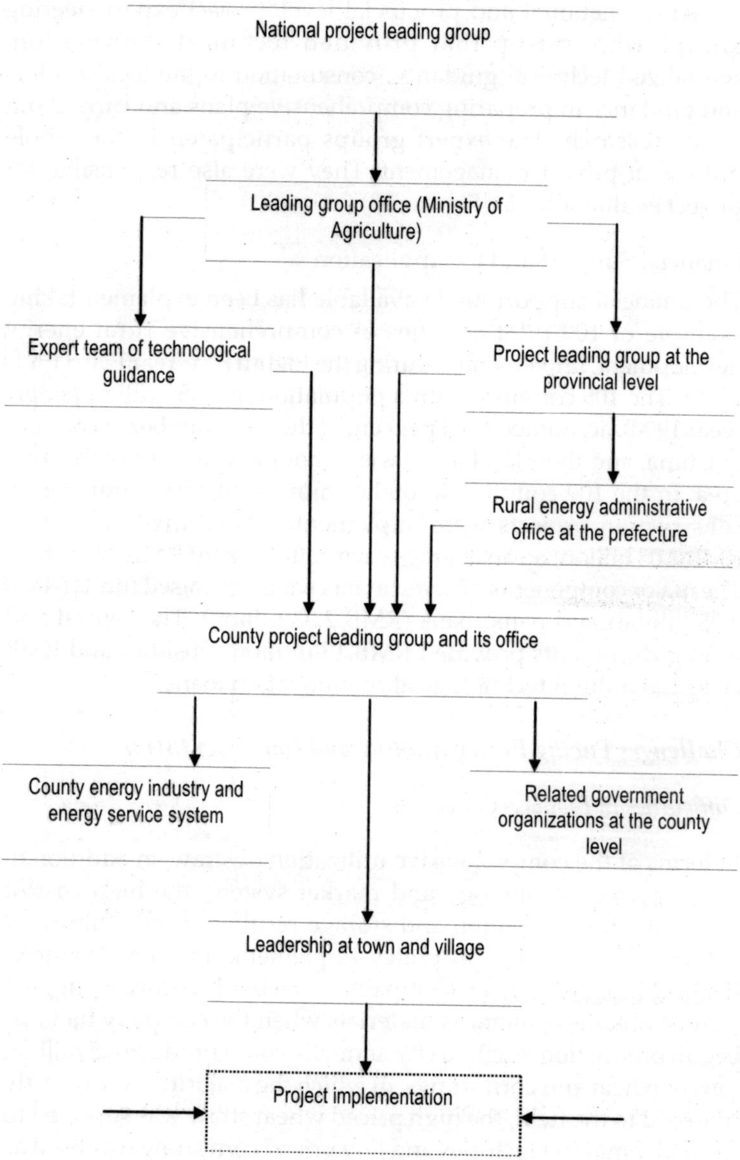

Figure 3.3: System of Leading Groups to Implement the Project[14]

At the national and provincial level, project expert steering groups were set-up that provided technical information, specialized technical guidance, consultation to the local leaders and guidance in preparing comprehensive plans and carried out policy research. The expert groups participated in the whole process of project management. They were also responsible for project evaluation (*See* Figure 3.3).

Financial Support and its Application

The financial support made available has been explained taking example of 109 pilot counties of comprehensive rural energy development, implemented during the Eighth Five Year Plan (1991-1995). The 109 counties, with a population of 57.5 million people (year 1990), accounted for 5 per cent of the total number of counties in China, and their land areas were about 2.6 per cent of the total area. In the 109 counties, a total of more than 5500 rural energy construction projects were implemented, total investment was RMB 7.03 billion; on an average each county spent RMB 69 million. The major components of investments were self-raised funds (RMB 3.68 billion) and bank loans (RMB 2.33 billion). The central and local governments provided RMB 19 million subsidies and RMB 60 to 100 million technological re-innovation loans.[15]

Challenges Facing Policy Making and Implementation

Difficulties in Biomass Collection

In terms of the comprehensive utilization of straw, in addition to the imperfect technology and market system, the high cost of collection, transportation and storage resulted in difficulties for enterprises as well as in policy implementation. For example, Jinshou Biomass Power Company in Hebei Province struggled against obtaining biomass materials when the company had just begun production. Jinzhou city annually could produce 0.5 million tons of wheat and corn straws, in which the majority were directly returned to the field, the high priced wheat straw was supplied to the paper making factories and low priced corn straw was used as feed for cows and went to biomass power company. The power company did not always buy wheat straw due to its high price. Thus, in summer the power company would only buy some wheat skins and wheat roots, and in the fall, the company would collect corn straw. The corn straw is high in moisture and sugar content, resulting in difficulties in storage. Moreover, the huge volume and low density of corn straw made it difficult to transport it. Moreover, collection of stalks and straws increased the farmers' work on field during a very short span of autumn harvest. The farmers, hence, did not want to undertake such efforts just to earn a meagre amount from the company for the collection of straw. Jinzhou Biomass Power Company could only collect 50,000 to 60,000 tons of straw. The deficit of more than 200,000 tons of straw had to be purchased from outside of Jinzhou. The company had to buy barks, cotton stalks from the places such as Xinle and Xintai, which are about 50 km away, which largely increased transportation cost. Xinle is well-known for its board manufacturing and thus, had more than 100 workshops of peeling tree skins. The barks became important raw materials for three nearby biomass power companies. The three biomass power companies of Wei county, Nangong county and Wuqiao county were set up in 2006 and 2010. The local price of bark was less than RMB 100 per ton in 2008 and it went up to RMB 185 per ton in 2012.[16] Similar problems were faced by Li Min Straw Cooperative (Chapter 5).

In spite of these difficulties, at national level, there have been continuous improvement in technology leading to considerable progress in China related to comprehensive utilization of straw. The "Report of National Straw Comprehensive Utilization and Burning in the Field" by the NDRC, shows that the area of China's arable land was 121.35 million hectares from which 817.45 million tons of straw was collected in 2012, of which 605.36 million tons (74.1 per cent) was utilized. Even then, the straw burning continued. This led to the government monitoring 4,664 summer harvest and 3,214 autumn harvest straw burning locations during the year 2012.[17] Even so, there are challenges facing policy making and implementation in biomass utilization.

Heavy Cost of Biomass Machines and Straw Transportation

Large quantities of straw collection for energy plants require big investment in machines such as the binding machine, grinder, dryer etc. The straw collection cannot happen manually. The companies/cooperatives which collect straw for reuse do not have enough money to buy all kinds of such machines.

It may be argued that other renewable energy technologies such as wind power and solar energy too require large initial capital investment for equipments. But, the cost of these could be brought down with scale economies. Such scale economies cannot work with biomass energy technologies. Besides requiring capital investment for setting up the plant, biomass energy plant also requires high working capital for collection of raw materials, as mentioned above. There has to be a major investment in equipment for the collection of raw materials. The operation also requires labor resulting in high labor costs. Besides, the dependability of raw materials, that is the straw, is low as it is tied to harvest. Availability is uneven across geographic regions. In all the biomass energy plants require transportation of straw across geographic spaces which increase the cost. After procuring large volumes of straw, these have to be stored before use and requires land area, which further adds to the costs. Lastly, the raw materials can be damaged due to rain, fire, and pests and the productivity of such damages materials would be low. Thus, the companies/ cooperatives may not store large volumes of biomass, which then creates uncertainty as to their availability.

Crop Rotation and Short Time for Biomass Collection

Double or multi-cropping has become a norm across China. Thus, corn, wheat and other crops are planted in rotation. This leaves a very small window of time between the harvest of one crop and sowing of the next crop. During the harvest season, farmers are busy harvesting and cannot spare time to collect straw and stack them in one place for the straw-users to collect the same.With the improvement in farmers' economic situation, they have no time and no economic incentive for harvesting straw and stacking them for further use. The cooperative/company reusing the straw as raw material cannot afford it, if they were to pay a high price for the straw. The harvesters and straw collection machines are used by the farmers at the time of harvest and so these machines are then not available to the straw cooperative/company. The straw waste does not get picked up and the famers burn the same in their field.

Policy Mis-match with Actual Situation

Some of the policies formulated with regard to straw do not match the actual situation on hand. For example, *the Interim Measures for the Management of Straw Energy Utilization Subsidies* of the Ministry of Finance in 2008, stipulated that the companies eligible for receiving subsidies have to meet the following conditions: (i) the registered capital of the enterprise to be RMB 10 million or more; and (ii) the annual consumption of straw to be more than 10,000 tons. Then, the subsidy would be RMB 150 per ton of biomass briquettes. The reality is, due to the high transportation cost, many enterprises engaging in the biomass energy tend to remain small and do not meet the conditions of the policy. Such companies/ cooperatives then claim subsidies through making false invoices, false and fraudulent sales and other unfair means. In 2014, the Central Government stopped the implementation of the policy. Instead, many provinces and cities raised funds on their own for straw briquette production subsidies, and the size of the enterprise was no longer a limitation. Because of the sharp decline in coal prices in recent years, briquette production further became more unprofitable.

In another situation, Hebei Province planned to promote the application of 1.3 million biomass stoves, with a subsidy of RMB 700 for each stove. In addition, the province decided to provide an additional subsidy of RMB 150 per ton of briquettes up to three tons of their use along with stove. However, in reality, none of the stove users could benefit from the briquette subsidy as there was not enough briquette supply. Thus, the local government had to subsidize coal briquettes instead of biomass briquettes. But, the farmers preferred not to use coal briquettes because of their low heat output upon combustion. The farmers continued to burn soft coal,which was much cheaper in addition to having high heat efficiency. Thus, a well-motivated policy failed in implementation stage due to the difficulties in collecting biomass and producing briquettes.

Most existing policies target individual projects. They do not consider the whole ecosystem necessary for any project to succeed. In case of comprehensive utilization of straw, policies for all ancillary activities, such as transportation, storage etc. have to be developed for the final goal to be achieved.

Multiplicity of Organizations—Multiple Reporting Requirements

Although the government at all levels have introduced a set of subsidy policies for straw-recycling enterprises, the amount of subsides is small. Moreover, the reporting procedures are quite cumbersome. A multitude of government organizations are involved in the implementation and monitoring of each project, thereby creating a situation of lack of coordination and duplicate as well as multiple reporting requirements for the enterprises/ cooperatives. For example, Environmental Protection Department is in charge of controlling straw burning; the Agricultural Department gives subsidies related to straw and biogas; Energy Bureau is mainly responsible for the straw power generation, heating and other energy utilization and the Financial Department provides support for the comprehensive utilization of straw with initial capital and preferential tax. The set-up, enforcement mechanisms and implementation efficiency of each of the departments is different. This creates problems for the reporting companies/cooperatives, which have to report to all of them and have to learn how to deal with each department. This also results into a lot of duplication of work. Also, the extent of enforcement of laws differs from one place to another. There has to be a single window reporting system for the biomass enterprises/ cooperatives.

Fragmented Subsidies

The subsidies, according to policies, are given by different departments, as discussed above. Hence, the enterprise/ cooperatives have to put in a lot of effort and paperwork in order to claim these subsidies. Instead, if there is a special fund created at the national level for the comprehensive utilization of biomass, it would be of great help. Also, depending on just local funds would lead to uneven implementation of the policies as some regions may have local funds and some may not.

Annexure 3.1

Straw Utilization Policies

Time	*Document title*	*Issued by*	*Purpose*	*Relevant Content*	*Notes*
1986	Opinions on Strengthening Rural Energy Construction	State Economy Commission	Guarantee rural energy supply	Development and demonstration of firewood-saving cooker, biogas, and straw utilization; Formulate rural energy long-term plan	In 1988, State Economy Commission was dissolved. In 1993, State Economic and Trade Commission was set up.
1994	Opinions on Strengthening Energy-saving and Comprehensive Utilization	State Economic and Trade Commission	Shift from extensive operation which is characterized by mass consumption of resources to intensive operation	Promote the development and utilization of biomass, wind, solar, geothermal and other new and renewable energies	In 2003, Ministry of Foreign Trade and Economic Cooperation and State Economic and Trade Commission were closed. Instead, Ministry of Commerce was set up to take charge of domestic and overseas trade and international economic cooperation.

(Contd.)

Time	*Document title*	*Issued by*	*Purpose*	*Relevant Content*	*Notes*
1999	Measures for the Administration of Straw Burning Prohibition and Utilization	State Environmental Protection Administration	Protect ecological environment, prevent stalk burning pollution, protect human health, and safeguard public security	Promote the comprehensive utilization of achievements of returning straw and stalk to field; the development of straw feed, straw gasification; works of straw and stalk burning prohibition and comprehensive utilization should be included into the different levels of environment protection and agricultural object responsibility; adopt strict inspection and assessment	In 2008, State Environmental Protection Administration was renamed Ministry of Environmental Protection in order to highlight the importance of environment protection; it clearly indicate the promotion of straw gasification technology
1999	Notice on Issues Concerning Further Supporting Development of Renewable Energy	State Planning Commission, Ministry of Science and Technology	Further support the development of renewable energy, accelerate the localization of renewable energy power equipment	Arrange state fiscal construction funding projects and national programs for S &T development; actively support renewable energy power generation projects, including biomass energy power generation.	State Planning Commission was in charge of overall economic management. In 1998, it was renamed as "State Development Planning Commission". In 2003, it was renamed NDRC, which guides the macro-control of the overall economic system reform

(Contd.)

Time	Document title	Issued by	Purpose	Relevant Content	Notes
2002	Science and Technology Outline of Sustainable Development	Ministry of Science and Technology	Promote the application of strategy of prospering the nation with science and education and sustainable development	Accelerate the upgrading of rural biomass energy utilization technology, develop biogas technology and solar utilization technology, analyze influences of international conventions like global warming etc. to relevant fields in national economic and social development	Begin to pay attention to issues on global climate change
2005	Opinions on Promoting Socialism New Countryside Construction	Central Committee of the Communist Party of China, State Council	Solve the problem of Agriculture, Rural Areas and Farmers	Especially promote comprehensive utilization of wastes; promote straw gasification and briquetting technology, cultivate biomass industry; strengthen countryside planning and living environment	Farmer innovators' technological achievements on stoves using straw and stalk briquettes as fuel are promoted
2006	Action Plan on Science and Technology	Ministry of Science and Technology	Promote new country-side construction through science and	Greatly promote the utiliza-tion ratio of biomass, improve ecology and save	Biomass energy utilization is related with ecology improvement

(*Contd.*)

Time	Document title	Issued by	Purpose	Relevant Content	Notes
	Promoting New Countryside Construction		technology development	resources; Focus on the recycling utilization of agricultural and forest biomass and demonstrative development of rural recycling economy; carry out rural resource conservation and the development and application of ecological and environmental protection science and technology	
2006	Interim Measures for the Administration of Special Funds for Renewable Energy Development	Ministry of Finance	In order to strengthen the administration of special funds for renewable energy development and improve the capital usage efficiency	This special funds could be used for: (i) science and technology research, standard setting and demonstration projects of renewable energy development and utilization (ii) renewable energy utilization projects in rural and pastoral areas	In 2015, Ministry of Finance issued the Interim Measures for the Administration of Special Funds for the Development of Renewable Energy again. It emphasized: (i) the demonstration, promotion of key renewable energy and new energy

(Ccntd.)

Time	Document title	Issued by	Purpose	Relevant Content	Notes
				(iii) renewable energy independent electric power system construction in remote area and islands (iv) promote the localization of production of renewable energy development and utilization equipment	technology and their industrialization demonstration; (ii) large-scale development and utilization of renewable energy and new energy and capacity building; (iii) public platform construction of renewable and new energy; (iv) Comprehensive utilization demonstration of renewable and new energy.
2007	The Eleventh Five Year Plan of Biomass Development	National Development and Reform Commission	Further Promoting the Development of Chinese Biomass Industry and Industrialization	Develop biomass briquette fuel technology; encourage producing briquette fuel by using agricultural straw and forest residues.	The development of biomass fuel is mainly to provide convenient, clean and high combustion ratio energy for rural and forest areas and to reduce the destruction of vegetation

(Contd.)

Time	*Document title*	*Issued by*	*Purpose*	*Relevant Content*	*Notes*
					caused by fuel consumption.
2008	Opinions on Accelerating the Comprehensive Utilization of Agricultural Straw and Stalk	State Council	Accelerate the comprehensive utilization of straw, realize its recycling and commercialization and promote resource conservation, environment protection and farmers' income growth.	Subsidize key technologies and equipment development related to straw power, straw gasification and straw collection, storage and transportation; give certain financial support to the application of returning straw to field, straw gasification technology and production of straw briquette fuel; encourage and guide social capital investment	It was quite common to burn agricultural straw and stalks in the rural areas; It polluted environment, threatened transportation, and wasted resources
2008	Interim Administrative Measures for Premium Subsidy Funds for Straw and Stalk Energy Generation and Utilization	Ministry of Finance	To accelerate the energy generation and utilization and provide application market for straw energy products	Straw energy production and utilization companies, whose registered capital is more than RMB 10 million and annual straw consumption is more than 10,000 tons, could get RMB 100 to 150 subsidy	Due to the restriction of transport distance, many of problems emerged during the implementation of this policy. It was terminated in 2014

(Contd.)

Time	Document title	Issued by	Purpose	Relevant Content	Notes
				for consuming one ton straw	
2009	Guiding Opinions on Compilation of Plan of Comprehensive Utilization of Straw	NDRC and Ministry of Agriculture	Accelerate comprehensive utilization of straw, realize the recycling and commercialization of straw, promote resource conservation, environment protection and increase farmers' income growth	Promote straw comprehensive utilization in areas which have abundant straw residues, tight crops rotation and heavy straw burning; try to achieve the straw comprehensive utilization ratio to 80 per cent by 2015	It points out that effective market mechanism and storage and transportation system have not been set up throughout the country; straw commercialization is low; specific policy measures of encouraging straw comprehensive utilization is lacking; the development of straw industry lags; shortage of supporting technology and equipment
2011	Interim Administrative Measures for Premium Subsidy Funds for Construction of Green Energy	Ministry of Finance, National Energy Administration and Ministry of Agricul-ture	Accelerate the development of rural renewable resources, optimize the structure of rural energy, promote clean and modern rural energy,	Biomass briquette fuel project is one of the most important fields supported by demorstrative subsidy funds	

(Contd.)

Time	*Document title*	*Issued by*	*Purpose*	*Relevant Content*	*Notes*
	Demonstration County		and improve farmers' production and living conditions.		
2012	Biomass Industry Development Planning	State Council	Develop new clean energy, relieve energy shortage, solve the problems of agriculture, farmers and rural areas	Actively promote the large-scale application of biomass gas fuel and briquette fuel; the total annual utilization of biomass energy would exceed 50 million tons of standard coal by 2015; reduce CO_2 emission by 95 million tons; the annual value of production could reach to RMB150 million	It proposes the relationship between biomass fuel and CO_2 emission reduction
2012	The Twelfth Five Year Plan of Biomass Development	National Energy Administration	Strengthen the comprehensive utilization of biomass energy, improve the use efficiency of biomass energy; create better resource, economic, social and ecological benefits; promote the	The annual utilization of biomass briquette fuel could reach 10 million tons by 2015; about 10 million households' energy consumption condition would be improved, among which 1.5 million households use biomass briquette fuel	National Energy Administration (vice-ministerial level) was founded in 2013. It is a national administration under the management of NDRC

(Contd.)

Time	Document title	Issued by	Purpose	Relevant Content	Notes
			sustainable development of biomass industry		
2012	Implementation Plan for Comprehensive Utilization of Agricultural Straw and Stalk during the "Twelfth Five Year Plan" Period	NDRC, Ministry of Agriculture and Ministry of Finance	Meet the challenges of climate variation, promote the comprehensive utilization of straw and stalk, accelerate the development of agricultural circular economy and emerging industry, improve living conditions of rural residents and increase farmers' income	In areas with high concentration of straw and stalk, on the issues on transforming straw and stalk into fertilizer, feed, base stock, raw material and fuel, pilot demonstration of comprehensive utilization of straw and stalk should be implemented. Widely promote straw and stalk comprehensive utilization technologies with large consumption and high technical content and additional value. A group of priority projects should be implemented	The relationship between comprehensive utilization of agricultural straw and stalk and CO_2 emission reduction
2013	Air Pollution Prevention and Control Action	State Council	Improvement and protection of air, environment matters a	Compared with that of 2012, the intensity of inhalable particles of	It is regarded as the strictest air pollution prevention and control

(Contd.)

Time	*Document title*	*Issued by*	*Purpose*	*Relevant Content*	*Notes*
	Plan		lot to fundamental interests of the people	prefecture level and above cities in 2017 will drop by over 10 per cent; the density of fine particulate matters in Beijing-Tianjin-Hebei region, Yangtze River Delta and Pearl River Delta will drop by 25 per cent, 20 per cent and 15 per cent respectively	action plan
2014	Action Plan for Energy Development Strategy (2014-2020)	State Council	To promote energy production and consumption revolution	Promote the construction of green-energy county, countryside and village; rural renewable energy to be developed in line with the local conditions; promote the clean and effective utilization of non-commercial energy and strengthen rural energy-saving work.	China's energy resource problem becomes increasingly severe; ecological environment problem is also serious. Pressures on adjusting energy structure, improving energy efficiency and ensuring energy security becomes higher and higher.

NOTES

1. *Source*: WHO database: http://www.who.int/phe/health_topics/outdoorair/databases/cities/en/, accessed on September 21, 2016.
2. On May 30th, 2006, Ministry of Finance issued the Interim Measures for the Administration of the Special Fund for Development of Renewable Energy.
3. Accessed on November 12, 2015, from http://www.theguardian.com/environment/2014/apr/25/china-strengthens-environmental-laws-polluting-factories#img-1
4. Xu, Jie and Zhenhong Yuan (n.d.) "An overview of the biomass energy policy in China", accessed on May 27, 2015 from http://www.besustainablemagazine.com/cms2/overview-of-biomass-energy-policy-in-china/
5. Xu, Jie and Zhenhong Yuan (n.d.) "An overview of the biomass energy policy in China", accessed on May 27, 2015 from http://www.besustainablemagazine.com/cms2/overview-of-biomass-energy-policy-in-china/
6. Sha, Fu; Zou Ji, & Liu Linwei (n.d.) *An Analysis of China's INDC*, *Source:* http://www.chinacarbon.info/wp-content/uploads/2015/07/Comments-on-Chinas-INDC.pdf, accessed on May 3, 2016.
7. "Report on Firewood-saving Stove Promotion Program in Rural China, National Planning Committee, February 10, 1983.
8. *Source*: Report "Firewood-saving Stove Promotion Program in Rural China", National Planning Committee and Ministry of Agriculture, February 10, 1983.
9. *Source*: Report "Firewood-saving Stove Promotion Program in Rural China", National Planning Committee and Ministry of Agriculture, February 10, 1983.
10. *Source*: Report "Firewood-saving Stove Promotion Program in Rural China", National Planning Committee and Ministry of Agriculture, February 10, 1983.
11. *Source*: Report "Firewood-saving Stove Promotion Program in Rural China", National Planning Committee and Ministry of Agriculture, February 10, 1983.
12. In April 1984, in order to strengthen the development of rural energy and further develop the rural economy for the aim of protecting the ecological environment, the State Council set up a rural energy leading group and its office. In 1986, the State Council decided to close this office. Instead, rural energy related projects were implemented directly by the State Council through setting-up group on energy savings that had regular meetings for the same. The participants in the meetings were the State Economic Commission, the State Planning Commission and the State Science and Technology

Commission, in which the State Economic Commission played a key role. The rural energy management office in the State Economic Commission was responsible for the promotion of new energy technologies in rural China. And the planning office of energy saving bureau at the State Planning Commission was responsible for policy research and preparing rural energy plans. Other government organizations jointly worked together with the State Economic Commission for rural energy development.

13. *Source*: Promoting Rural energy projects accessed on June 20, 2016 from http://max.book118.com/html/2015/1112/29302785.shtm
14. *Source*: Promoting Rural energy projects,, accessed on June 20, 2016 from http://max.book118.com/html/2015/1112/29302785.shtm
15. Promoting Rural energy projects, http://max.book118.com/html/2015/1112/29302785.shtm, access on 20 June, 2016.
16. *Source*: Income and expenditure account of a biomass power company, Hebei Daily, 7 August, 2012.
17. NDRC, Ministry of Environmental Protection and Ministry of Agriculture, Notification on National Biomass Comprehensive Utilization and Incineration, Document No. 516, 2014.

4

Liu Yongquan: From Gasifier to Biomass Stoves

Context

The farmers continue to use biomass for their domestic energy use, in particular for heating and cooking. The traditional cooking stoves emit fumes and are not efficient. Some farmers are, therefore, in constant search for better domestic energy options and hence, they take initiative to innovate on the existing technologies. Liu Yongquan, a farmer of Hunghua City, Hebei Province, is one of the farmer-innovator, who first developed a straw gasifier and then developed a biomass stove. It is important to innovate but diffusion of the said innovation is much more important. In Mr. Liu's case, government subsidies on the product at the time of sale were available to him for diffusion of his innovation. The innovation has to be commercially produced for its wide scale diffusion and for this local entrepreneurs are required. The government took an initiative to link Liu with a local manufacturer, who was financed by the local government, so that the production could start without much hassle. The local government thus, assisted this farmer-innovator, first through financing a manufacturer to commercially produce Liu's product and then provided subsidy to the buyers at the time of purchase. The local government, therefore, played a very strong role in supporting this farmer-innovator.

Liu is one of the pioneers in gasifier development in China. But, he did not have an opportunity to learn from the others and use the others' research achievements for reference. Initially, he had to find his own way, acting blindly. But, with dogged perseverance, he made slow progress that attracted the attention of the local government. Both the local government officials and organizations supported Liu in many different ways. As mentioned above, the local government financed diffusion of his product. But, prior to that, the local government sent him for training, invited experts to help his research and also helped him in patent application for his innovation. Liu's research and innovation went through three stages—research on his own without any support or knowledge, only following his own instincts; government support in research and then, cooperation with private companies for commercialization of innovation. Before we present Liu's case, we describe the backdrop of the city and the region he is located in and present the facts about the availability of biomass resources in the region.

Huanghua City, Hebei Province

Hebei Province has taken proactive steps in preparing action plans for reduction in air pollution, rural energy improvement and comprehensive utilization of biomass energy. In 2013, the Province prepared three action plans: (i) 'Country Improvement Action Plan', which included action plans for the straw and stalk energy generation and utilization; (ii) 'Air Pollution Prevention and Control Action Plan' and (iii) 'Rural Energy Saving and Emission Reduction work'. In 2014, RMB 350 million special funds were invested to ensure that 0.3 million households could benefit from the straw and stalk energy generation and utilization[1].

Huanghua city used to be a county under Cangzhou city, Hebei Province. But now, it is a complete city with an area of 1,544.7 square kilometres (kms) and population of 426,000 in 2009. The per capita income of the farmers in Huanghua in 2009 was RMB 6,592 annually, which was higher than the national rural resident per capita net income of RMB 5,153 (China, NBS, 2010). Huanghua has 327 administrative villages. The villages have water supply, automobile and transport, telephone, electricity and cable TV facilities. The economic condition of the local people is good and they use agricultural machinery for seeding and harvesting.

In 2009, Huanghua city had a total cultivated area of 83,311 hectares, including 25,742 hectares of corn acreage with a production output of 154,452 tons and 4,890 hectares of cotton with a total output of 5,281 tons (Huanghua Statistics Bureau,

Huanghua City in Hebei Province

Hebei Province in China

Map 4.1: Huanghua City in Hebei Province and Hebei Province in China

Table 4.1: Basic information of Huanghua city

Aspect	*Unit*	*2009*	*2008*
The whole city area	Sq. kilometers	1,544.70	1,544.70
Arable land	Ten unit of area	7351.95	7,351.95
Agricultural population at the end of year	Person	325,377	320,870
Non-agricultural population at the end of year	Person	113,094	111,730
Electricity used in village	Ten thousand kW	60,971	56,584
Rural total income	Ten thousand RMB	5,533,125	4,945,297
Per capita net income of farmers	RMB	6,592	5,880
Rural residents per capita disposable income	RMB	6,541	5,631
Rural residents per capita consumption expenditure	RMB	2,849	2,422

Source: Huanghua Statistics Bureau (2009: 2).

2010). The price of cotton straw in the region varied from RMB 0.08 per kg to RMB 0.12 per kg.

Similar to other rural areas, cooking fuels of Huanghua rural area has also diversified. Although, household electrical cooking appliances have become more popular recently, less-efficient stoves, small boilers and self-made heating equipments are still commonly used. These equipments mainly use cheap and low-grade coal as fuel. As discussed in Chapter 1, while the households move up the energy ladder, they do not give up their earlier energy sources and for many years to come, there is fuel stacking, meaning that a particular household may use multiple fuels (Liu *et al.*, 2013). Table 4.3 too, shows that the rural households use multiple fuel sources. Also different fuels are used for the same purpose in different seasons. For example, straw is used for cooking and heating under the bed in winter. But, gas and electricity are used for cooking in summer.

Efforts to Innovate Gasifier

Self Efforts

Liu Youngquan, born in 1966, is a farmer of Hou Jie town, Huanghua city, Hebei Province[2]. In 1991, Liu and his wife came to Huanghua from his home town, Shanghe County, Shandong Province. To make a living, he initially went in for farming, in addition to doing other small, odd jobs like selling

Table 4.2: Population and Resources of Huanghua City

Year	*Population in End of the Year, 10,000*	*Agricultural Population, 10,000*	*% of Agricultural Population to Total Population of City*	*The Natural Population Growth Rate (%)*	*Food Production, Ton*	*Cotton Production, Ton*	*Oil Production, Ton*	*Arable Land, Hectare*	*Net Annual Per Capita Income of Peasants (RMB)*
1980	29.9	28.6	95.7	11.50	102,247	51	4,373	51,353	154
1985	32.7	30.9	94.5	6.60	115,235	2,753	7,909	51,027	547
1990	35.8	33.4	93.3	20.00	137,518	1,514	6,998	50,525	868
1995	36.9	33.4	90.5	7.90	182,826	1,754	2,966	50,121	2,531
2000	40.7	34.9	85.7	16.00	179,686	97	2,138	49,473	2,840
2005	41.7	28.0	67.1	5.96	164,524	4,198	2,800	47,882	3,616
2009	43.9	21.0	47.9	9.11	190,693	5,281	4,072	49,013	6,592

Source: Huanghua Statistics Bureau (2009).

Table 4.3: Fuel usage in the rural areas of Huanghua

Winter	*Cooking*	Straw is used for cooking and firing under bed to produce heat[3]. Honeycomb coal for steaming buns, cooking porridge and to boil water. Induction cooker for purposes that require high heat, as honeycomb coal produces low heat. Natural gas for cooking lunch due to its ability to produce high-temperature heat quickly.
	Heating	▪ Self-made central heating powered by one stove used for 3 months during winter for a household of 2-3 members. Estimated 1 ton of coal is used. For a household with 3 or more rooms and 4 or more members, 2 to 3 stoves required for the self-made central heating. ▪ 400 pieces of honeycomb coal required to power one stove for the winter. ▪ In late autumn and early spring "Kang" bed used. The stove heated by straw and stalk, for two months to provide heating and fire to cook. ▪ Kang not used in the noon as the temperature is satisfactory for activities. ▪ Kang used during the evening for cooking dinner and provide heating for the beddings.
Summer	*Cooking*	▪ During the summer electricity and natural gas instead of coal. ▪ Electric rice cooker is used for rice or porridge. ▪ Induction cooker and gas burner are used for cooking food. ▪ Microwave oven is used to heat meals. ▪ Electric grill is used to make pan-cakes. ▪ Solar water heater is used for boiling water for bathing ▪ Some villagers cook with biogas.[4] ▪ For a family of 2-3 members for cooking food only, 15kg of natural gas is enough.

Source: 2012 May, Field Study in villages of Huanghua City.

clothes, books, garlic and even cashmere. He even worked as a pedi-cab driver to help the others in transportation. Liu, being a restless personality, liked trying out new things. If something sparked his interest, he would stick to it and complete the work with utter diligence. Liu's friendly face, warm-heartedness and guileless nature belied his tough and strong character within! He was a man of firm strength and beliefs.

Liu noticed, as a part of his daily life, that the biomass waste lay scattered all over the village, which not only made the village filthy and look untidy but also created a situation of fire hazard. More importantly, Liu felt disturbed that so much of biomass was wasted and could not be properly used to benefit the poor farmers, who then had to purchase energy from the market. Liu realized that if he could find a technique to use the biomass, he could sell it and make some money to improve his family's living standard.

Life is full of accidental chances. One day in 1998, by chance, Liu came across an article in a newspaper that gave information on successful development of a large gasifier in a laboratory in Tsinghua University, Beijing. At that time, gasoline costed RMB 0.75 per litre while liquefied petroleum gas (LPG) costed over RMB 30 per 15kg in Huanghua. The annual average income of a household was only about RMB 1,000. Farmers found LPG expensive and they directly burnt biomass and coal for domestic energy use. Liu naively believed that he could "draw a tiger with a cat as a model", that is, he could produce a small sized gasifier for family based on the model that was developed in the Tsinghua University laboratory. If the model succeeded, he could make some money.

Being a farmer with just three years of schooling, he could not understand the difference between a laboratory model and real prototype. Nor could he gauge the huge risk involved in the Research and Development (R & D) of a gasifier. Naïve as he was, he went to the Beijing with his two friends. But, on reaching there, they did not go to Tsinghua University to meet the professors involved in the innovation of gasifier. Instead, they went to a briefcase company (one that operated out of briefcase and hence fake!) located in Tsinghua campus and purchased from the company a set of drawings for constructing a gasifier. Liu spent several hundred RMB for this purchase. This small company also demonstrated to Liu and his friends the use of gasifier. In the late 1990s, there were many reports of development of straw gasifier in the newspapers and magazines, which attracted attention of many people, mainly the rural residents. Some organizations and individuals advertised in the papers for this technology transfer. Many people purchased such technologies and were cheated. Something similar was to happen to Liu.

Back in the village, Liu developed a prototype gasifier from bricks with the help of the drawings he had purchased from the fraudulent company. But, the results obtained by Liu were disappointing. The main problems were: (a) The operation of the straw gasifier was too complex to be managed by any common farmer; especially the process of igniting the gasifier, which was complicated. (b) This straw gasifier had a very specific requirement of fuel; the straws used as feed had to be cut to a length of less than five cm, which added to the farmers' workload and did not make the gasifier feasible for regular use. (c) Worst, the gasifier produced heavy smoke, dirty tar and a strong foul smell while in use. Almost all gasifiers face the problem of crusting of tar in the gasifier over time. The working theory of a gasifier is that the incomplete combustion of biomass produces different kinds of flammable gases. When these gases pass through the connecting pipes of the gasifier, the temperature of gases goes down, resulting in the formation of tar. The tar has a strong, peculiar smell and causes environment pollution as well. (d) Liu's gasifier did not create a fire strong enough for cooking and heating.

This first experiment of Liu, therefore, failed. His friends got discouraged and gave up. Liu's temperament never let him succumb to any adverse circumstances. He was hopeful that further improvements on the gasifier would correct its flaws and it would be successful. He mistakenly believed that the continued improvements on the gasifier would finally pay off. For quite a long time, repeated trials and errors and failures became Liu's daily routine. Indeed, these were trying circumstances for a common farmer like Liu.

After struggling alone for a few years, in 2003, Liu was able to sell some of his gasifiers to the farmers of his hometown in Shandong Province. Unfortunately, and in fact inevitably, the gasifiers did not work well and Liu had to take them back to Huanghua. Liu had no choice but to go back to further research on gasifier.

Liu was obsessed with the idea of the gasifier and its research. He invested all his money in research and at one point, even his wife's possessions! The family disregarded all of Liu's work as a waste of time and money. His friends and family considered this obsession to be extravagant, particularly when he did not have any resources to carry on and was staking the family's future on something, which they considered as having no future scope.

Neither his family nor his friends understood him. The final breaking point came when he brought back home, all the gasifiers he had sold in Shangdong Province. His wife could not contain her indignation towards him, and the conflicts within the family, which had been going on for long, finally took its toll! His wife, along with their two daughters, took away all their savings and went back to her hometown in Shandong Province. Liu was thereafter, left with no money for his research. He had little opportunity for borrowing money from others. His research went through a difficult phase and he could not even afford to feed himself.

Despite the many odds and struggles to carry on the research, Liu had a strong belief in himself and his ability to undertake research successfully and make a gasifier. He was also convinced and happy with the thought that the gasifier, which he would make, would help the rural households. But, his penniless plight during 2003 shook his faith in himself and he was unsure about the path he should take. To survive, he worked as a taxi driver during daytime. In the evenings, he engaged himself in the gasifier improvement research. He tried different ways of solving the tar problem and the ensuing problem of smell. None of these efforts succeeded. At most, he succeeded in separating the tar from the gasifier but he could not eliminate it. Even worse, the separated tar resulted in secondary pollution. Apart from these, Liu's gasifier had other shortcomings, such as incomplete burning, a short service life of the gasifier and so on. Faced with economic problems and the technical bottleneck, Liu was confused. Finally, a relative suggested a way out.

Getting Government Support (2003-2005)

One day in 2004, Liu's relative—a college graduate, who often helped him in searching for information from the internet, suggested that Liu should put his research achievements on the internet which would possibly attract the potential supporters and partners. Liu's relative hoped that through this effort, Liu could continue his research. It was a period when the internet was flooded with false claims of magnificent achievements of gasifier. On typing "gasifier" in Baidu search engine, people could read more than 1000 pieces of news/ads on gasifier. The advertisements' claims went thus: "gasifier is an environmental friendly product, easy to make money for the dealers"; "free training, experts give support"; "technology transfer and guaranteed success in gasifier production", and so on. The addresses of those companies were either located near the well-known universities, such as Peking and Tsinghua Universities, or in the office buildings/villas. All the advertisements mentioned that they were selling products developed by the professors of Tsinghua or Peking Universities. Actually, they hardly produced the products and were just briefcase (fraudulent) companies. Because of the tar problem, many dealers suffered financially.

After long-term efforts on improving the gasifier, Liu had found that the flaws of gasifier were not visible within a short time. After some 1-2 months of use, many customers had to give up its use because of the tar problem. The tar problem did not occur if the biomass burnt fully inside the gasifier. The producers showed the customers gasifiers where there was full combustion and tar was not formed. Also, demonstration would be for a short period, during which the buyers would not find any problem. On the contrary, the customers were impressed with the use of biomass-waste as fuel in the gasifier. For all rural households, biomass-waste was a nagging problem. The gasifier also has some problem at the time of igniting. But, the gasifier sellers would keep it ignited before the buyers came and hence, the buyers could not see the full process of operating a gasifier. Also, it was never clearly mentioned that the gasifier required biomass to be cut into small sizes before being used as fuel, which took effort and was time consuming. Only when the customer purchased the gasifier and operated it for a long period of time, that the problems with its use begun to appear.

Liu was in a deep dilemma as to which path he should take! Should he also fool the customers? He was deeply pained by the tricks the dealers and manufacturers played with the customers. He believed that the customers were ultimately the poor farmers who should not be cheated. On the other hand, he also wanted to sell his gasifiers and make some money, given that he was in a dire financial situation.

Liu was a smart person. He decided to take a new approach for marketing his innovation. He decided to first grab attention of the customers on the Baidu search machine. For every click on a product on this search engine, the seller had to pay Baidu some amount. The normal practice was payment of RMB 1 for every click and that was how all products were sold. Liu, not having the required financial liquidity at his disposal, agreed to pay RMB 0.5 for every click. This was the cheapest price that Baidu offered. Further, he also decided to tell the truth about the problems of the gasifier to the customers, while putting his product for sale on the internet. People were attracted to Liu's site because of something different on the site than all the other promotions. At the same time, when they clicked on his product, they could see the video of a very brightly burning gasifier. The videos also had promotional material with the users praising the gasifiers and stating how wonderfully well they worked! Through this smart arrangement, Liu killed two birds with one stone—informing people about the gasifiers along with the problems and marketing his product at the same time. This worked well for him.

Soon, the dealers from all over the country came to Huanghua[5]. Liu applied the marketing skills he learned from the company in Beijing, selling the gasifier drawings. Interestingly, the dealers could watch his burning gasifier, only if they paid a fee of 100 RMB. Liu's mysterious behaviour aroused dealers' curiosity. Liu sold both gasifiers and manufacturing instruction. The price of instructions varied from one to two hundred to several hundred RMB.

At that time, a major problem faced by the gasifier market in China was duplication. Many people, especially the poor farmers who dreamed of becoming rich quickly, believed that gasifier making was easy technology. Hence, they spent several hundred RMB to buy the drawings, the video explaining how to produce gasifier, and a sample gasifier. They produced gasifiers by themselves but faced many technical problems. Some people gave up and some people became gasifier innovators, improving the gasifier design in many different ways. Many dealers had to become gasifier innovators because various problems came up when the customers using their gasifiers approached them with problems. Some people who bought manufacturing instructions from Liu also became gasifier technology innovators later. According to Liu, there were dealers from over 100 counties throughout China, who bought products from him and made various modifications on the gasifiers.

Since a lot of people from all over China approached Liu to watch the demonstration and purchase the gasifier drawings, it attracted the attention of the New Energy Office of Huanghua Agriculture Bureau. They contacted Liu. There were no existing government policies/programs that could directly support Liu's research. However, the then Director of the local Agricultural Bureau, Zhao Enting, personally gave Liu Yongquan RMB 1,000 to encourage him to continue his research. Liu was invited to give a speech to a farmers' assembly in Huanghua city. Liu used his own inspirational story to encourage and inspire farmers to become entrepreneurs to increase their financial stability. Interestingly, and an out of box thinking, the local government sent a bus to Liu's hometown in Shandong to fetch his wife, children and other relatives to be present at the mass rally. Liu's wife was touched by his efforts and she realized that Liu was respected and encouraged by the local government. Her respect for Liu went up and she decided to stay back with her children in Huanghua and restart her family life.

The local agriculture bureau's support to Liu for research and entrepreneurship caught the attention of the local media, the newspapers and television, who started noticing Liu and his work, which eventually led to increased publicity. The local government arranged for him to consult experts, attend exhibitions, study tours and training. They also encouraged him to join the competitions organized by the provincial agriculture bureau and helped him apply for government project supports.

The government support made a strong impression on Liu Yongquan. He not only realized the importance of internet and the integration of external resources, but also deeply appreciated the support of national policy on energy saving technology. Later on, in his work, Liu started paying attention to marketing himself and his innovation and also towards the establishment of a network for the purpose of his cooperation. Liu realized and had also experienced that the government strongly supported energy saving techniques. Thus, he repeatedly sought government support for his work. It is important to remember that in 2005, the national government passed a legislation called Renewable Energy Law of the People's Republic of China, which laid emphasis on using biomass for the purpose of energy production. It was also realized that direct burning of biomass created local air pollution and hence the national government was also keen to promote clean energy in rural areas. Gasifier technology came in handy in these endeavors and hence Liu was able to get support in many different ways from the local government.

Liu wanted support from the government for carrying on research and improving his technology, which he had been unable to do on his own. He approached the local government for the same and in 2005, the newly established energy office of the Huanghua agricultural bureau, invited Liu to help find solution to three major technical problems—(i) First, to generate a stronger fire. Liu's gasifier had an initial combustion furnace that was in an anaerobic condition and the fire produced was relatively weak. So, by adding a blower to the furnace, more oxygen was forced into the chamber to help increase the intensity of the fire. (ii) Liu's gasifier also had initial ignition problems. Since, the blower was added this ignition problem was also solved. (iii) The gasifiers had problems of residual tar. A filter was installed. This led to the burning of tar twice, which reduced the residual tar output to some extent and also reduced emission of foul smell. Finally, Liu applied for a utility model patent with the help of the Huanghua Science and Technology Bureau in March 2006, which was granted. Liu, therefore, becomes an IPR patent holder. Once Liu's gasifier was modified, the farmers found it to be useful. So, some of them learnt from him, officially or informally, and some even infringed on the IPR and began to assemble such gasifiers.

Photo 4.1: Liu's Gasifier[6]

Source: http://www.youboy.com/pics9359288.html

Cooperation with Companies (2006-2008)

This is a phase when Liu starts on a new trajectory, of developing cooperation with private companies to market his innovation for wider diffusion. He cooperated with two such companies.

Cooperation with Long Xiang Company

In 2006, the Huanghua Agriculture Bureau successfully applied for a project to Hebei Agriculture Bureau under the government's policy of New Village Construction. The application was for obtaining subsidy of RMB 200 on the selling of 1000 units of Liu's gasifier[7]. Liu did not have enough money for production. Thus, the local government put Liu in contact with Long Xiang Company to produce gasifiers. The cooperation arrangement was that Liu would take 20 per cent shares of the company by his technology investment and in addition earn a salary. The local government provided Long Xiang a funding of RMB 120,000 to purchase production equipment, such as punching machine, press machine and steel plated shears. With this help, Long Xiang soon produced the first batch of straw gasifiers. The government selected more than 10 pilot villages from amongst the New Village Construction for the gasifiers' promotion. In May 2006, the Huanghua Agricultural Bureau also held a news conference on straw gasifier to promote its selling[8]. In 2006, 600 units were sold in total. But, due to immature technology and the defects in the stoves, such as residual tar and foul smell, farmers soon abandoned the use of Liu's gasifiers.

Along with the government, Long Xiang and Liu actively promoted their products. More than 4,000 gasifiers were sold nationwide, in areas such as Henan, Shandong, Guizhou Provinces, and Yinchuan city in Ningxia Hui Autonomous Region. The marketing strategy aimed at mainly attracting stove dealers to sell the gasifiers and at the same time demonstrating the functioning of the gasifier in the exhibitions everywhere.

Liu's gasifiers were also selected and used by the rehabilitation project of the Three Gorges Reservoir. The Cangzhou city government—Huanghua earlier belonged to Cangzhou—provided a financial support to the tune of RMB 150,000, for purchasing the gasifiers and donated them to the rehabilitation project. At that time, there were many gasifier manufacturers in the market. Mr. Yang, the Director of Energy Office, Hebei Province, recommended Liu's gasifiers to the Cangzhou government. He said that the Hebei Energy office had once introduced 200 gasifiers procured from Zhangjiajie city, Henan Province, but they had failed.

Soon, Long Xiang earned more than RMB one million because of Liu's innovation. Long Xiang used the money in further expanding the production line, as it believed that the market potential for this product was huge. Liu did not benefit monetarily from the expansion and continued to get his regular salary. But, Liu had a sense of accomplishment and felt pride in his achievement.

Unfortunately, Liu's pride soon disappeared. The gasifier had some weaknesses in theory; for example, the flammable smoke would inevitably produce tar while passing through the connecting pipe due to the decreasing temperature. This tar produced foul smell. Although diligent efforts were made towards rectifying those problems, they could not be solved. The live demonstration shown to the consumers was deceptive in nature, because during the short span of demonstration they never realized, nor could they detect the problems of residual tar or the foul smell; they only saw the strong burning fire and its resultant advantages! All the shortcomings of the gasifier were noticed only after the consumers used it for some time.

Soon, the dealers and users came to Long Xiang, wanting to return the gasifiers and demanded a refund. Due to this, Long Xiang lost several hundred thousand RMB. At the end of 2006, the cooperation between Liu and Long Xiang ended. Long Xiang claimed the media exaggerated Liu's research achievement, which resulted in Long Xiang taking a wrong production decision.

When interviewed regarding the same, Liu had a different opinion. He said that both himself and Long Xiang ought to take some responsibilities in the latter's failure. Liu argued that: (i) he had warned the leaders of Long Xiang in theory, the shortfalls of his gasifiers but they had not taken his warning seriously. They did not try to understand the gasifier market in depth and see if any hidden risk could be involved. They were highly optimistic due to its short-term external flourish in the gasifier market and expanded production immensely. (ii) The live demonstration of how the gasifier worked showed only the good side of his products.

It took time for consumers to find the defects in the product. In another word, their sales have a time-lag problem. Although Liu knew of these technical shortcomings, for the sake of business interests, he had allowed the product to be launched in the market. (iii) This partnership also had a lack of clarity on the IPR matters. While the company had applied for an IPR for this gasifier in the name of company, Liu thought that this was his IPR and that the company had infringed on his IPR without paying him. The company was of the opinion that it had paid Liu his legitimate share for the IPR. Thus, partnership ended. This experiment showed, in particular the misunderstanding on the IPR ownership, how important it was to spread basic legal knowledge among the masses.

Cooperation with Haotian Company

After leaving Long Xiang, Liu Yongquan rented a workshop from Hualin Machinery Company to continue his modification on the gasifier. In Hualin, Liu met one of his important innovation partner—He Junhai, who found Liu's innovation interesting and left Hualin and joined Liu.

In 2006, the project supported by Hebei Agricultural Bureau, as discussed earlier, was to subsidize the selling of 1000 gasifiers. But, only 600 units were sold that year. Thus, in 2007, the local government of Huanghua planned to complete the project. Again, the local government introduced Liu to another company, Haotian, for jointly partnering in the gasifier production. Liu was invited as the general engineer. Ms. Wang Junfang, the owner of Haotian believed that the gasifier had market potential. In fact, Wang had relatives working in government departments. Through them, Wang learned that, although the media had written off the straw gasifier, the government was keen to encourage the research and production of straw gasifiers, which meant that the straw gasifier still had a promising future. In 2007, Haotian sold 400 gasifiers in the pilot-villages, with the government subsidizing each unit with RMB 200.

Since the beginning of 2007, with the media continuing to disclose the technical defects of the gasifiers, the unhappy customers kept returning Liu's products. At the beginning of 2008, Liu's cooperation with Haotian stopped. The main defects of the gasifiers revealed by the media were:

(i) Unresolved problem of tar deposits and other wastes resulting in foul smell and environmental pollution.The gases produced through gasification of straws, had a complex composition. To use it, the gases had to be filtered for usage. However, this process itself produced large amounts of waste gas, tar, wastewater and many harmful gases. And these filtered wastes could not be decomposed, causing serious environmental damage.

(ii) Secondly, the process of using the gasifiers was complicated. The feed required for the gasifier had to be of high density and the biomass had to be cut into pieces of less than 5 cm length. This required the farmers to have cutting equipment. Besides, the feed for the gasifier had to be completely dry before use and hence the users either needed access to dry biomass or had to have a large space to dry it. In many villages it was not easy to find a large space for drying the biomass. The problems with its ignition remained unresolved in spite of expert advice, as discussed earlier. Heavy smoke was produced at the time of ignition or while adding biomass to it.

(iii) The misleading advertising in the media cheated the customers, who thought that the technical requirement of straw gasifier was very low. Hence, many people started its production on their own. Some speculators, taking advantage of national policy on renewable energy, made false claims about the straw gasifier. This created a bad impact in the society. Some enterprises, under the influence of inappropriate propaganda, blindly introduced the gasification technology and eventually went bankrupt. For example, a company in Tongzhou County, Beijing, introduced the gasification technology purchased from a company in Hunan Province. They invested more than one million RMB in gasifier production but could not sell them and finally, the company became bankrupt. A company in Chongqing, also introduced the gasifier production technique procured from a company in Hunan. In 2006, they sold 21,000 units nationwide. Due to the tar problem, they had to call back their products, resulting in a loss of more than 10 million RMB.

Working on Semi-gasifier (2009-2011)

Comparison between Gasifier and Semi-gasifier

In 2008, the media began to promote the concept of semi-gasifier. Liu Yongquan shifted his focus to the research on semi-gasifier. He successfully developed the semi-gasifier that year[9]. In 2008, Liu sold 1200 to 1300 gasifiers and semi-gasifiers in total (For the differences between gasifier and semi-gasifier, *see* Table 4.4). About half of the products were semi-gasifiers. According to different specifications, the prices ranged from RMB 300 to RMB 1200, based on the types of stoves. Most of them were sold to the cities in Hebei Province, such as Xingtai, Handan and Chengde. Some products were even sold to the far-off areas in the south of China, such as in the provinces of Guangdong, Hubei and Guangxi. The major marketing channels were through dealers nationwide. However, in 2008, the local government did not provide support to Liu for selling the gasifier because the media again started highlighting the defects of the same.

Photo 4.2: Liu's Semi-Gasifier

Photo Credit: CIE, TUFE team.

Table 4.4: Comparison of Gasifier and Semi-gasifier

Features	*Gasifier*	*Semi-gasifier*
Appearance	Add-bin and cooking part are separated; a pipeline connects them.	Add-bin and cooking part are integrated as a whole.
Burning features	All raw materials are gasified, can not see fire	Half gasification and can see fire
Sources of fuel	Smashed biomass	Briquettes
Problems	Tar and bad smell; Complicated operation process	When flameout at night, still produced little of tar. The users had to often add briquettes and remove the residues due to the low caloric value Not enough supply of briquettes in many villages
Application	Gasifiers were used in the locations such as barbershops, bathhouses, where flameout was not needed.	Many people used the semi-gasifiers to burn coal, instead of briquettes because it was energy-saving.

Briquettes' Making

Semi-gasifier use briquettes as fuel. Cotton stalks have high oil content and its density is close to wood fiber. Because of high density, 1.2 to 1.5 tons of cotton briquettes can produce almost the same heat as one ton of low quality coal. Corn straw can be condensed to 80 per cent its original volume. Two tons of corn briquettes produced heat equivalent to one ton of low quality coal and 2.5 tons of corn briquettes could produce the same heat as one ton of good quality coal.

In 2010, the price of cotton briquettes in Huanghua was about RMB 600-665 per ton and that of corn briquettes was RMB 450-500 a ton[10]. At that time, the price of the worst quality coal from interior Mongolia was RMB 750-800 per ton. One ton of good quality coal costed RMB 1500-1600. The cost of burning briquettes and burning coal were almost the same. Thus, financially, use of briquette was more viable. But, the basic hurdle was promoting the use of briquette among the villagers! This could be resolved either by seeking financial support from government for the farmers who used briquettes or banning the burning of low quality coal, which was largely used by the farmers. Farmers used corncobs as well for direct burning and did not require briquetting. In 2010, Huanghua corncobs were 0.5 RMB a kg and corn straw was 0.4 RMB per kg. Other briquetting materials such as sawdust, peanut shells, leaves and barks were also used. Sawdust could be used directly, but could not last long. For example, burning sawdust directly lasted for half hour. But, if the sawdust was briquetted, the fire would last for two hours. There was, therefore, a requirement for preparing briquettes for semi-gasifiers.

Photo 4.3: Briquettes of Cotton
Photo credit: CIE, TUFE team.

Photo 4.4: Briquettes of Saw Dust
Photo credit: CIE, TUFE team.

Semi-gasifier Promotion by Government

The government decided to promote semi-gasifiers, which would use briquettes from biomass as fuels. The semi-gasifiers did not have the problems like that of gasifiers (Table 4.4). Liu began to produce semi-gasifiers in 2009, in his small workshop and he sold them to the provinces of Liaoning, Shandong and Inner Mongolia. Dealers from other cities all learned from Huanghua's practices and tried to get financial support from their local governments according to the government policy of New Village Construction. In the same year, about 2,000 stoves were sold in Huanghua, out of which, 500 stoves got government subsidies. The subsidies varied from RMB 200 to RMB 500 depending on the model.

The Huanghua government planned to subsidize 10,000 semi-gasifiers in 2010. Unfortunately, Liu's workshop was too small to produce 10,000 units. Again, the Huanghua Agricultural Bureau put Liu in contact with another private company, whose owner was named Sun Chengguo. Sun was interested in cooperating with Liu Yongquan because: (i) Liu's technique was more developed than the others, which received good comments not only by the users in Hebei Province but also from people in and around China. (ii) Liu was a local innovator and his innovation was in line with the national industrial development policy. Hence, Liu's semi-gasifier qualified for the subsidy, both at Hebei Provincial and Huanghua city levels. (iii) Since 2007, the Huanghua government began to focus on New Village Construction. Thus, keeping the village clean through the reuse of agriculture waste became an important government priority.

Selecting Pilot Villages

In November 2009, the Huanghua Agriculture Bureau organized an on-the-spot meeting at Zhaozizha village, Changguo Town. The meeting aimed to promote Liu's semi-gasifiers. The mayor of Huanghua made an announcement that the government planned to subsidize 10,000 semi-gasifiers. On an average, each stove would receive RMB 200 of subsidy. The government selected 20 pilot villages for the introduction of the semi-gasifiers. The main criterion for pilot village selection was that the villages should be spread evenly all across Huanghua County. Thus, villages from east, west, south, north and some from the middle of the city were selected. The minority ethnic villages were also included. But, in reality, the methodology of selecting scattered villages, largely increased operational cost of the project and became the key reason for the failure of the project's implementation, as discussed later in this section.

The other criterion for pilot village selection was a history of initiatives taken for innovations, by the village leaders and the farmers. One of the pilot villages was Zhaozizha, which was the hometown of the director of the Huanghua Agriculture Bureau. In 2010, nearly 5,000 semi-gasifiers were sold in the pilot villages and in 2011 another 5,000 sets were sold with government subsidies. Sun Chengguo's company benefited.

In 2010, many models of semi-gasifier were sold in the pilot villages, such as model 40, 80, 100, 120 and 200. The model number indicates the area that it would heat. For example, Model 40 referred to a stove whose heating area was 40 sq. m. On an average, the government provided a subsidy of RMB 200 for each stove, to the producer, to reduce the price. So, if the market price of Model 40 was RMB 480, the farmers in the pilot villages were required to pay only RMB 280, because of the subsidy. The market price of Model 60 was RMB 759 and the farmers had to pay only RMB 520. Table 4.5 lists the prices of several semi-gasifier models.

Table 4.5: Prices of some semi-gasifiers in 2010

Purpose	*Heating Area (in sq. m)*	*Number of Radiators*	*Price before Subsidies (RMB)*	*Price after Subsidy (RMB)*	*Group Purchase Price (RMB) (50 sets or more)*
Cooking and stove	40	1 set	460	260	220
Cooking and heating	60	2 set	700	500	480
Cooking and heating	80	3 set	820	620	600
Cooking and heating	80	3 set	950	750	720
Cooking	100	4 set	1,000	800	770
Cooking	100	4 set	870	670	640
Cooking	120	5 set	1,100	900	860
Cooking	200	6-8 sets	2,200	2,000	1,900

Note: Cooking stove means it can be used for cooking and heating.

Source: from Liu Yongquan.

Zhaozizha Village – Pilot village for Semi-Gasifiers

Zhaozizha village was one of the pilot villages for semi-gasifier application. The village had 199 households and the population was 872. In 2009, 124 (62 per cent) households bought these stoves. In 2010 the annual per capita income was over RMB 5,200, which was about the average per capita income of Huanghua County. The main crop of the village was corn and not cotton, because growing corn was easy work as compared to growing cotton. The villagers worked in the factories nearby and earned salaries. Many villagers had their own small workshops. The people with good economic condition preferred working in the factories, or managing their own small businesses, in order to save time. For them, saving time was more important than the cost of energy. They did not care if gas and electricity were a bit expensive and preferred to use it, rather than save money and use energy that forced them to put in more time. Since the farming was highly dependent on weather, agriculture income was low and hence farming was not preferred as an important means for living. In contrast, the low-income families or the elderly people had more time on hand and were not averse to spending more time on cooking, as the application of semi-gasifiers would entail. Further, the village also had families that reared livestock and worked on farms, and they used biomass for feeding their animals. So part of the families were interested in using the semi-gasifiers, while many others were not. Hence, only 124 (62 per cent) households bought these stoves.

At that time, there was no briquette supply in the local market. Moreover, the technique of briquetting machine was not competent enough. Traditionally, the briquetting machines were used for making briquettes for livestock feeding. The key parts of the briquette machine, such as grinder roll and millstone were not strong enough to briquette biomass for the purpose of fuel. The high density of briquettes needed a strong grinder roll and millstone. The briquetting process broke down many a times and people frequently had to change the key parts, increasing the cost of the process.

The local government supported the marketing of semi-gasifiers because they burned straw briquettes, and not coal. Therefore, in order to get the government subsidies, Sun had to produce briquettes. Sun Chengguo procured several machines on a trial basis from the briquetting machine producer in Shijiazhuang, the capital city of Hebei Province. He had to transport the big machine from one village to another village, so that the farmers could convert biomass into briquettes. The regionally balanced selection of pilot villages increased the project operation cost, since the briquetting machine had to be transported from one village to another, so that the villagers could convert their straw into briquettes and then use it for the semi-gasifiers which they would purchase from Sun with the help of government subsidy.

In Zhaozizha, the briquetting machine was put in the village school. Villagers only had to bring the straw to the school and it would be pressed for free. The villagers ran the briquetting machine but they were not skilful. In addition, the briquetting machine itself had its own problem and did not work well. For instance, the machine easily broke down, had low working efficiency and high electricity consumption. The corn briquettes were light in density and could not burn long. Moreover, the briquetting machine was not under the ownership of anyone in the village, so no one took the responsibility to look after the machine. The machine also suffered a lot of wear and tear due to the weathering effects of rain and wind. In the fall of 2010, due to such condition of the briquetting machine, the producer took it away. Left with no choice, in 2011, villagers went back to burning coal. Although straw briquetting created many problems, the residents of Zhaozizha placed a high value on Liu's semi-gasifiers.

The opinions of residents of Zhaozizha village on Liu's semi-gasifier were[11]:

- Initially the semi-gasifier was designed to use straw briquette both in the night and during the day. But, the fact was, the villagers burned straw briquette in daytime and coal in the night because the briquettes could not last the whole night.
- While burning briquettes in daytime there was no smoke and bad smell.
- A small blower made the ignition easy and fire strong. The strong fire made cooking easier and faster.
- The stove design consisted of a narrow top and a wide bottom, so it was good at containing heat. The semi-gasifier

had a high thermal efficiency and saved coal (the villagers used coal because they did not get enough briquette supply).

- Semi-gasifier was especially suitable for burning bituminous coal. While the common stove produced smoke while igniting bituminous coal, Liu's semi-gasifier did not give out smoke. The smoke got sucked into the stove and reconverted into fire when ignited.
- The stove heated and reached a high temperature quickly. For example, after ignition, in about five minutes, Liu's stove would reach a certain degree of temperature. Whereas the other traditional stoves, took about ten minutes to reach the same temperature as Liu's.
- In 2009, the villagers used their own biomass for briquetting for free. Thus, on an average, they saved half of the coal consumption as compared to earlier years. Generally, a stove would need one ton of coal for heating purposes. Since the villagers used briquettes in the daytime and coal during the night, they could save half a ton of coal.
- The semi-gasifier saved coal compared to other stoves. A teacher at Zhaozizha, owned a house consisting of 5 rooms. He said that during the winter of 2010, they used less than 1 ton of coal by using Liu's semi-gasifier, whereas in 2009, they had consumed more than 1 ton of coal, while using another well-known national brand of stove.
- The briquettes produced/available were of a lower quality as they did not have the requisite high density and could not burn as long as compared to burning coal. If coal could burn for 4 hours, the same weight of briquettes could only burn for 2-3 hours. Moreover, compared to coal, burning briquettes produced a lot of soot. The villagers had to clean the chimney 3-4 times during one winter.

Learnings from Zhaozizha as Pilot Village for Semi-gasifier

This pilot village experiment for semi-gasifier offered some learnings in general and also to Liu. Liu realised that the semi-gasifier needed further improvement because the briquettes could not last the whole night after being ignited. But the users believed the stove was of good quality. Liu had used straw briquettes as fuel for the semi-gasifier, in order to address the issue of tar and the resultant bad odor, with the understanding that it was not to be used overnight. But, the villagers wanted to run the semi-gasifier the whole night. Hence, they solved the problem by combination of fuels—use of straw briquettes during daytime and use of coal in the evenings and night. Liu's stove had a higher efficiency in burning of coal than the traditional coal burning stoves! But at that time, the policies did not support the energy saving stoves that burnt both coal and straw briquettes.

Just as in any other rural part of the world, in rural China too, the inhabitants of the same village cooperated with each other, observed and learnt from each other and believed in word-of-mouth. Generally, with regard to diffusion of any innovation in the villages, such as that of the new and innovative semi-gasifiers, burning the briquettes etc., the villagers observed and followed each other and the new technology would be diffused through word of mouth. This is what our data analysis presented in Chapter 2 also reveal. But, that was not the case in the pilot village of Zhaozizha where, the households had strong connections either with their relatives or their neighbors and hence the diffusion of the new innovation was limited to the known circles of early buyers of the new technology. In this village, all the residents were not close to each other. Thus, the people who lived in the eastern side of the village, bought semi-gasifiers, but those who lived in the western part of the village hardly bought these semi-gasifiers. Zhaozizha is a big village with a population of more than 1000 people. The people who lived in the west hardly came to the eastern side of the village.

When we interviewed the common farmers of Zhaozizha, it was learnt that they did not have much information about the village in general, like the population of the village, how much land they owned etc. Only the village leaders and the village accountant had this information. The research team from Tianjin University of Finance and Economics, Tianjin, China observed that most of the villagers did not show much interest in semi-gasifier and briquettes. They were not interested in learning about this new technology. They were satisfied with the working of their stoves and did not trust the working of the semi-gasifiers. Also, as mentioned earlier, some were using LPG stoves and others electricity and were not interested in semi-gasifiers.

The case of Zhaozizha pilot village throws up important issues for discussion. The government policy sometimes is dogmatic. For example, selection of a village for pilot project has to be based on the ground reality rather than on some dogmatic criteria. For example, the success of a pilot project, such as for semi-gasifier or any other, would be successful only if the local residents are willing to participate. This was not the case for this project, as the villages were selected based on their location. Thus, all the residents of the village did not participate in the pilot project. Half the village was unaware of the ongoing pilot project and was not even interested in this technology. Those who used this technology benefited, which led to benefits related to environmental protection and saving energy. Unfortunately, others did not benefit since they did not participate.

Producing Stalk-briquettes in Nandagang Farm

While the success of Liu's semi-gasifier was limited in Huanghua, one farmer named Liu Lexun in Nandagang farm, located about 15 km from Huanghua, was contacted by the entrepreneur Sun Chengguo for partnership in the semi-gasifier business. Nandagang farm had 0.1 million Mu (6667 acres[12]) of cotton land. One mu land of cotton cultivation can produce 200-225 kg of dry cotton stalk. The main use of the cotton stalk at that time was as firewood. The nearby villagers took cotton stalks back home from Nandagang for free.

Farmer Liu Lexun was smart and eager to try new things. He decided to grow cotton on 1000 mu of land in Nandagang farm. Attracted by the large quantity of cotton stalk of Nandagang, Sun Chengguo offered to provide Liu a briquetting machine, so that the latter could produce cotton stalk briquettes on his Nandagang farm. Sun Chengguo would then purchase these briquettes from Liu Lexun and sell the same to the villagers, who bought semi-gasifiers in the pilot villages. In September 2010, Sun introduced a briquetting machine into Liu Lexun's cotton farm. Liu and his friend, farmer Zuo Deqiang, worked together on briquette production. Due to the inappropriate design of the machine, the parts of the millstones were frequently damaged in the production process. Liu Lexun and Zuo Deqiang studied the machine carefully and identified the problem. They modified the machine accordingly and since then that machine has worked well. Later on, they also helped Sun Chengguo to modify his three other briquetting machines. Since then, the briquette quality and its yield have improved. The density of cotton briquettes made by Liu Lexun and Zuo Deqiang was about 1.1-1.2gm/cm^3, the total cost was about RMB 550-560 per ton. They sold to Sun Chengguo at the price of RMB 600 per ton. Adding the transportation cost, Sun sold the cotton briquettes to the villagers at RMB 640-650 per ton.

By July 2011, Liu Lexun and Zuo Deqiang had produced a total of more than 200 tons of cotton stalk briquettes. Overall, Liu Lexun and Zuo Deqiang did not earn much money but they also did not lose money. According to Liu Lexun, they could have made better profits had there been a market for the cotton stalk briquettes, which at that time was not the case. Their briquetting machine had a capacity to produce, on an average, 8-9 tons of briquettes in a day but they produced only 3 tons. The output was also low, as the machine had to be stopped for repairs now and then, due to certain technical problems and hence its optimum capacity could not be utilized. Moreover, lack of market for the briquettes also deterred its optimum use. The costs of briquetting mainly include that of labor, electricity, transportation and waste. The cost of briquette production varied in different places. Table 4.6 gives the briquette production costs details of Liu Lexun and Zuo Deqiang.

The main problems in cotton stalk briquetting and suggestions by the farmer innovators are:

- A large place was needed for the briquetting machine to function properly. Ideally, it should be placed in a workshop.
- The briquetting could be done well only if proper moisture was maintained during the process and the farmers had difficulty in controlling the same. Although Liu Lexun and Zuo Deqiang could modify the machines, they failed in solving the problems of controlling temperature during its operation due to their low formal education.
- At that time, the cost of burning coal was the same as the cost of burning briquettes and hence, there was a need for financial support from the government in order to attract the farmers to buy briquettes.
- It would be good if a machine could integrate the functions of crushing and briquetting.

Table 4.6: The cost of cotton stalk briquettes production

Item	*Explanation*
Labor cost	The labor cost in Huanghua was quite high. In 2010, while a man earned RMB 100-200 a day, a woman earned RMB 80 a day. The labor cost of crushing and pressing was about RMB 110 per ton of briquettes.
Electricity consumption	According to Liu Lexun and Zuo, producing one ton of briquettes required 560 kwh of electricity. In 2010, they paid a little more than RMB 0.6/kwh, which was the price for agricultural purpose, which was cheaper compared to RMB 0.8 for industries.
Transportation cost	Depending on the distance from Nandagang, to the pilot villages, the transporting fee varied between RMB 30 to 50 per ton.
Wastage	For example, after the rains, the straw rotted, the crushed straw powder was blown away with wind, the straw naturally lost weight after they dried.
Others	At the beginning it costed nothing to use cotton stalks but they might have to pay money, if later they consumed in large quantity.

Source: Liu Lexun and Zuo Deqiang

Improvement on Semi-gasifier

Compared to the original gasifier, the semi-gasifier was much more technically sound and practical and could solve the problem of tar and resulting foul smell, to a certain extent. But, Liu Yongquan's first generation of semi-gasifier still had some problems, for example, banking the furnace in the night would cause tar. Banking the furnace meant covering the fire with ashes or fresh fuel to restrict air from reducing the combustion rate, and thus preserving the fuel for future use. This also ensures that the heat in the furnace (here gasifier) is preserved and it is easy to start the furnace (gasifier) again.

When the temperature reached 1000-1200°C, tar would naturally be decomposed. Tar would be produced if the temperature were lower than 1000°C. When the temperature is low, adding a catalyst can solve the problem of tar formation. For example, at 750°C, using nickel base as catalyst can decompose tar; when temperature is at 900°C, dolomite is needed to decompose tar. The main hurdle was that the cost of using a catalyst was too high. Thus, although Liu Yongquan tried many ways to use a catalyst, he could not get a satisfactory solution.

To avoid banking up furnace in the night, Liu changed his products' purpose from heating to cooking function. The markets targeted were mainly in south China. Additionally, places like the bathhouse, barbeque, small restaurants and others which needed longer time burning time, without banking up in the night, became the target markets. Liu also developed some new products to meet the market need/demand. For example, in 2011, he developed a semi-gasifier for summer. This stove could use a small pot. An attached oven could toast sweet potato, crispy bun slice etc.

Liu's semi-gasifier had been tested by the testing center for new energy-saving products, Hebei Province in 2009 and 2010 but not in 2011[13]. Liu's products met the requirements. The testing report was valid for only one year, which meant that testing was required every year. There were two reasons to test the products, one was to get the professional data for further research and another was for the purpose of marketing. A testing certificate/ report from the concerned authority or department helped in attracting the potential buyers.

Cooperation with Xinhuo Company (2014)

Once again, Liu Yongquan entered into cooperation with a company for producing semi-gasifiers. In early 2012, entrepreneur Sun Chengguo became bankrupt and he did not have adequate working capital to run the operations of his company. Liu, therefore, had to once again find a new job, which he found in a stove company in Liaoning Province. His partner, He Junhai, started work in a company in Hebei Province. In 2014, respecting the suggestion by the Energy office, Hebei Province, Liu joined Xinhuo, a new energy company in Quzhou county, Handan city, Hebei Province. As the technology manager, he was responsible for developing, improving semi-gasifier and designing different kinds of energy-saving stoves for the market. Mr. Zhu, the owner of Xinhuo had another company that prepared special designs of energy saving equipment and then installed them in big companies such as steel companies, coal companies etc. He earned some money through that business. Since 2012, Mr Zhu's business had suffered due to recession in steel and coal mine industries.

Mr. Zhu had to look for new business opportunities. His company had once received government support of RMB 5 million for manufacturing energy saving devices. Zhu, thus believed that the government supported energy saving industry and that government money was easy money for business development. In 2013, he came to know that Hebei Province would provide subsidy of RMB 700 per unit for marketing of 0.5 million units of semi-gasifiers from 2014 onwards for three years. In addition, the project would also provide support to the tune of RMB 150 per ton of briquettes. The policy also stated that the stove company had to provide three tons of briquettes to the buyers of one semi-gasifier.

Hebei Province is located next to Beijing and Tianjin, the two large national level cities and important centers for international business for China. Besides, Beijing was also the political capital of the country. It was incumbent on Hebei Province, to reduce emissions, so that the air quality in Beijing and Tianjin improve. This led Hebei Province to specially provide large incentives to the farmers, to quit burning coal and biomass and move towards cleaner energy fuels. Supporting semi-gasifiers was one of the policies adopted by the province.

Attracted by the promising future, Mr. Zhu invested in a new company, Xinhuo—a new energy company for semi-gasifier production. He did not understand the semi-gasifier business and did not have technicians for the same. Once again, the local government stepped in and introduced Liu to Mr. Zhu. As a team, Mr. Zhu, Liu, and another partner, Yubo, worked together at Xinhuo. Yubo was good at marketing. He also helped Liu in new product development.

This policy of promoting semi-gasifier was made in 2013, but, its implementation begun in the latter part of 2014. Mr. Zhu was a novice in understanding the ways the government functioned. He thought that since the policy was announced, it would be immediately implemented. He jumped into the production of semi-gasifiers against the advice of Liu. The traditional stove companies in Hebei and other parts of China waited for the clear picture with regard to policy implementation to emerge, before beginning their production. Since the big stove companies did not immediately responded to the policy announcement, Mr. Zhu thought that he had good opportunity at hand. To please the government officials, he invested large sums of money on buying 20 robots and briquetting machines for biomass briquettes production. These largely increased his production cost. In addition, Mr. Zhu thought that the bidding for the contracts for manufacturing semi-gasifier devices for the pilot villages would be organized at the provincial level and his company being big and modern, would win the bids. But, the bidding happened at the county level and many small companies with low production costs won the bid.

Now, the small producers did not have capacity to produce so many semi-gasifiers. So, they all went to Renqiu city, Hebei Province, for purchasing semi-gasifiers. Renqiu was the stove production center in China. Due to a sudden increase in demand, many stove producers increased the price. Some of them did not have the techniques in semi-gasifier production, but in the greed of making good profits, they produced low quality semi-gasifiers. In such a confused situation, Xinhuo did not have any advantage in the competition. Mr. Zhu was in short on finances and could not run his business. He did not pay Liu and his team as per the contracts. Once again, Liu's partnership with a company for diffusion of his technology did not work out well, due to lack of experience of the company owner!

In 2015, the Hebei government learned from the lessons of 2014, and improved their implementation policy such as starting the bidding quite earlier compared with 2014, so that the companies could have enough time to sell and install semi-gasifiers, before the farmers got ready for winter heating. During the year, many big traditional stove companies started switching over to the semi-gasifier business. All of them easily won the contracts. Liu and his team could not get money from Xinhuo, so they left and started their own business in Renqiu. They helped big companies in stove marketing.

Diffusing Energy-saving Stove Technology in India (2015)

In earlier 2015, invited by National Innovation Foundation (NIF), India, Liu and Yubo went to India to make a presentation on energy-saving technology. The research team of Tianjin University of Finance and Economics, followed Liu's case for years. They understood the value of Liu's innovation. TUFE's team has had a long-term cooperation with India's National Innovation Foundation (NIF).

Conclusion

Innovation Journey

Liu's innovation and entrepreneurship journey is an epitome of Chinese grassroots level innovators struggling for survival, as well as the epitome of the development process of energy-saving stove in China. Initially, Liu developed the gasifier, failed many times and then shifted to semi-gasifier design and marketing. Around 2014, the briquetting technique developed fully and became sound and that was useful for diffusion of semi-gasifiers. Table 4.7 sums up Liu's innovation and entrepreneurship journey.

Innovation Network

In the process of innovation and entrepreneurship, many a times, the government linked/set up Liu with other companies. As an individual innovator, Liu knew that a strong innovation network would help him and make up for his weaknesses in experiences, capabilities and knowledge. Thus, he continually sought various partners. Table 4.8 gives the Liu's network of partners. Not all the partnerships he made have been discussed in the chapter—only the important ones have been discussed in details. Indeed, this long journey of innovation and then attempts to diffuse innovation through commercial route cannot be single-handedly taken.

Larger Policy Implications

Nearly all the rural households at this time, in the mid-2015, used traditional stoves for cooking and heating in China, irrespective of their household incomes. Some households, particularly the poor households, used them for all domestic energy needs such as cooking, water heating and room heating, the higher income households used it only for certain limited purposes. The situation creates 'energy stacking' as the households adopt new energy sources, while still continuing to use the traditional sources. China is transiting rural households into urban living, under the program

Table 4.7: Liu's Innovation and Entrepreneurship Journey: From Gasifier to Semi-gasifier

Time	*R&D process*	*Government support*	*Marketing*	*Issues for discussion*
1998-2002	Personal strives for perfecting straw gasifier	No		
2003	Produced several products	Began to support	After products were sold, they were returned due to their bad quality	The importance of internet, cooperation and marketing
2004-2005	Improve products continuously	Received subsidies for selling; Helped Liu in solving technique problem	Selling drawings and gasifiers	
2006	Cooperated with Long Xiang but failed the same year; Continued to improve products	Subsidies for selling gasifier and helped promote the products	Because of tar and resulting foul smell, many villagers gave up use of gasifier	How to understand IPR issues? How to balance the grasping of commercial opportunity and the long-term development?
2007	Begin to cooperate with Haotian	Continued to provide subsidy	Same as above	
2008	Succeeded in developing semi-gasifier and end the cooperation with Haotian	No	Continued to sell gasifier and began to sell semi-gasifier	

Time	*R&D process*	*Government support*	*Marketing*	*Issues for discussion*
2009-2010	He Junhai joined Liu on semi-gasifier improvement; Started the cooperation with Sun	Subsidy to product selling, on site promotion meeting	Media reported the short-comings of gasifier; Semi-gasifer marketing	How to make the government policy more suitable to the real situation?
2011	Continued to modify semi-gasifier; Sun failed due to liquidity issues	No	Targeting the restaurant, barbershop	Innovation diffusion depended on many factors, such as related technique, equipment, government support, transportation condition, etc.
2014	Joined Xinhuo company, Hebei Province; Briquetting technology became mature	Hebei provincial government subsidized 0.3 million semi-gasifiers' marketing and selling of straw briquette	Policy implementation did not work well	What would the proper time for a company to enter a certain market?
2015	Started their own business; Invited by the National Innovation Foundation, India to share the innovations	Hebei government subsidized 0.5 million semi-gasifier units' sale	Liu's business did well	How to protect the intellectual property of grassroots innovators in innovation diffusion? Process of transition from a grassroots innovator to an entrepreneur?

Source: By the authors.

Table 4.8: Main Partners of Liu Over a Period of Time

Sl. No.	*Name*	*Period of partnership*	*Cooperation Content*	*Notes*
1.	Liu Xiaodong	2006	Online marketing to demonstrate Liu's innovation	Liu Yongquan's nephew
2.	Guo Jiye	2009	Technical guidance, policy consulting	Knew each other in a stove-training program of 2009; In 2013. Liu and Guo worked in the same company in Liaoning
3.	Wang Jinbao	2007	Stove installation and marketing	Sold Liu's products; A stove dealer and then stove innovator
4.	Qi Bin	2007	Provided technical service; marketing Liu's products; Liasioning Liu with government projects	
5.	He Junhai	2009	Most important partner of Liu in innovation	Worked together with Liu since 2009
6.	Yu Bo	2007	Most important partner in technology promotion; good at stove marketing	Began to sell Liu's gasifier in 2007; Joined Liu's team in 2014 in Xinhuo, and then started their own business together.
7.	Wang Jiwei	2012	Stove production	Owned his company in Renqiu, Liu had cooperation with him in stove parts production
8.	Li Chunyou	2013	Stove production	Owned his company in Renqiu, Liu had cooperation with him in stove parts production
9.	Hou Xiaoliang	2013	Briquetting production	Providing briquettes to Xinhuo
10.	Su Wentao	2012	Helped in developing electron circuit plate used in semi-gasifier	Senior electrical engineer; Yo Bo's cousin

Source: By the authors after discussions with Liu.

of New Village Construction, wherein, the households are being encouraged to shift to using electricity for all domestic purposes and the biomass waste of these villages are being transported to be used as fuel in power plants. But, in the transition phase of China's development, for some years to come, traditional cook stoves with some modifications based on local innovations, will still be in use. This chapter is the story of a farmer in Huanghua city of Hebei Province, who has made tremendous efforts to innovate gasifiers and then semi-gasifiers to ease the efforts of the farmers in cooking and heating activities. Hence, although the government's emphasis is on centralized solutions for use of biomass, something that is even evident from the policies discussed in Chapter 3, there will be a need to continue support to decentralized solutions.

Scholars Gan and Yu (2008) argue that the current government strategy, investment policy and industrial interest over-emphasized on biomass burning power generation as part of the clean energy development trajectories, which may not lead to the most cost-effective outcomes in terms of investments, resource use and social development objectives. They suggest that there are large potentials in developing and disseminating household-based biomass technologies in rural areas, especially with energy-efficient modern biomass stoves, which can produce far more economic, social and environmental benefits than biomass power plants. The decentralized solution to use renewable energy resources would, therefore, meet multi-objectives. They, therefore, recommend that the government policies should be aimed at providing incentives for decentralized technological solutions for the rural households such as assisting rural households to access renewable energy technologies, modern biomass stoves etc. This would lead to a win–win situation at the global, regional and local levels with regard to environmental protection, sustainable resource management and related social benefits, particularly for the poor in remote communities. To some extent, such a policy support has been made available by the government as this case of Liu Yongquan illustrates.

The farmer, Liu Yongquan, started his efforts in 1998 and has persevered till 2014 (when the case study was documented), that is, for a long period of 16 years, although, with modest success. Three attempts by him to commercially diffuse his innovation failed, initially because of limitations of technology but thereafter, because of the lack of business experience of the entrepreneurs with whom he partnered for the purpose.

Farmer Liu Yongquan could persist for so long, in spite of his failures at perfecting the technology and then commercially diffusing his innovation, because of the active support of the local and provincial government on one hand and the national laws on energy conservation (1997), promotion of renewable energy (2005) as well as policies on New Village Construction. The Energy Conservation Law of 1997 (*See* Chapter 3), lay emphasis on increasing energy efficiency of all devices and it is applicable to even cooking stoves used in rural China. But, the impetus to renewable energy under the Renewable Energy Law of 2005, has envisaged the use of biomass for energy production and particularly, the use of agriculture waste such as stalks and straw directly. One way to deploy the agricultural waste is through using them as feed in the thermal power plant and thereby reducing the use of coal, thus reducing carbon emissions. Another way is to make the existing cook stoves more efficient by using the briquetting and gasifier or semi-gasifier technologies. Liu has contributed to developing this technology. But, because of these laws and policies of the Government of China, provincial funds were made available for supporting his activities. He obtained direct funds for his research from the Huanghua city Energy Office. But, then the subsidy available for promoting renewable energy was made available only to those companies that were manufacturing the gasifiers or semi-gasifiers, at the time of sale of the product. The local government announced the number of units that it would subsidize. Subsidy on purchase was an incentive for the rural households to purchase the new technology. The local government also served as the innovator's liaison with the local entrepreneur so that the innovation could be commercially diffused. Although, Liu Yongquan himself did not benefit from such marketing subsidies; the companies did benefit for a short while. Liu had to use his own funds for innovation. Liu's case supports the findings in Chapter 2 that the innovators did not have access to finance for their efforts.

Despite many efforts, Liu has not been able to perfect the technology. The two major problems, that of formation of tar and ensuing foul smell from the gasifier and semi-gasifier stoves remain. Then there is also the problem of the feed for such stoves. In gasifier stoves, the biomass fuel used, has to be cut to a certain size before being used, while the semi-gasifier requires briquetting. Both are time consuming. Briquetting itself is a technology and the machines used for this purpose have to produce briquettes of certain density, to be able to keep the semi-gasifiers burning through the night, when used for the heating purposes. Tar formation can also be contained by using some catalysts, which are expensive for farmers. Besides, before using the new technology, the farmer/users have to be appropriately trained. There is, therefore, a need of capacity building at the grassroots level, using the funding from Science and Technology (S&T) Bureaus at the local level.

Moreover, most of the local entrepreneurs (as per this case study) were not successful, as they did not have the requisite knowledge to understand the local market, nor did they have the ability or understanding as to when to make investments. They too, require training for developing an astute business sense. This role can also be performed by the local or at best the provincial government. In a large country, such as China, when these technologies are going to continue as options for rural households, there is a need to improve the technology, improve the production of such devices, and develop local entrepreneurs who could commercially diffuse such devices locally. Since 2014, China has made Environmental Protection Law, 1989 more stringent by inclusion of PM 2.5 standards. These are more difficult standards to follow. The key question, therefore, which arises is, whether such grassroots innovations and innovators such as Liu, would be able to develop techniques to control emissions of PM2.5 from the burning of biomass.

NOTES

1. Lei Hanfa and Yang Meiting, "Eco-utilization of Straw and Stalk", *Economic Daily News*, July 8, 2014.
2. In 1986, Huanghua County was renamed as Huanghua City (county level).
3. If cotton stalks are used as fuel of Kang bed-stove, about 1,500 kg cotton stalks are needed for one winter. But, young people of the village instead prefer common beds and heating sleep on common from self-made central-heating.
4. In 2009, the policy of appliances to the countryside was implemented in Huanghua City. Farmers could get subsidy from the government for purchasing certain appliances. In the same year, the city Agricultural Bureau selected several pilot villages to promote biogas,

which is also subsidized by the government. Some villages built a big community biogas plant. For example, there is a large biogas plant at Xipai Village of Changguo Township, which is used by 300 households. Shen Hua Group invested in this plant. The biogas was not free. Villagers could purchase biogas in exchange of straw and/or stalk or with money, at price of RMB 1 for $1m^3$ biogas.

5. Mrs. Yu Bo, an important partner of Liu Yongquan later, also came to cooperate with Liu after seeing the internet advertisement.
6. Liu's gasifier too looks like this picture from the web.
7. In October 2005, "Guidelines of the Eleventh Five-Year Plan for National Economic and Social Development" was passed in the Fifth Plenary Session of the Sixteenth Central Committee of the Party. Village cleanness problem was listed in it. Straw and stalks abandoned around rural houses not only pollute environment but are also a hidden risk of fire. For example, according to the Huanghua Fire Department, more than 900 fire cases were reported each year. Amongst them, one-third were caused by straw and stalks. If the house fires caused by straw and stalk burning were accounted for, the proportion of fires caused by straw and stalk would reach half. After the implementation of New Village Construction policy, the numbers of fire cases reduced largely.
8. During the news conference, when the government only focused on the marketing of gasifier and did not give enough attention to the innovator, Liu felt sad.
9. He Junhai joined Liu Yongquan while Liu worked on developing the semi-gasifier. He used to work as a quality inspector for ten years at Hualin Company. He showed interest in semi-gasifier when he welded stoves for Liu. He decided to quit his job in Hualin and join Liu although Liu could only pay him a bit more than 1000 RMB per month. Another reason he decided to work with Liu was that he thought Liu was a honest man and could be trusted. In the later innovation, he played a very important role.
10. Data from the fieldwork.
11. In May 2010, the research team at Tianjin University of Finance and Economics (TUFE), Tianjin, China, interviewed 12 villagers who used Liu's semi-gasifier. In May 2012, the TUFE team visited Zhaozizha again to study the using effect of semi-gasifiers.
12. 15 mu is one acre.
13. In 2011, the products were not tested because Sun's company was in trouble. The reason why the gasifier was not tested was because there was no related testing standard. Only stoves burning coal and straw briquettes had testing standards.

5

Making and Marketing Briquette Machines and Biomass Pellets

Chapter 4 presented the case of farmer Liu Yongquan, who developed a gasifier and a semi-gasifier with some moderate degree of success. But, the innovation's success was based on use of briquettes. The gasifier and semi-gasifier use briquettes made from biomass as fuel. The semi-gasifier innovated by Liu, found government support and companies were roped in by the government to market these devices. But, the companies also had to arrange for supplying of briquettes either by getting some farmers to produce briquettes from straw or make available a briquette making machine in the villages that were selected as pilot villages for the semi-gasifiers so that the resident farmers made their own briquettes for the semi-gasifier. This chapter discusses the case of a farmer, Suo Wenbin, who developed a small briquette machine for easy use. The case of Lu Min Straw Utilization Cooperative is also discussed which commercialized the process of straw pelleting with some success amidst difficult times, where many such other cooperatives did not succeed.

Sue Wenbin's Case of Small-sized Briquetting Machine Innovation

Research Motivation

Suo Wenbin was born in 1956 in a small mountain village in Changzhi, Shanxi Province. He was clever and tenacious. After he graduated from middle school, Suo was enlisted in the army. After retiring from the army, he began to work in an agricultural machinery institute under the aegis of Changzhi City Agricultural Machinery Bureau. He learned technical knowledge about agriculture machinery on his own during his spare time.

As mentioned in Chapter 4, the research in straw gasifier was quite popular since late 1990s. Many grassroots innovators were involved in the modification of gasifiers. Like Liu Yongquan (Chapter 4), Suo was also affected by the gasifier-innovation boom and began to modify the biomass gasifier in 1998. His several different attempts using different methods to modify the gasifier failed. Like Liu Yongquan, he too faced the problems of tar and resulting foul smell from the gasifier. The problems resulted from a basic design flaw in the gasifier. The effect of the problems could be reduced, by modifying the gasifier design, but the major problems of tar and foul smell could not be completely eradicated. Suo worked on modifying the gasifier design for ten years till the time the media began exposing the basic defects of the gasifier design. The media also campaigned to expose these defects and appealed to the people not to be cheated anymore by any of the companies selling the gasifier design. Realizing the fruitlessness of his efforts, Suo gave up work on improving gasifier and began work on modification of the briquetting machine in 2008.

The choice of research on briquetting machine was not arbitrary. Suo had observed in his earlier long-term research efforts that there was an internal connection between tar production and biomass humidity. He was sure that the tar problem could be solved if he could use briquettes as fuel. At that time, the briquette making technology was not well developed and efficient. Suo understood that if a briquetting machine could successfully make briquettes with low or no humidity, it might very well lead to the reduction in tar output while using the gasifier. Hence, although he was very much interested in improving the gasifier technology, he first wanted to develop a briquetting machine that was small and could easily be used by the farmers.

Changzhi was rich in biomass but the briquette making machines sold in market at that time was huge. These machines required large quantities of biomass for efficient use. Big briquetting machines were, therefore, not suitable for the local use. A small sized and cheaper briquette making machine was adequate for the quantity of biomass generated by one village. Such a machine could then promote decentralized briquette making,

Changzhi City in Shanxi Province

Shanxi in China

Map 5.1: Changzhi City in Shanxi Province and Shanxi in China

Photo 5.1: Large Briquette Making Machine
Photo Credit: CIE[1], TUFE team

Photo 5.2: Small Briquette Making Machine of Suo Wenbin
Photo Credit: CIE, TUFE team

resulting in the decentralized implementation of the renewable energy program, whereby each village would be able to sustainably use its available biomass to produce briquettes.This cut the cost of transporting biomass to far away locations where larger briquetting machines were located and transporting back the briquettes to the villages. The smaller machine could also reuse all the locally available biomass. The briquettes could then be readily available with the village households to be used as energy fuel in gasifiers.

Changzhi City is very cold during winter and heating is required for about 4 months in a year. On an average, for an area of 60 sq. m. to be heated, a household would burn 4-5 tons of coal in a winter. It costed more than RMB 3000 in 2008. Since 2001, the coal price had increased to RMB 1100 to 1200 per ton for good quality coal and to RMB 800 per ton for inferior quality coal, i.e. A household would, therefore, spend between RMB 3,200 to 6,000 per year just for heating requirements during the 4 months of the year. This was quite expensive. A cheaper source of heating fuel was now necessarily required for the rural households in Changzhi City.

Whenever Suo visited his village, he repeatedly heard the residents saying: "Thirty years after reforms and opening up of trade, farmers' lives had greatly improved. They could afford to build big houses but could not afford to keep them warm. They prepared fried pork using firewood and wrapped themselves in blanket to watch TV!" This vividly described how important it was for the local farmers to have cheaper fuel!

The coal for heating was available from the numerous coal mines in the Shanxi Province. But, after frequent coal mine accidents and reports of exploitation of the workers, Shanxi Provincial Government closed the small mines in 2008. The availability of coal became a problem. The price of coal went up and the low-income households of the area could no longer afford to purchase coal. The availability of wood also had declined as it was already mined for cooking and heating purposes. In order to solve the heating problem in winter, from 2011 onwards, the Shanxi Provincial Government started to subsidize fuel for poor farmer households for heating. The subsidy standard was "one ton coal for each household". The subsidy period was from 2011 to 2015. However, one ton coal was not enough as 4-5 tons of coal was required for the 4 months period. Hence, finding an alternative to coal as heating fuel had become imminent!

If a small, straw pellet machine were to be developed, it would be much cheaper. The entire village could share one machine. Straw waste in rural areas could also be made good use of. Using of straw pellets instead of coal, would greatly relieve the heating problem during winters in the rural areas.

The second problem that Suo wanted to solve was elimination of pollution created by the agricultural waste lying around. This had also been one of Liu's (Chapter 4) objectives for developing the gasifier, so that the biomass lying around as waste could be recycled for a very useful purpose such as heating the living spaces in the farmers' houses.

Changzhi City's rural areas abound with corn stalks due to its suitable natural environment. In 2006, the corn was cultivated on 2.64 million mu of land; in 2007 it was 2.73 million mu; in 2008, it was 2.84 million mu and in 2009, the number reached 2.88 million mu.Corn was the main agricultural crop. For example, in 2009, the corn plantation accounted for 68.4 per cent of the total cultivable land available for agriculture in the areas of Changzhi (Zhang *et al.*, 2012: 4). Suo Wenbin, estimated that one mu of corn could produce nearly 500 kg dry stalks. The total dry stalks production per year in Changzhi city would, therefore, be about 1400 to 1500 tons. Of these, only one-third to two-fifths were utilized and the rest were burnt. Since the stalk-burning was prohibited as per the air pollution laws, many farmers subverted the law and burned stalks in the dark and windy night. Thus, large areas of land with dry stalks would be burnt, assisted by the winds, which helped in spreading the fire quickly in addition to dissipating the smoke too! The leftover corn stalks in the field were collected by the poor farmers for their household use. There was, thus, a massive waste of corn-stalk biomass resource.

To reuse straw the local government promoted straw mulching from 2011 onwards. Straw mulching requires moisture. However, since this area receives less rainfall, the straws could not rot quickly. Also, the quantity of straw being, it could not rot in a year's time, before the next seeding cycle. Hence, the farmers had no option but to burn stalks in 2012, despite the promotion of straw mulching activity by the government. Hence, the illegal nocturnal burning of straw continued.[2] There was a strong need, therefore, to find an alternate use of the crop straws and this motivated Suo to innovate a small briquetting machine for the use of these straws.

Innovation Process

Suo developed a small straw pellet machine on the base of existing straw pellet feed machine. He said: "I'm so obsessed with this innovation. It's like my child!" He named his QQ (a Chinese chatting software) as "QiuSuo"(means "seek"). In 2008, Suo purchased a straw pellet feed machine from Zhangqiu city, Shandong province. He modified it to compress straw pellets, which could be used as fuel in the straw gasifier. At that time, modifications to the machine had slightly reduced the problem of tar residue. Since 2009, Suo began to develop a smaller straw pellet machine. Suo himself undertook the R&D. A technician of Changzhi Productivity Promotion Center assisted him[3]. They together prepared the machine drawings in the office and built the machine at a factory manufacturing grain machinery in Changzhi.

In 2009, Suo tried to improve the wear resistance of the machine gear. In the beginning, he used gears meant for trucks. Later, he made the gears himself. But all efforts failed. The main parts of a straw pellet machine are compression rollers and refiner plates, which faced maximum wear and tear. If the pellets were to be prepared for animal feed, the density of the pellets could be kept low, which would not result in any major wear and tear of the machine. But, the fuel pellets were required to be of high density.This meant that the compressor roller and the plate had to take higher levels of stress leading to increased wear and tear. The main innovation required here was with regard to increasing the service life of the compressor roller and the refiner plate. This was the first innovation tried by Suo.

In the same year, Suo took his innovation to join The 3rd China Clean Stoves Expo. Mr. Hao Fangzhou, Director of China Alliance for Clean Stoves, suggested that he research more on semi-gasifier. Considering there were lots of people doing this research and very few on small straw pellet machine, Suo decided to pursue a dogged research to develop a small straw pellet machine. Suo's efforts paid off and in 2010, he was able to improve the wear resistance of gears that operate the roller and the refiner plate of the pellet machine.

In 2011, he made three more innovations/improvements on the straw pellet machine:

(i) **Reduce noise**: The electric control cabinet's vibration caused much noise. Dust shaken off by the vibrations also affected the working of the machine. In the original machine, the controlling cabinet was exposed to air, making loud noise while the briquetting machine was working. Suo used a big iron box to cover both the electric control cabinet and the machine. This modification solved the noise problem.

(ii) **Installing temperature sensor and current sensor on motor to prevent them from burning out[4].** When compressing straw into pellets, high output and quality would be achieved if the temperature is high. However, high temperature would also reduce the service life of compression roller and refiner plate. Suo installed a current control device on the machine. If the current exceeds 40 Amp, electricity would be cut off automatically after 15 seconds. After setting controlled temperature in the electricity meter of motor and refiner plate, the machine would turn off automatically if it exceeds 200°C.

(iii) **Improving the material quality and manufacturing technique of refiner plate and compression roller and increase their hardness.** This innovation was meant to increase the life of the plate. After improvement, both sides of the refiner plate could be used. If one side is worn out, the plate could be turned upside and used again. The whole refiner plate would be quenched[5] at one time. The thickness of quenched plates could reach to 4.5 mm[6]. Thus, the hardness of the whole refiner plate could remain uniform.

In 2012, Liu Haibing, from Li Min Straw Utilization Cooperative, found that the power of straw pellet machine was too low. He suggested Suo to change the power of the machine from 15 KW to 18.5 KW. Although the output was improved, energy consumption almost remained the same.

In 2013, Suo again made three further improvements on the machine.

(i) **Dust-free processing:** Suo installed a closed box over the machine so that dust would not blow out and spread around. The outer box also made the machine visually aesthetic besides being safer for those using it. The cost of this box was RMB 55,000.

(ii) **Double-speed gearbox:** The improved machine could compress pellets from both, corn stalk and sawdust. The cost of both these raw materials was almost the same. The corn stalks were too light to fall easily within the machine. The speed of the main axel had to be fast enough for the stalk to fall inside the machine fast. But, the pellet machine's gear box speed was fixed. Suo added a small gearbox to the outside of the machine to control (increase or reduce) the speed. The sawdust was heavy and could be compressed with normal speed. The user could adjust the speed by operating the gears. This small gearbox could speed up the machine when the corn stalks had to be compressed. This innovation led to year-round use of the pellet machine. The corn stalk was available only during some months and using the pellet machine would not be feasible if it were designed to use only corn stalk. Other raw materials feed also needed to be used for pellets during those months of the year, when corn stalk supply was not available.

(iii) Liu Haibing, the Director of Limin Farmers' Cooperative, Changzhi, found that smashed straw and stalk would drift after being fed into the machine and one person was constantly needed to use a stick to press them down. He realized that because a scraper inside the feeding chamber was straight, it obstructed the smashed straw and stalk to fall directly into the chamber. So, Liu bent the scraper at an angle and after this improvement, no additional worker was required.

In 2014, Suo developed the technology of integrating five straw pellet machines together. If one briquetting machine broke down or was damaged, it could be repaired without affecting the working of the other machines. Output could be adjusted according to the production requirement. The total cost of using these five machines together was less than RMB 200,000.

Characteristics of Small Straw Pellet Machine

Compared to large machines, the small straw pellet machine developed by Suo has many advantages. It is cheaper and easier

Table 5.1: Technological Innovations by Suo on Small Straw Pellet Machine

Year	*Innovation*	*Notes*
2009	Tried to increase the wear resistance of gears, but the effect was not obvious	Wear resistance of gears was poor; Briquetting rate was low; Low yield; Big noise.
2010	The service life of gear was greatly prolonged after introducing reducer produced by a company from Zhejiang province	
2011	Installed the electric control cabinet into the machine; Installed temperature sensor and current sensor on motor; Improved the material quality and manufacturing technique of refiner plate and compression roller	Began to cooperate with Li Min Straw Utilization Cooperative; The machine was listed in the catalogue of agricultural machinery purchase allowance of Shanxi Province; one machine could be subsidized by RMB 20,000; the subsidy period was from 2011 to 2012; the market price of one machine was RMB 51,000; One refiner plate could be used to produce 150 to 200 tons of pellets and could continuously be used for 300 hours.
2012	Changed the machine power from 15 KW to 18.5 KW	The output was improved, but energy consumption remained same.
2013	Dust-free processing; Double-speed gearbox; Changed the straight scraper into a slant one	Suo drafted a local standard of straw pellet machine for Shanxi Province and submitted to Shanxi Bureau of Quality and Technical Supervision; the standard has passed the experts' primary examination;
2014	Developed five straw pellet machines which could be used at the same time	Designed for a factory of Puyang, Henan province[7].

Note: All the innovations have not been discussed in the text.

to repair as compared to the large pellet machine. It is quite suitable for rural areas for decentralized pelletization. Table 5.2 presents different aspects of comparison between the small and large pellet machines.

Table 5.2: Comparing Small and Large Straw Pellet Machines

Aspect	*Large straw pellet machine*	*Small straw pellet machine*
Price	High; Average price about RMB 100,000	Low; Average price is about RMB 50,000
Floor space required	Large; at least 15 to $20m^2$	Small; less than $10m^2$
Output	High; Over one ton pellet produced each hour; output is decided by production time;	Low; about 350 kg pellets produced per hour; output could be increased through parallel use of several machines[8];
Mobility	Immovable. Raw materials have to be transported to the machine increasing transportation costs.	Each local household has several Mu fields, but are scatteredin location. Thus, straw collection cost is quite high. Small machine can be placed near raw material production areas so as to reduce transportation cost.
Ease of maintenance	Machine stops working even if one part is broken.	Convenient to maintain. Suo's innovation allows repairs and working of machine simultaneously.
Power requirement	Requires High Tension power supply to operate minimum 120 KW machines. Existing power supply cannot be used. Special transformer has to be installed[9].	Existing power supply system of the village can be used; works for equipments requiring up to 20 KW. Small machines are in this range.
Power consumption	120 KW is needed to produce one ton pellets	55 to 60 KW is needed to produce one ton pellets.
Operation	Relatively complex	Simple; farmers can operate the machine according to instruction book. Phone-call instruction is enough to help them solve problems.
Target consumer	Sell to others	Both could be sold to others and for self-use; For example, villagers could use straw pellets produced by themselves; timber factories could use their sawdust to produce fuel pellets and then use their fuel pellets for their own heating, wood drying and cooking.

Source: Based on discussions with the farmers.

Product Diffusion

By the end of 2014, Suo had sold 50 small straw pellet machines developed by himself to various buyers that included nearby production brigades, few individuals, a Beijing-based park management company (Chao Yang Park in Beijing) and most importantly, to a straw utilization cooperative in Changzhi. Some customers bought the machine for organic waste recycling, for example—the garden waste. As stated earlier, it also helped in saving energy costs, transportation costs of disposing organic waste, including the agriculture waste, and meeting with the national law and policy of not burning the biomass to reduce CO_2 emissions. The Li Min Straw Utilization Cooperative of Changzhi bought Suo's machine to produce straw pellets and for sales in the local market. In particular, these pellets were in demand for heating water for tea restaurants. The examples of application of Suo's straw pellet machine are given in Table 5.3. In comparison to the efforts put in by Suo Wenbin, the product did not find successful diffusion.

Table 5.3: Application of Suo's Straw Pellet Machine

Year of purchase	*Buyer*	*Main application*
2011	Li Min Straw Utilization Cooperative, Changzhi City	Produce sawdust and corn stalk fuel pellets for sales.
2013	Chao Yang Park, Beijing; It covers an area of 5,000Mu. About 200 tons of waste-branches produced every year. Dealing with these branches costed almost RMB 200,000	Smashed branches and compressed them into fuel pellets for the heating and water-boiling of staff dormitory. Thus, coal-burning could be discontinued.
2012	Nearby villages' production brigades of Changzi County, Changzhi City, Shanxi Province	Nearby villages' production brigades bought one straw pellet machine for each village. Straw pellets were collectively produced and then distributed to villagers for free.
2013	Nantong Yong Qi Art Treasure Co. Ltd., Jiangsu Province[10]	Compressed sawdust into pellets and used them as fuel for water-heating and timber drying.

Source: Fieldwork.

Setting up Changzhi Productivity Promotion Center

Suo Wenbin set up Changzhi Productivity Promotion Center. The purpose of the centre was to cooperate closely with the cooperatives in the area and provide them technological and managerial guidance. The Center also helps the cooperatives to gather information about various government schemes and projects so as to apply for available subsidies. As we shall see later, this Center strongly supported the Li Min straw utilization cooperative and was one of the reasons for the success of the latter.

Li Min Straw Utilization Cooperative

Development Process

Li Min Straw Utilization Cooperative uses small straw pellet machine developed by Suo Wenbin to compress straw and sawdust into pellets and sell them in the local market. Li Min Straw Utilization Cooperative of Changzhi County (hereinafter referred to as 'the cooperative') was founded in March, 2011. It is located at Nancheng Village, Beicheng Township, Changzhi County. The cooperative has members from six households related to the main person, one Liu Haibing. These members are Liu's father, Liu's younger brother and three other relatives. In 2012, it was selected for government support as a provincial level demonstrative cooperative. Thereafter, its member-strength increased to 50 households. The cooperative decided to restrict the membership to households of Nancheng village only, so that it was convenient to manage it. The cooperative is mainly involved in the production and sale of corn stalk and sawdust briquettes and pellets.

Liu's father owned a foundry. After graduation from middle school, Liu and his brother worked in his father's foundry and learned machinery operation and maintenance techniques. In 2009, due to the government-enforced laws, the foundry was closed down on the grounds of environment pollution. Liu and other family members had to seek a career change. Attracted by news reports about straw utilization, Liu spent nearly one year surveying the straw processing industry in Baoding, Hebei Province, Shijiazhuang city and Yuncheng city of Shanxi Province. Although, everyone whom he met stated that the future of straw processing industry was promising, they also said that it was difficult to manage the enterprise. Liu decided to give it a try. Table 5.4 is the development process of the cooperative.

Table 5.4: Development Process of Li Min Straw Utilization Cooperative

Time	*Events*
2011	Encouraged by the promising future, Liu and others founded Li Min Straw Utilization Cooperative;Rented a bankrupt local coal cleaning plant and transformed it; It begun production in the same year[11] Began to cooperate with Changzhi Productivity Promotion Center.
2012	At the beginning, it only produced briquettes. Later, it also produced pellets; The cooperative produced and sold products at the same time. All its products were sold out this year; Local government departments, such as Business Administration Bureau, Agricultural Bureau, Environmental Protection Bureau and Science and Technology Bureau, began to pay attention to the cooperative and provided encouragement and all possible support; Selected as provincial level demonstrative cooperative; Improved straw pellet machine.
2013	Improved straw pellet machine; The real investment of the cooperative reached RMB 2 million by the end of 2013. The cooperative got into financial trouble; The coal price fell at the beginning of 2013. Selling straw fuel could not just not give any return but was a loss-making activity; Hope of bright future forced Liu to carry on; Liu and other members used money they had earned from other sources to support the cooperative.

Source: Discussion with Liu Haibing

Liu Haibing and the others decided to set up a cooperative and not a company. The reasons for the same are as follows:

(i) Local farmers are quite familiar with cooperatives. Every village had several cooperatives. Even Liu's village had a vegetable cooperative, a planting cooperative, a transportation cooperative and an agricultural machinery cooperative.

(ii) The procedure to get cooperative business license at industrial and commercial bureau is simpler than that of a company.

(iii) Cooperative having business related to straw utilization is tax exempt. The process is that the cooperative pays tax first and then the tax is refunded back to the cooperative.

(iv) The rule of minimum capital requirement for setting up an enterprise, is not applicable to cooperatives. Liu and others could not put together enough funds to meet the minimum capital requirement for starting a company.

(v) A local businessman named Feng, found business opportunity from national level policies supporting straw recycling. He persuaded local farmers to set up dozens of straw recycling cooperatives. The founding of Liu's cooperative was also because of this encouragement from Feng.

Production and Operation of Cooperative

Machines of the Cooperative

Liu Haibing, sold some of the equipment of his father's foundry and purchased necessary equipments for producing different types of straw-fuel successively (Table 5.5). The cooperative first bought a straw briquetting machine. Later, because of the market demand for straw pellets, they bought a straw pelleting machine. And they started the cooperation with Suo Wenbin and his Changzhi Productivity Promotion Center. Due to the underestimation of market risk and non-availability of sufficient raw materials, the cooperative could not utilize the installed capacity. Some machines remained idle. The production capacity of the cooperative's machines was 10,000 tons briquettes every year. But, actually they could produce only half of that capacity. This also increased the cost of production of the cooperative to some extent, which further affected the business.

Raw Materials

The main material used by Li Min Cooperative, to compress briquettesi, was corn stalk. After the corn stalk was exhausted,

Table 5.5: Machines of Li Min Straw Utilization Cooperative

Machine	*No.*	*Costing*	*Purchase information*	*Notes*
Straw briquetting machine, one large and one small	2	Large straw briquetting machine cost RMB 170,000 and subsidy was provided to the tune of RMB 30,000 by government; small one costed RMB 98,000 and the government gave of subsidy of RMB 15,000; Total actual expense was RMB 223,000	Bought in 2011 from Shijiazhuang, Hebei Province	Small straw briquetting machine could produce 800kg briquettes per hour, while large one could produce 2 tons; Mass production of corn stalk fuel would need briquetting machine; Due to insufficient raw material, machines were left unused later.
Straw pellet machine	2	The price was RMB 51,000, in which government subsidy was RMB 20,000; The subsidy period was 2011 to 2013. In 2013, the subsidy policy was cancelled and the market price was back to the original RMB 51,000.	Bought in 2011 from Changzhi Grain Machinery Factory	Two machines could compress 5 to 6 tons of pellets per hour; One reason for purchasing these machines was most boilers used pellets as fuel. Another reason was sawdust could be used to produce pellets, if stalks were not available.
Dryer, one small one large	2	Small sized was RMB 11,000; large one was RMB 48,000; total cost RMB 59,000	Bought in 2011 from Henan Province	Added a conveyor belt to the dryer; Since there was not enough raw material, the bigger dryer was hardly used.[12]
Straw collecting and bundling machine	1	Cost RMB 117,000, government subsidy RMB 50,000; actual cost came to RMB 67,000	Bought in 2012	There was only one small tractor; Did not have enough money to buy tractor that could tow straw collecting and bundling machine forward. The machine not used.
Small sized loader	1	Cost RMB 30,000	Bought in 2011	In the past, 5 to 6 labors were needed to work for half a day for loading. After using small sized loader, the same work could be finished in half an hour by one laborer.
Pulverizer	3	NA	—	The cooperative has 4 to 5 pulverizers.

Source: Field study at Li Min Straw Utilization Cooperative by TUFE Research Group.

sawdust was used. Sometimes, herbal medicinal plants residue available from the nearby pharmaceutical factories or corncob residue of xylitol factories were used. In order to reduce costs, Liu and others combined various proportions of different raw materials in such a way that the calorific value of fuels required by customers was not changed.

<u>Corn stalk</u>

Corn is the major crop of Changzhi County. About 26,000 Mu of land is used for corn crop cultivation in Beicheng Township alone. Beicheng Township is where Li Min Straw Utilization Cooperative is located. Corn is planted and harvested only one time a year. One Mu of corn stalk produces 500 kg of dry stalk. The total corn stalk produced every year in Beicheng Township alone, was 13,000 tons. The entire corn stalk has to be harvested and collected within a three-month period to prepare the farm for the next crop cycle. The cooperative did not have enough machines to harvest and collect the corn stalks of the township. As a result, the cooperative could collect only one-third of the total corn stalks. Another 30 per cent was damaged due to exposure to natural elements, like the sun and wind. The cooperative could produce only 3000-4000 tons of stalk briquettes every year. The farmers have to clear up their fields by February, so that the spring sowing can start. Since the cooperative could not lift all the corn stalks, the farmers had to burn the ones still standing on their fields. The purpose of starting the straw utilization cooperative was not fully met.

Farmers do not charge the cooperative any costs for lifting the stalk, but, the cooperative has to bear the cost of handling and transportation, which costed RMB 200 in 2013, which, however, are not significant. Further, the cooperative did not generate employment round-the-year. In winter, after the corn harvesting, about 30 people worked at the cooperative. But in off-season, only 7- 8 people worked because there were not enough raw materials for production.

The storage of corn stalk required a large area and it was also very expensive. Corn stalks need to be smashed before being compressed. The cost of smashing one ton of corn stalks per hour included RMB 24 as electricity charge and another 6 to 10 RMB as labor cost. The price of corn stalk briquettes per ton was RMB 650 (price in 2011 and 2012).

Sawdust

The work of collection of corn stalks and production of briquettes lasts for about six months in a year. During the remaining six months, sawdust pellets are compressed. Timber factories in and around Changzhi County, could produce 3 to 4 tons of sawdust everyday. In the past, sawdust was discarded in the drains and ditches near the factories. Not only was such a useful resource wasted, but it also polluted the environment. Realizing the commercial potential of sawdust, the timber factories began to charge the cooperative for the sawdust. Pine sawdust is the best raw material because it does not have fine dust, so there is no residue and hence no tar and smoke after burning. Its utilization ratio could reach 98 per cent. Its combustion value is similar to that of coal. Another advantage was that the sawdust did not require smashing before compression and hence land area was not required by the cooperative for its storage.

Sawdust is often relatively moist as compared to stalk. Sometimes, its moisture content is more than 35 per cent. So, it has to be dried before use. The dryer could use straw pellets as fuel. Additionally, only a fan is needed. So, the electricity consumption is low. But, the drying process increased labor costs.

Products

The main products manufactured by Li Min Cooperative are fuel briquettes, that used corn stalk as its major raw material and fuel pellets that used sawdust as the main raw material (Table 5.6). For example, GuYun Tea Market of Changzhi, which is 17 km away from Li Min Cooperative, used to burn coal for heating. It began to cooperate with Li Min Cooperative from 2012. The Cooperative provided it with fuel pellets. About 100 tons of fuel pellets are needed during the entire winter season for heating the 2,000 sq. m., two-storied building.

Production Cost

Production of biomass briquettes or pellets is almost unprofitable. Table 5.7 gives the cost analysis of sawdust pellet production of Li Min Straw Utilization Cooperative. It shows that the business is not profitable.

Table 5.6: Main Products of Li Min Straw Utilization Cooperative and their Use

Product	*Raw Material*	*Target Market*	*Production Time/Cost*	*Note*
Briquette	Corn stalks that are cut into 5 to 6 cm small sections.	Rural market, common biomass stoves.	Short production time and low cost	Used as fuel and feed; Stalk moisture should be 30% to 40% for feed briquettes and 20% to 25% for fuel briquettes
Pellet	Sawdust	Boilers of urban areas[13] and self-ignited and self-feeding biomass stoves	Long production time and high cost	–

The factory price of sawdust pellet per ton is RMB 900 (2011). In 2012, the price increased to RMB 1,050. The factory price increased due to increase in the labor costs. The difference between the factory price of the product and the selling price of the product is very low. Therefore, the factory could hardly make any significant profit. In 2013, when the coal prices drastically reduced, the demand of briquettes and pellets declined and the factory incurred a loss.

Difficulties and Possible Improvement

The endeavor of Lui Haibing and others of the cooperative has been fraught with many difficulties. They faced many technical problems in the production process. They could solve some of them, while for some others; they had to take help from Suo Wenbin. We discuss below, first, some of the difficulties they faced and thereafter, the solutions they found or could have found.

Difficulties

The straw cooperatives in general have faced many difficulties. Li Min Cooperative too faced numerous difficulties as discussed below:

Table 5.7: Production Cost of One-ton Sawdust Pellets

Items	*Notes*	*Cost (RMB)*
Electricity	Power consumption is 55-60 kw/h.	About RMB 50.
Labor	One woman is enough for machine operation. One machine can produce 300kg pellets per hour. If production time in one day is 8 hours, total production is 2.5 tons pellet.	In 2014, labor cost for one woman was RMB 70 per day. Labor cost for producing one ton pellets was RMB 30.
Wear and tear of key mechanical parts	Key parts are refiner plate and compression roller, which cost together RMB 200. One unit of these two parts could produce 150 to 200 tons pellets.	Refiner plate and compression roller cost RMB 12 per ton.
Raw material collection	Major raw material for pellets is pine sawdust; sawdust collection cost includes buying expense, manual loading fee and transport.	In 2011, cost of one-ton pine sawdust was RMB 400; In 2012, it increased to RMB 450 due to the increase in labor cost.
Packing bag	One bag cost RMB 0.8. One bag could fill 25 kg.	40 bags required for 1 ton; cost RMB 32.
Transport	Buyers pay transportation fees.	Cost included in the market price of pellets.
Machine maintenance	About 20 to 30 minutes are needed to clean and maintain the machines.	RMB 50.
Capital cost	Buy equipment, rent place, build factory and collect raw material.	Li Min Cooperative, for example, made capital investment of RMB 2 million till end of 2012. The capital cost per year came to about RMB 200,000. In 2012, the cooperative produced 3,000 tons of briquettes and 1,000 tons of pellets. The capital cost per ton was RMB 50.
Management cost	The cooperative needs one manager, one salesman and a person to cook lunch for workers.	RMB 15.
Others	Moisture content of pine sawdust is about 35%. It should be dried to 20% to 25% before compression.	Weight loss cost RMB 40.
Total		RMB 750-800

Source: Lecture given by Suo Wenbin in TUFE on November 5, 2014.

Collection of Raw Materials

The cost of collection and transport of stalk is high. The period within which the stalk has to be collected is short. This collection needs to be done after the corn is harvested and before the sowing season of the next crop in spring. This means that the collection and transport costs go up if all available stalk has to be collected. Secondly, while collecting the stalk, dust and other dirt also gets collected which then has to be cleaned out before putting the stalk in the briquetting machine.

Collection of stalk is labor intensive and if the farmer asked to gather the entire stalk and collect it at one place, to be later lifted by the cooperative, the farmer also finds it difficult to do so. He would prefer to burn the stalk where it is lying, rather than laboriously collect it all in one place, to be picked up by the cooperative. The cooperative by itself cannot go to various parts of a farmer's farm to collect the stalk, as that would consume a lot of time resulting into increased labor and costs. The cooperative itself does not have that much funds to deploy in stalk collection. Thus, the Li Min Cooperative faces a situation where it does not have adequate raw materials to generate output to make the cooperative economically viable.

Inadequacy of Capital

Raw materials collection and storage requires capital, both fixed capital as well as working capital. The cooperative did not have adequate funds to purchase the required machines. For example, the cooperative purchased two straw bundling machines using borrowed capital. But, they could not raise funds to purchase a tractor on which the bundling machine requires to be fitted. The cooperative, not being able to offer collateral guarantee, was unable to borrow funds for the tractor from a bank. Hence, due to insufficient funds, the cooperative could purchase only part of the required machines.

Lack of funds also resulted in another situation. The Cooperative purchased machines that were available at low prices because of government subsidies on some of them. However, not all these machines were necessarily required! Hence, the limited funds that they had were also inappropriately used. For example, subsidy was available for large briquetting machine or pelletizing machine that had a production capacity of 10,000 tons per year. But, since such large quantities of raw materials were not available, such large machines were of no use and hence the subsidy available was not rightly utilized. In case of this cooperative, the machines were utilized only up to 50 per cent of its capacity. This happened with almost all the machines that the cooperatives purchased, including the grinders.

Space

Using stalk for briquetting is a land-intensive activity. Stalk storage requires a large area. During winters, farmers' lands are left unused. The cooperative would rent these lands to store stalks. The rent for one Mu of land per winter was RMB 700-800. Again, this posed an issue.

Electricity Costs

The electricity company lists stalk processing as a commercial activity in their tariff rates. Hence, the cooperative was charged the same electricity rate as that for a large company. The tariff for power consumption for commercial purposes in 2014 was RMB 0.78 kwh, while for agricultural activities, it was only half that of the commercial rate[14]. It would have been appropriate if this Cooperative were treated as an agricultural business entity rather than a commercial business unit.

Labor Costs

When the cooperative was started in 2011, the labor costs for an adult man or a woman was about RMB 70 to 80 per day. In 2013, the labor cost increased significantly; it more than doubled for young male laborers and increased to RMB 100 (per day) for those above the age of 60 years[15]. A young male, even if offered RMB 150, was not willing to work. At these high wage rates, it was difficult to sustain straw briquetting cooperatives as viable financial entities. Due to this, the cooperative entrepreneurs were willing to take whatever subsidy was available from the government—for example, the purchase of non-useful machinery.

Difficult Production Environment

Stalk processing pollutes the surrounding air due to the fine dust that it produces.The production process is labor-intensive and tedious. Given such an environment, it was difficult to attract laborers to work. Only those who could did not find any work or were totally unemployed joined the cooperatives as laborers.

Potential Risk

Dry stalks can easily catch fire and such production units require good fire safety measures. Once again, this increased the costs.

Lowering of Coal Prices

The stalk briquetting could become a viable business only if there is a demand for these briquettes as a local energy source. Demand for straw-briquettes depends on the availability as well as price of other competing fuels. If coal was not available, as it was discussed in case of the village to which Suo Wenbin belonged, the village residents would create a demand for straw briquettes. Moreover, if coal became more expensive, the villagers would substitute it with the straw briquettes. This was the scenario in 2011. But, in 2013, coal prices fell sharply from RMB 1,100 to RMB 600-500 for good quality coal. For black coal, i.e., the bituminous coal, the prices fell from RMB 800-700 to RMB 500-400. The rural households found coal to be cheaper. And coal is easier to use than the straw briquettes! Thus, the business of the Cooperative declined and its financial viability took a beating. Thus, this cooperative suffered because of some macro level phenomenon on which it did not have any control.

Policy

The government policies are meant to protect such small enterprises from market fluctuations. That did not happen. Further, the government subsidy policies for large machinery benefited only those enterprises that could undertake production on a large scale. In order to benefit from the government policies, the straw briquette production would have to be centralized and also be undertaken on a larger scale. But, as illustrated in this chapter, straw fuel production is not suited for centralized production. It is expensive to opt for mass production due to high costs of collection and transportation. Further, large enterprises would also require large land parcels for storage of stalk. During the current scenerio in China, especially in the rural areas, decentralized solutions would be more effective but these require policy support.

Options for Cost Reduction

Other similar straw recycling cooperatives need to learn from Li Min Cooperative's experience. They could reduce their production costs and increase profits in the following ways:

(i) Technological improvement can reduce the wear and tear of key machine parts and thereby, the costs of production.
(ii) To have a thorough understanding of market dynamics and thus be able to predict better the market prospects of the business. This would help them avoid unnecessary early investments such as purchasing unnecessary machines/equipments not required for the scale of production that is viable financially.
(iii) The enterprises could use cotton stalks and/ or caragana, which is planted in the desert areas to fix the soil and prevent soil erosion, as raw materials for briquetting. Since these are plantations, cost of collection may be less. However, that does not solve the problem of agricultural waste, which in any case has to be reused, given that the law prohibits its burning.
(iv) The electricity costs can be reduced if the electricity companies consider this activity as related to agriculture and not a commercial one. This would reduce production costs to some extent and increase the potential of profits.

Conclusions – Reasons for Li Min Cooperative's Survival

The key question then arises as to why the Lu Min Straw Recycling Cooperative survived against all odds when many others (about a dozen) in Changzhi County went bankrupt by 2011. Li Min Straw Recycling Cooperative also confronted the difficulties discussed in the section above but survived due to the following reasons:

Box 5.1: Caragana Microphylla as Resource

Caragana microphylla (common name is Little leaf Peashrub) is extensively planted in provinces of north China, namely Shanxi, Inner Mongolia, Shaanxi, Gansu and Ningxia. It is useful in breaking wind and fixing sand. For example, in Shanxi Province, by the end of 2012, 11 cities, including the biggest city, Xinzhou City, had this shrub planted over 167,600 hectares in total. In fact, three cities, Xinzhou, Lvliang and Shuozhuo had the largest areas under the Caraganal Microphylla plantation. The city of Xinzhou had 93,600 hectares of land covered under the plantation of this shrub and comprised 55.85 per cent of the total planted areas of Shanxi Province. In second position was Lvliang, which had 32,700 hectares or 19.51 per cent of the total planted area in the province. Shuozhou City comprised 10.26 per cent of the total planting area of Shanxi, which totaled to 17,200 hectares. These three cities comprised 85.62 per cent of the total land distributed for the production of Caragana Microphylla in Shanxi Province.

According to the report of Shanxi survey team from the State Statistics Bureau (Qiao, 2011), the Caragana Microphylla grows well in high-density plantation and it can reach a height ranging from 1 meter to 1.5 meters. After the experiment of such high-density planting of Caragana Microphylla, the harvesting yield was 900kg per Mu. In comparison, this plant in its natural habitat on the barren mountains grows to 1 meter in height and yields 200kg per Mu. Thus, evidence shows that Caragana Microphylla, which is a very hardy plant, can grow well, both in regulated environment and unregulated barren land, where it naturally grows.

Every three years, the Caragana Microphylla plant must be cut 5cm above soil to ensure minimal growth. From 2011, Shanxi government has provided a subsidy of RMB 65 per Mu for cutting of Caragana Microphylla by machine. In 2013, the government allocated RMB 10 million subsidies to 26 counties and four cities including Datong, Shuozhou, Xinzhou and Lvliang. A common issue amongst farmers was that they did not know what to do with the top end of the Caragana plant. They, therefore, threw it and thus littered the surrounding mountain areas. The dry waste of this plant is inflammable and therefore, there was a risk of mountain fire during the winter months.

Technical Knowhow Among Core Members

All the main members of the Cooperative themselves worked in the maintenance room of the foundry factory. They all had worked with technology. They had built factories and had repaired machines themselves. They did the same when this Cooperative was set up. This led to significant reduction in the initial costs. For example, they only spent RMB 300,000 to level the ground for the construction of the factory, since they did all the major work themselves. They put in equity in through their sweat! If this work was done through hired labor, the costs would have doubled. Further, they themselves repaired the machines. When the refiner plate of the briquette machine was damaged, they changed it on their own. Each change of refiner plate would otherwise have costed RMB 2,000. Due to this, they only had to pay the cost for the new plate and not the labor charges for changing or repairing the plates. Moreover, since they were familiar with the machines of the earlier foundry, they reused some of the old machines, thereby reducing initial costs.

Basic Management Skills of Core Members

Liu Haibing's father was the founder of the foundry. He had over 30 years of experience in business management, when the cooperative was started. Liu and his brother also did some managerial work in their father's foundry. As suggested by Suo Wenbin, Liu Haibing, being an extrovert, enthusiastic and friendly in nature, took up the responsibility for marketing as well as all other external coordination. Liu Haibing's brother, being quieter and an introvert took the responsibility of production. Their father had contacts with the government and his responsibility was to obtain financial support from the government. Each core member of the Cooperative has their individual strengths and they took the work responsibility accordingly.

Government's Financial Support

Since its foundation, the cooperative was able to get financial support from the local government in many different ways. This Cooperative partnered with the Changzhi Productivity Promotion Center. The latter was set up by Suo Wenbin, who provided information to Liu Haibing and others about the government projects under which they could apply for funds. In total, the Cooperative obtained government grants worth RMB 1,700,000 in 2011 and 2012 (Table 5.8). Different local government departments contributed towards this grant as shown in Table 5.8.

All this support, focused on the National government's strong shift towards CO_2 reduction strategies, one amongst which was to shift towards renewable energy. Li Min Cooperative and many other straw utilization cooperatives would assist in promoting renewable energy. Each local government has to promote the National government policy and hence the various local

Table 5.8: Government Financial Support to Li Min Cooperative (RMB 100,000)

	City Business Administ-ration Bureau	County Business Administ-ration Bureau	County S&T Bureau	County Environment Protection Bureau	County Agricultural Bureau	Total
2011	0	2	5	10	0	17
2012	5	5	5	0	2	17

Note: Environment protection bureau charges polluting enterprises and then uses this fund to support environmental protection enterprises. S&T bureau supports S&T projects and improvement of briquetting machine. Business administration bureau supports demonstrative cooperatives.

Source: Provided by Liu Haibing and SuoWenbin

government bodies, at the city and the county level have given financial support to this Cooperative since 2011.

Support from Changzhi Productivity Promotion Center

The Changzhi Productivity Promotion Center has closely cooperated with the cooperative. The cooperative obtained technological and business managerial guidance from the center. It also received help from the center in applying for government projects to benefit from the subsidies available.

Inspiration from Other Successful Local Cooperatives

Besides, Liu Haibing and others received encouragement from the nearby successful cooperatives. During the interview, Liu Haibing mentioned many times that big cooperatives of the county and nearby counties were awarded the status of national demonstrative cooperatives and got financial support from the government. For example, there is a planting and breeding national demonstrative cooperative that got one million RMB from national funds in 2012. Another straw recycling cooperative, which was founded by a company from Beijing, met with the government subsidy policy requirement on straw fuel production. It got RMB 150 per ton subsidy for producing straw fuel[16].

Thus, although the cooperative has faced many difficulties, its driving forces have been promising prospect for its business and recognition from the government. The Li Min Cooperative has persisted in its efforts to produce straw briquettes and pellets. Its promoters have realized the importance of their work in the national goal of partial transition to renewable energy.

Cooperation with Changzhi Productivity Promotion Center

The cooperation between Li Min Straw Utilization Cooperative and Changzhi Productivity Promotion Center has led to a win-win situation for both. The Cooperative uses Suo's straw pellet machine and provides technological improvement feedback and suggestions to the Promotion Center. In addition to providing help on the improving and upgrading the technology for Suo's machines, the Cooperative also helps in training the customers purchasing Suo's machines. In return, Suo helps the Cooperative get government's project grants and provides the latter technological and business management guidance.

The Cooperative's supports to the Centre are with regard to:

(a) *Testing and improving small straw pellet machine* – The Cooperative gives suggestions to improve the machines and then tests the machines once improved. "Because we used to repair machines, it is not so difficult for us to improve the straw pellet machine" said Liu.

(b) *Test and display the Centre's products for promotion purposes* – Liu's Cooperative is the experimental base/platform of Suo's Productivity Promotion Centre. The Centre puts on display the various stoves, straw pellet machines, and straw collecting and bundling machines bought from all over the country, at the Cooperative. Thus, in addition to display and promotion of various machineries, the Cooperative also carries out a number of experiments on them.

(c) *Help train customers* – Tai Hang Grain Machinery Factory is responsible for the manufacture and sales of small straw pellet machine developed by Suo Wenbin. Customers who purchase these machines are required to go to the Cooperative to learn the operation techniques of the machine. Liu Haibing and his partners also repair machines or give telephonic guidance to the customers who need assistance in starting the machine or dealing with some problem in the machine's functioning. Liu Haibing's team uses its own production experience to train customers.

The Centre supports the Cooperative with regard to:

(a) *Technological guidance* – Suo Wenbin always provided technological suggestions to Liu. For example, the straw briquetting machine of Li Min Cooperative was producing 430 kg of briquettes per hour and had reached the maximum available power load of 50 Kw. Whenever a machine reaches its maximum power load, its working life reduces. When this was brought to Suo's knowledge, he advised Liu and his team to reduce their output to 350-400 kg of briquettes per hour. This would help maintain or prolong the service life of the machine.
(b) *Managerial guidance* – Suo frequently provided sound managerial support to the Cooperative. For example, he advised Liu, to distribute work amongst his father and brother and himself in accordance with their personal skills and strengths. As discussed hereinbefore, Liu's brother was given the responsibility of production and Liu being good at communication was in charge of marketing. Since Liu's father owned a foundry and held prestige in the society, it was suggested that he should be responsible for liaisoning with and obtaining funds from the government.
(c) *Policy proposal* – Suo worked in the government department. He was familiar with the national and local policy information. He provided Liu and his associates relevant information regarding the policies and helped them apply for the funds.

This case, therefore, suggests that more than technological innovations, there has to be institutional as well as managerial innovations for successful diffusion of innovated technology. There is a need for appropriate government policies. There is a need for education among innovators. Lastly, there is a need for cooperative spirit. Market alone will not give answer to the successful diffusion of a technical innovation.

NOTES

1. Center for Innovation and Entrepreneurship, Tianjin University of Finance and Economics.
2. When the TUFE research team interviewed some farmers in Changzhi City, the latter categorically stated that they would be happy if someone or some agency would collect and take away their stalks from their fields. They were willing to give away the stalk for free. That would save the stalk from being burnt, protect the environment from air pollution and help farmers by clearing out their fields for the next round of seeding and crop growing. In addition, the farmers were also looking for support in ploughing their fields, which however, did not have any connection with the issue of agricultural waste management. The farmers, therefore, stated that they had no problem with implementing as well as assisting in the implementation of the national laws and policies. But, with regards to straw waste disposal, they had no option but to burn it. The TUFE team has visited just before the seeding season and the farmers were preparing the fields, after burning the stalk, for the next cropping season.
3. Suo set-up Changzhi Productivity Promotion Centre in 2010. He is the director. It is a private, non-business organization (under Changzhi S&T Bureau. It aims at providing information and technology support for agricultural machinery companies of Changzhi. It has a stove centre, which is responsible for the promotion and demonstration of biomass stove and straw pellet machine.
4. If too much raw materials were fed at a time, it developed large resistance. The motor then had to work hard, through more power supply. This created friction and heat and burnt the motor as well as the electric current sensor.
5. Quench hardening is a mechanical process in which steel and cast iron alloys are strengthened and hardened. These metals consist of ferrous metals and alloys. This is done by heating the material to a certain temperature, depending on the material.
6. Refiner plates produced by common machinery factories only have 2 mm quenching. Common steel is used in the middle, which reduces the plate's hardness greatly. Once the plate's surface is worn out, the plate cannot be used any more.

7. This factory has a 15m square area of closed workshop. They dug a hole in the wall and connected the machines with crushers. Thus, smashed materials would flow into those five pellet machines directly. Straw pellets would be conveyed to an elevator through a conveyor belt to filter out dust. Generally, the briquetting ratio of straw pellets is 95 per cent. Pellets would fall directly into packaging boxes.
8. There is a sawdust pellet production enterprise in Tianjin. It is located in a large timber market. There is sufficient raw material. The price of one-ton sawdust was about RMB 800 (in 2014). The market price at that time was RMB 400. This enterprise invested 3 million RMB and bought two production lines. In 2014, products could not be sold because the price of coal was only RMB 500 per ton while the production cost of sawdust pellets was more than RMB 800. So the enterprise had to stop production.
9. The power of the main motor of a machine, whose output per hour was one ton, is about 90 kw to 120 kw. If other auxiliary apparatus like cooler and conveyor are included, the power required could reach 150 to 160 kw.
10. Head of this company also combined a semi-gasifier and a hot water tank together to replace small boiler. Thus, need for a person to attend to the boiler was done away with. This saves the cost for one laborer for this small company. The company collected sawdust for a week and then compressed it into fuel pellets. The company saved RMB 50,000 worth of coal in one year. In 2014, a rosewood furniture factory learned this technology. After one-year application, it saved over RMB 100,000 worth of coal (this factory is relatively larger). Use of straw pellet machine not only saves on the cost of coal but also protects environment. If leftover materials from timber factories are burned directly, 10kg is needed. But if compressed them into pellets, only 5kg is enough. Besides, inadequate direct burning would cause lots of smoke. Stoves that burn pellets do not emit smoke as the entire feed is fully burnt. These machines are fully automatic, which saves the cost for one hired-labor to continuously feed the machine.
11. The coal cleaning plant that belonged to Liu Haibing's father was closed by the government due to environment pollution. Many local factories which were dependent on coal were forced to close down by the government on environmental grounds.
12. During the initial years of the Cooperative, Liu believed that high productivity briquette machines needed to be matched with dryers. So they bought two dryers at a time.
13. Since stalk has dust and sugar, residues are produced. So straw pellets are generally used for rural heating and cooking. Manual cleaning is needed every 3 to 5 hours. Sawdust pellets do not produce residues. They are used in urban areas. Liu Yongquan added a dam-

board in semi-gasifier. Drawing the dam-board outward every few hours would help residues fall down.

14. In November 2014, TUFE research group found that local straw recycling cooperatives were charged according to agricultural power rate during field studies in Haian County and Rudong County, Jiangsu Province.
15. During the field study in 2014, in Hainan County, Jiangsu, research group noticed that only women and old men work in straw cooperatives. They worked about 9 hours a day. The lunch was free and was of good quality. Each one earned RMB 70-80 per day according to their work ability. The younger age group of the population was not willing to work in this activity due to low wages.
16. In 2008, China introduced supporting policies on straw industry. Enterprises or cooperatives whose annual straw fuel output reached 10,000 tons could receive subsidy of RMB 150 per ton.

6

Innovations in Mushroom Production Chain – Case of Gao Dedian

Context

Changde City (Map 6.1), is the place where Gao Dedian, has innovated on the production of mushroom cultivation and has then disseminated the technology locally. As a big agricultural city (the production of major agricultural products of Changde, *see* Table 6.1), Changde City has a long history of mushroom production due to its climatic advantage[1] and known history of technology. Many types of mushrooms are grown in Changde, which include Oyster mushroom, Agaricus Bisporus (button mushroom), Needle mushroom, Ganoderma Lucidum (reishi mushroom), Cordyceps Militaris (a fungi with medicinal use), Agaric (red mushroom with white spots) and Lentinula edodes (black mushroom). Oyster mushrooms comprise 50 per cent of the total mushroom production. In 2012, the output of fresh edible mushroom was 90,000 tons[2]. The production value was more than RMB 0.6 billion[3]. More than 31,000 households were engaged and if 2 persons from each household are considered to be engaged in the mushroom production, the number of individuals employed in this industry would be over 60,000[4]. Compared to 2011, the output of 2012 was 10,000 tons more, the production value increased by RMB 0.1 billion and the number of mushroom growers increased by more than 2,000 individuals[5]. In Hunan Province, mushroom production industry is ranked 6th amongst the different agricultural industries, following crop, cotton, edible oil, vegetable and fruit production industries. Mushroom production in 2011 was 720,000 tons, with a production value of RMB 5.5 million and farmers' income of RMB 3 billion[6]. Hunan Province plans to achieve the goal of engaging 1 million people in mushroom production, output reaching 1 million tons and the production value reaching RMB 10 billion.

Table 6.1: Production of major agricultural products of Changde City, 2011

	Planting Area (1,000 hectares)	*Per Hectare Yield (kg)*	*Total Output (tons)*
Total sowing area of agricultural crops	1184.47		
Grain crops	651.53	377	3,680,250
Grain	622.20	385	3,590,223
Rice	585.91	393	3,452,850
Wheat	11.22	158	26,595
Corn	23.27	306	106,713
Broomcorn	0.27	168	1,810
Beans	17.64	135	35,674
Potato	11.69	310	54,353
Oil plants	301.85	124	561,331
Cotton	94.20	101	142,615

Source: Changde Statistics Yearbook in 2012, Changde Statistics Bureau

Various biomass wastes are used for mushroom production in China. Agricultural waste such as the stalks of cotton, cotton shells, corn-cobs, saw dust, tree branches and twigs, and animal waste such as that of livestock and poultry are all used for mushroom cultivation (Table 6.2). Gao Dedian has diversified the base used for mushroom cultivation and has given this technology to the other producers. This chapter presents his case history, his various efforts and finally his various achievements in innovating the mushroom cultivation in Changde City.

In Changde City, traditionally, cottonseed hulls have been used as substrate for mushroom production. Also, the mushroom production occurred under artificial conditions. Gao Dedian replaced cottonseed hulls with straws and created natural conditions inside the green house for mushroom production. He called his technique as 'Straw transforming into Oyster Mushroom' Technology, also called supernatural production technology of mushroom. This is the starting point and major contribution of

Hunan in China

Changde in Hunan

Map 6.1: Hunan in China and Changde in Hunan

Table 6.2: Biomass wastes used in Mushroom Production in China ('000 ton)

Crop-Waste Type	*Year*				
	2008[7]	2009	2010	2011	2012
Agriculture waste (cotton shell, corn cob) & stalk ('000 ton)	10,150	11,160	12,270	13,380	14,490
Saw dust, tree branches & twigs ('000 ton)	9,290	10,200	11,308	12,417	13,529
Others (including livestock and poultry dung, wheat bran, gypsum etc.)	3,360	4,470	5,479	6,598	7,685

Source: Data provided by Ma Yongchun.

Gao Dedian's mushroom innovation. 'Straw transforming into Oyster Mushroom' refers to the production of Oyster mushrooms using long straws as the main raw material that reproduces the natural environment of mountains suitable for the growing of wild mushrooms. After several cycles of Oyster mushroom production, all long straw rot and create natural environment like situation.

The Mushroom industry in China contributes significantly to the GDP and employment ratio of the country (Table 6.3). The same is true for Hunan Province and Changde City, wherein this case study is located (Tables 6.4 & 6.5). The total mushroom production in the whole of China, in 2012, was 28,280,000 tons (28.3 million tons) and was valued at RMB 177,206 million (RMB 177.21 billion). Mushroom production employed 20 million people in 2012 (Table 6.3). Hunan Province, in comparison, produced 750,000 tons (Table 6.4) (2.65 per cent of the total mushroom production in China).

Table 6.3: Mushroom Production in China

	2005[8]	2006[9]	2008[2]	2009[2]	2011[10]	2012[11]	2013
Production ('000 Ton)	13,350	14,740	18,000	20,200	25,717	28,279.9	
Value of Production (Million RMB)	98.93	99.87	100.29	110,300	140,000	177,206	
Employment (Million)*	15.78	16.54	17.98	18.85	19.95	20.00	

* includes full-time and part-time workers.

Source: Data provided by Ma Yongchun.

Table 6.4: Mushroom Production in Hunan

	2011[12]	2012[13]
Production ('000 Ton)	720	750
Value of Production (Million RMB)	5,500	5,800
Employment* ('000 persons)	700[6]	710

* includes full-time and part-time workers.

Source: Data provided by Ma Yongchun.

The value of mushroom production in Hunan Province in 2012 was RMB 5,800 million (3.27 per cent of total of China) and gave employment to 710,000 people. In Changde city alone, 62,000 people were employed in mushroom production in the same year and produced mushroom valued at RMB 600 million (Table 6.5).

Table 6.5: Mushroom Production in Changde

	2010[14]	*2011*		*2012*	
	All	All	Oyster	All	Oyster
Production (000' Ton)	>50	80	40	90	45
Value of Production (Million RMB)	300	500	–	600	–
Employment*	40,000	60,000		62,000	–

* Includes full-time and part-time workers including those from families of mushroom growers.

Source: Data provided by Ma Yongchun.

Different Innovations by Gao

The Beginning

Gao was born in 1956 in a small village in Hubei Province, neighboring Hunan. After marrying a girl of Hongyun Village in Changde City, Hunan Province, he shifted to this village. Hongyun belongs to Dingcheng District, Changde City, Hunan Province. Dingcheng is the capital of Changde and Hongyun is located at the outskirt of Dingcheng. Gao received a lot of help from the village residents when he was new to the village and always wanted to reciprocate and express his gratitude to them by helping the poor of the village in the future by making efforts to improve their standard of living. After he graduated from high school, Gao did many odd jobs to make a living—he worked as a mason and carpenter and also pulled handcarts for three years. Gao often went to the nearby Changde library to read newspaper and magazines to seek business opportunities.

In the early 1980s, he built the first green house for pepper in the village and introduced new varieties of peppers developed by the Hunan Academy of Agricultural Sciences. Six months later, Gao earned RMB 7,000[15] from the crop and this motivated the other residents of the village to learn the technique from him. Gao taught them patiently. This led to the spread of greenhouse pepper production throughout the village. With the increase in production, the pepper price gradually dropped to RMB 0.4 from RMB 1 per half kg (1 *jin*). Gao then learned bean sprout propagation technique from Yichang in Hubei Province. Within one year, he earned more than RMB 10,000, once again motivating the residents of the surrounding villages to learn from him. Again, Gao unreservedly taught the farmers the bean sprout propagation technique. As the saying goes "Once the apprentice mastered the technique, the master has to master a new technique." Gao, was once again, forced to do something different.

One day in 1986, on a visit to the Changde library, Gao came across an article titled "To become rich, grow oyster mushroom" published in Hunan Science and Technology News, which inspired him. He carried out a market survey and found that oyster mushroom sold well in the local market. Considering Hongyun village was close to Changde downtown, which is good for sales, Gao decided to grow mushrooms. He borrowed money to participate in a training program of mushroom growing at the Hunan Academy of Agricultural Sciences. This was the first training program of this kind in Hunan. After training, Gao started experiments with growing edible mushrooms, but soon, he encountered some obstacles.

Traditionally cottonseed hull was used as raw material for mushroom production. But its price was high and it was difficult to buy. Its price had gone up to RMB 0.4 per kg. In addition, Gao had to buy cottonseed hulls in Changsha, the capital city of Hunan Province, which is about an hour's journey by road. Secondly, production of mushrooms is a complicated process; it requires the sterilization of cottonseed hulls, otherwise, there is risk of contamination. Thirdly, mushroom inoculation was done in sterilization box, which Gao could not afford. Fourthly, mushroom seeds aged easily, greatly increasing the cost of production. Gao realized that for producing mushroom, the problem of raw material had to be solved first. In desperation, Gao tried to use straws as the main raw material in place of cottonseed hulls in an attempt to imitate the mushrooms' natural growth environment conditions and reduce the production cost.

Gao selected the straw as experimental material because Changde produces a large quantity of rice and there is abundance of straw. Wild mushrooms grow in nearby mountains, which happen to be very popular amongst the local villagers. Its shortage had increased the price of wild mushrooms in the local market. Wild mushrooms are tastier than the ones produced using cottonseed hulls. One day, Gao observed that large edible mushrooms had grown around the base of a rotten tree. Analyzing this phenomenon he understood that crop waste and weeds could provide the necessary nutrients for the mushrooms to grow. This natural growth environment for wild mushrooms looked promising.

Gao was motivated to innovate a new technique for wild mushroom production in his village. But innovation required finance, which he did not have Moreover, R & D for any innovation is an iterative process and there many be many failures before success is achieved. Till such time that the experiment succeeds, the innovator has to go on, thus requiring continuous finance.

Gao's first experiment of using 1,200 kg of straw and 900 kg of weeds and vines which he used as substrates or base medium for production of oyster mushroom, failed. Several successive attempts too resulted into overwhelming failures. Gao then made a second attempt by renting 3,000 kg of straws from a leader of the neighboring village. This too, did not succeed. He consulted experts at Hunan Academy of Agriculture Sciences, who told him that it was futile to try and that it was impossible to grow mushrooms using straw. After repeated failures, he had spent all his savings in addition to RMB 2,000, which he had borrowed from friends and relatives. His family survived on his wife's income, who worked as a shoeshiner in Changde. His friends taunted him, saying that when scientists could not succeed, how could a farmer succeed! Gao was confused and did not know what to do.

Indomitable as he was, Gao sold three of his houses and developed his 4.5 acres of wasteland into a mushroom growing experiment-base. He built a simple shack at the edge of the plot for his family and continued experiments in the plot land. Heavy rains on September 8, 1988, brought Gao unexpected hope. Humus from the soil was swept onto the mushroom growing land by rain and Gao then covered this substrate under a plastic film. Thereafter, fat mushrooms, tasting like wild mushrooms, sprouted from the rotten straw substrate under the humus soil. The reason for this was that humus from the soil contained many microelements needed for the growth of mushrooms. Gao had succeeded in his experiment! He realized that just straw was not adequate as substrate; nutrients had to be added to the straw.

Using Gao's technique, one Mu (1 Mu ≈ 6.67 acres) field could produce at least 7,500 kg worth oyster mushroom. Considering the market rate of 1 kg of mushroom to be RMB 4 in the late 1980s, one Mu of land could provide a gross income of RMB 30,000. If the total cost per Mu for the production of mushroom by using straw was RMB 4,000 (*see* Table 6.6), the net income per Mu would be RMB 26,000[16]. Generally speaking, one worker could manage about three greenhouses (one greenhouse covers one Mu field). The annual net income per worker would be RMB 78,000 if the worker had 3 Mu of land for this purpose.

Simplifying Seed Production Techniques

After the success of "Straws becoming Oyster Mushrooms", Gao

Table 6.6: Cost of investment for mushroom production[17]

Item	*Cost (RMB)*	*Notes*
Rent of land	500	
Raw materials like straws etc.	1,000	5,000 kg raw materials are needed for each Mu field; 50 kg raw materials cost RMB
Spawn[18]	1,500	500 kg spawns are needed for 5,000 kg raw material; the cost per kilogram is RMB 3
Other things such as plastic film	1,000	For 5,000 kg raw materials
Total	4,000	

Source: Provided by Gao Dedian.

began to improve mushroom breeding techniques[19]. To produce mushroom, spawn culture should be first-bred. But traditional method had three problems. Firstly, raw material was difficult to be procured. Secondly, the process was quite complicated. Thirdly, standards for the working environment for producing mushroom spawns were quite high. Gao's innovations include improvement on breeding tools and materials for oyster mushroom production.

Innovations in Raw Materials Used

At that time, traditional chemicals used for breeding mushrooms, were not only expensive but also difficult to purchase. So Gao used common materials easily available in the rural areas and inexpensive breeding materials like rice (or millet, or grain, or corn, or sorghum), glucose, gypsum, plant ash, dried worm-cast powder, rice-rinsing water, cottonseed hull, lime and dried soil from vegetable fields. Most of Gao's innovations happened due to his detailed observation. Since Gao did not own a microscope, he had to observe the progress of hypha[20] by his eyes. He derived his own understanding of the hypha growth; if the hypha was white and thick, it meant that it grew well and if it was yellow and thin, the mushroom suffered from over nutrition or under nutrition. Initially, the formula developed for the micronutrients was approximate. But, subsequently, he was able to develop the formula with exact measure of each element. He then promoted his formula with measurements of the ingredients in grams. He did not stop here and continued to innovate the use of raw materials.

(a) First change: From rotten stump to dried vegetable field soil to dried earthworm excrements. One day, Gao noticed a dense mushroom growth on a rotten stump. He surmised that rotten stump might contain various nutrients for the growth of mushroom. So he soaked rotten stump in water and used this water to replace the microelements used in substrate. But the results did not turn out to be promising.

Once, he noticed that mushroom that grew on a stump, which happened to be accidentally covered with some soil, tasted extremely good. This gave Gao the idea to use vegetable garden soil in place of wood fiber on the tree stumps to grow mushroom, which he executed with success. Later, Gao did some research which[21] established that the vegetable garden soil contained microelements for the growing of mushroom.

The use of earthworm excrement was also found by accident since the color of earthworms is very close to that of the soil. Once, when he used vegetable garden soil, Gao mixed it with some earthworm excrement. He found the result was much better. Since then, he used dried soil in vegetable field and worm excrements together.

Gao had observed that there was a layer of thin membrane over the earthworm's stomach, which covered its excrement. The thin membrane would disappear if the earthworm were to be exposed to the sunshine. On one cloudy day, Gao was forced to use earthworm excrement soil dried in the shade. The result turned out to be very good. Since then he began to use this kind of soil.

According to Gao, about five or six universities' textbooks quoted this technology. Besides, Gao also found the method to cultivate earthworms. That is, collect earthworms from wild and cultivate with wheat bran. Thousands of earthworms could be cultivated per quarter.

(b) Rice replacing potato and agar: Because potato contains a lot of starch, traditional mushroom seed production often used potato as substrate. Agar was added to solidify the potato juice. But the process was complicated and required high levels of operational skill. Gao pondered over alternatives and came up with a method of adding nutrient solution of earthworm excrement into rice to replace potato. Since rice is sticky, agar is not needed. The process got simplified. Steamed rice was used for the purpose. The hypha survives only in rotten or cooked things so steamed rice served the purpose. Secondly, rice is steamed and not boiled, which preserved its nutritional contents.

(c) Use of gypsum to separate rice grains: Use of rice as substrate brought a new problem—rice being sticky, the grains stick together after being steamed. Hypha that grows on it sticks to the substrate and it is difficult to take out the ripened hypha. This necessitated the addition of some material that would keep the steamed rice grains separate. Gao had noticed that the locals used flour to keep the noodles and dough-twists separate and thought of using it to keep the grains separate. But, that could not have worked here as the flour would stick to the steamed rice. Looking for alternatives, Gao learnt from magazines that gypsum has mineral elements that can act as a stabilizer. He experimented with gypsum and succeeded in keeping the rice grains separate.

***(d) Use plant ash to supplement potassium*:** Hypha is quite sensitive to potassium. If it lacks this element, it would bend. Gao observed this phenomenon during his experiment. After consulting a professor from Hunan Agriculture Science Academy, Gao learned that soil in Changde was acidic and contained various microelements, but the proportion of potassium was relatively low. Traditionally, in order to make hypha grow well, KSO_4[22] was added. Plant ash contains a lot of potassium. So Gao tried to use plant ash to replace.

***(e) Use edible sugar to replace glucose*:** Glucose required for conventional seed production technology was not easily available in the remote rural areas. So Gao used brown sugar and white sugar to replace it. He used brown sugar in winter and white sugar in summer. Gao learned this during a training he attended on mushroom cultivation technology in Hunan Agriculture Science Academy. During the training program, one of the trainees asked a question to the trainer about replacement for glucose, which was not available in the rural areas. The trainer stated that instead of sugar, glucose could be used. The trainer further stated that brown sugar was warm and suitable for winter use while white sugar was cold in nature and suitable for summer use. The trainer's explanation left a deep impression on Gao, who then applied that for mushroom growing.

Innovation in Operationalizing the Process

(a) Production of medium/substrate: Because of the improvement of raw materials, the original troublesome process of medium/ substrate production became simple. And the success rate of inoculation (seeding[23]) was also greatly improved. In the past, the contamination rate of inoculated test tubes was 20 per cent to 30 per cent. The success rate of this new inoculation method was 100 per cent[24]. The conventional method of substrate (medium) production was: (i) potatoes were peeled, cut into slices, steamed, ground into juice and the juice filtered; (ii) potato juice was heated and poured into tubes to which KSO_4, K_2SO_4[25], $MgSO_4$[26], and agar were added, with care taken so that the juice did not stain the tube wall[27]; and (iii) the tubes were then put into pressure cooker for sterilization and then kept in an inclined position to increase the growth area of spawns.

Gao improvised on this method. He (i) put the mixture of rice and gypsum into the tube; (ii) then he mixed the earthworm excrement, plant ash, and white sugar or brown sugar (use white sugar in summer and brown sugar in winter) into a bowl, added water to it and stirred it, allowing the solids to settle at the bottom and poured the liquid thus enriched into the tube; and (iii) he then steamed the rice in the tube for the spawns to grow in the rice-based substrate.

(b) Extracting spawn: The process of extracting spawn[28] from the mushroom was also simplified. The traditional method was to repeatedly sterilize the surface of mushroom leaves, cut parts of spawns with a sterilized knife and insert the spawns into a test tube. Gao believed that mushroom leaf did not contain spores[29]. So he peeled off the surface of the mushroom leaves directly in a sterile area, and cut parts with spawns and put them into the test tubes. Gao's method eliminated the repeated sterilization process. The success rate in general mushroom research institutes was around 80 per cent while that of Gao had reached100 per cent.

Simplifying Operation Environment

Traditional methods used an inoculation box for mushroom inoculation. These boxes were usually closed. Such a process of inoculation could easily be carried out in a laboratory but was impossible to implement on a farm in rural areas. Further, the mushroom growers could neither afford nor know where to buy these devices. Plus , the cost was very high. At least RMB 80 worth chemicals were needed everyday. The price of alcohol, which is used for sterilization, was also high.

Gao invented a fully-open mushroom inoculator, which had almost no cost. Gao created an area above the stove as sterile area. The stove used briquettes, which were easily available as fuel. The inoculation of the mushrooms was carried out in this indigenously created sterilized area. This fully-open mushroom inoculator enabled mushroom inoculation operation without electricity, chemicals and alcohol lamp. A single person was required to manage it. It could be operated both indoors and outdoors at any time. It was more than 10 times faster than the traditional method. Its success rate could reach to 100 per cent. This full-open mushroom inoculator was successfully invented in 1995 and was granted a national utility model patent in 1998.

Photo credit: Gao Dedian

Photo 6.1: Full-open Mushroom Inoculator

(a) Recreating equivalent of sterilized box: Traditional inoculation method used an inoculation box. Potassium permanganate and formaldehyde had to be mixed in a bowl and then put into the inoculation box. The box had to be sterilized by ultraviolet radiator and alcohol lamp before and after the operation. The process was not simple. The inoculation box together with ultraviolet radiator and alcohol lamp would cost about RMB 1,000. Only 30 to 50 test tubes could be put into the box at one time. Besides, obtaining potassium permanganate in the rural areas[30] was also difficult.

Gao wanted to simplify the process. He started with simple methods. One day in 1993, Gao read an article about using steam to produce seed in *Rural Know-all Magazine*[31]. It said that steam produced from boiling water could expunge germs from air, creating a sterile area that was similar to the sterile inoculation box. During his training, Gao had learnt that bacteria would die if the temperature increased above 50°C. He experimented with this method but this method could not solve the problem of contaminated inoculation shovel. Alcohol lamp could not burn if it was too close to water vapor. If too far, inoculation shovel would be contaminated again before entering the steam zone. And the success rate of vapor sterilization was only about 30 per cent[32]. This problem had to be solved.

One day in 1996, when Gao was cooking, the flame accidentally burned his eyebrows. This enlightened Gao. Fire could kill bacteria in a short time! Instead of boiling water to create sterile area, he used fire. Because liquid gas was too expensive, Gao used a briquette stove to produce a sterile area. Initially, he inoculated directly over the stove, which offered a limited sterilized area. Gao then designed an iron plate with a hole in the center and jagged edge. He put his plate on the stove to expand the sterilized area.

(b) Sterilizing inoculation tools: Initially, Gao sterilized inoculation tools directly over the stove fire. But the high temperature of tools would kill spawns when they were picked from the mushroom growth. One day, while browsing through a book Gao saw a picture of a penholder. He studied the structure of pen-holder and designed a shelf like a pen-holder to place inoculation shovel, tweezers and other tools. The shelf was made with insulation plywood. Inoculation shovel, when put on this shelf would always remain in the sterile area. The hot shovel was put into a sterilized wine bottle for cooling. This method could both sterilize the shovel and prevent spawns from death because of overheating.

Gao's inventions are simple and practical. They greatly save production costs. For example, Senyuan Wild vegetable Cooperative of Huayanxi, Changde, which is located 30 km away from Hongyun Village, got Central Government funding under a program called '1,000 Mu Mushroom cultivation base new project of Ding District, Changde City'. From the funds made available, RMB 60,000 were used for building mushroom breeding workshops. In 2013, Gao was appointed to this cooperative as S&T correspondent. He taught this simple inoculation technique to members of the cooperative. Thereafter, these workshops were abandoned.

Imitate Natural Environment to Grow High-yield Mushroom

Traditional technique of mushroom cultivation was to use bags for fruiting. That is, mushrooms were fruited from two sides of a bag[33]. Because there were fewer and fewer nutrients left after each round of mushroom growing, the mushroom yield from each bag declined. These bags were discarded. Gao found that mushrooms could grow from the cuts in the discarded mushroom growing bags if these bags were covered with top-soil. This meant that the spawns were drawing nutrient from the soil. Inspired by this, he abandoned the use of spawn bags and begun to grow mushrooms directly in the field. This new technique created an environment that imitated the natural growing environment of mushroom.

Gao's mushroom production formats, which imitated the natural growth conditions, as found in the wild, are of three types: cold frame type, block type (rectangular substrate) and three-dimensional cultivation. After several trials and errors, Gao settled at 25 per cent of vegetable garden soil and 75 per cent straw, as the medium or substrate on which the mushrooms should be grown. This material was then spread on the large mushroom growing bed. A total of three layers of spawns and two layers of growing material were spread on the mushroom growing bed. Then, a plastic film would be covered over them to form a cold frame. This method could enable hypha to absorb nutrients from the soil. And mushrooms produced by this method would be larger, plump, and with high yield.

Photo credit: Gao Dedian

Photo 6.2: Cold Frame Format

Photo credit: Gao Dedian

Photo 6.3: Block Type Frame

Block-style cultivation method is similar to cold frame type. The difference between them is that the former is with the shape of a block while the latter is large pieces (Both block type and cold frame type refer to rectangular substrate. The difference between them is that block type substrate is smaller than cold frame type substrate. Block type substrates could be put in the cold frame.) These two formats not only produced delicious mushrooms but also improved work efficiency. For example, in case of bagging method, a person needs a day to bag one ton of growing materials, whereas in the case of block or cold frame type, it just needed half a day! The problem in case of these two formats is that large amounts of input materials are needed[34] in case of the latter.

In order to improve land utilization, Gao adopted three-dimensional cultivation in greenhouses. Three-dimensional cultivation includes using vertical surfaces too for cultivation. Gao improved this cultivation pattern. He created pagoda-shaped structures and spread the spawns and growing materials on these structures. The structures, being stable, do not collapse and improved yield.

Gao also improved the processing technology of straws while imitating the natural conditions for the production of wild mushroom. The traditional method of using straw for mushroom production, involved soaking the chopped straws in special concrete ponds with 4 per cent limewater for three days and three nights. These were then taken out, drained and washed with clean water until its pH level reached 8 before being used. This method was not only costly but also wasted time and labor. Instead, Gao sprayed 5 per cent lime-water over the spread of straws. Then piled them and then sprayed them again with lime from the top. He then covered them with a thin plastic film and used them after fermentation[35].

Bagging Machine for Mushroom Substrate[36]

Traditionally, the mushrooms were bagged by hand. Three persons were needed for this traditional method. One person opened a bag. The second person put substrate into it and the third one tied up the bag[37]. To improve work efficiency, Gao found some plastic buckets, the same size as the bag, from waste recycling station. He fixed these buckets to one corner of a desk and covered the plastic bag over the bucket. Through this method, the bagging efficiency was greatly improved.

One day in 1990, enlightened by the working principle of the briquette-making machine, Gao thought of a new idea. He spent some RMB and bought a second-hand motor (a new one cost over RMB 200) from the waste recycling station. He asked a mechanic (this mechanic also produced small agricultural machinery) from

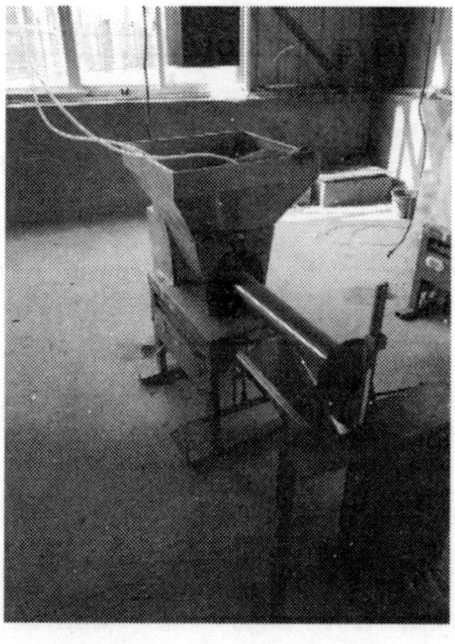

Photo credit: Gao Dedian

Photo 6.4: Bagging Machine

his village to help him make a mushroom bagging machine on the working principle of briquetting machine. Plastic buckets moved mechanically on this machine on a belt, which increased the bagging speed. But bags still had to be tied by hand.

Gao always kept himself updated about mushrooms and technology through books and magazines such as Rural Know-all Magazine, Rural New Technology and various others. These magazines carried many advertisements. One such advertisement was about a kind of automatic bagging machine, which could fill 1,000 bags per hour. Its cost was over RMB 10,000.The common mushroom cultivators could neither afford it, nor was the requirement as high as 1000 bags per hour. Gao began inventing a small and simple bagging machine.

One day in 1992, a sausage salesman visited the village with a portable, mini sausage machine. Gao observed that this machine could encase quite a long sausage. Struck by this idea, he again sought out the mechanic and assembled an automatic mushroom bagging machine. The total cost of this machine was RMB 600-700, including the motor, which costed RMB 200. Gao gave away detailed drawings of his bagging machine to everyone who participated in the training program of mushroom production technology[38], so that they could make one on their own after returning home. Gao, subsequently made additional improvements to the bagging machine. Table 6.7 shows the

Table 6.7: Improvement process of mushroom bagging machine

	Labor required	*Bags filled per day*	*Working efficiency (one person works for 8 hours per day) per person per day*	*Improvement over manual bagging process (by one person per day)*
Before improvement	3	450, each bag filled 1kg substrate	150	
After the first improvement	3	570	190	Could prepare 40 more bags
After the second improvement	3	630	210	Could prepare 60 more bags
After the third improvement	1	100 bags per hour	800	Could prepare 650 more bags

Source: Provided by Gao Dedian.

improvement in the process of bagging with the help of Gao's machine, whereby one person could fill 650 more bags per person per day. This bagging process tremendously increased productivity.

Multifunctional Steam Generator

Steam was generated by briquette stove and pressure cooker to sterilize mushroom spawns. However, adequate steam generation required many types of equipment. Also, when the steam flow was high, it was difficult to known how much water remained inside the steam-generating equipment. Gao's multifunctional steam generator, required fewer devices but could generate more steam. It had a water level indicator and more water could be added when required. The steam generator, could not only be used for sterilizing mushroom spawns, but could also be put to various uses. For example: (i) Vegetable seedlings need to be cultivated in a greenhouse. It needs relatively high temperature and humidity. This steam generator could be put in vegetable greenhouses to increase the indoor temperature and humidity. (ii) Steam generated by this device has such a high temperature, that it can be used to boil soybean milk, which is then made into Tofu (bean curd). (iii) The generator could burn more than 5,000 kg crop stalks, wild grass and vine. It could soften straws in a short time and change them into the rotting growth material used for growing of mushroom.

This multi-functional steam generator got the national utility model patent in 1999.

Initially, Gao put in a lot of effort to generate more amount of steam. First, he used kettle, but only a small amount of steam could be produced. Later, he painted the bucket filled with water for heating. But the effect was still not good. One day in the early 1990s, he saw a workshop using three large oil drums filled with water to produce steam for making tofu. Gao went to the scrap-yard and bought a large oil drum and made a few changes to the drum.

(i) He put a steam pipe and an injection pipe on the top of the oil drum. Despite the small amount of steam, it could generate more than paint bucket;

Photo credit: Gao Dedian

Photo 6.5: Innovation in Sterilization Area

(ii) Gao noticed that fire tends to spread to the surrounding areas, but could not be made full use of. So, he asked a welder to add a hollow tube within the oil drum. Thus, it increased the heated area of water. The hollow tube could inhale the fire just like cupping and it could also prevent fire from spreading to the surrounding.

(iii) In order to further increase the amount of steam, Gao added another four bent tubes at the bottom of the oil drum. He also changed the flat bottom to concave so the heat could not be dissipated.

The cost of the steam generator was about RMB 230. The oil drum costed RMB 60. (This price was in 2013. It could have been half a decade or so earlier.). The tubes costed about RMB 20. And the labor cost of welder was RMB 150. Trainees who participated the training could make this device themselves or ask local craftsman to make it according to Gao's drawing.

Mosquito and Pest Killer for Mushrooms, Vegetables and Fruit Trees

Gao's invention of mosquito and pest killer for edible mushrooms, vegetables and fruit trees gained the national patent for utility models in 2011.

One day in 2001, one of Gao's apprentices informed Gao about pest attack on one of his three-year old mushroom greenhouse. After field study, Gao found that when mushrooms fell on ground, they rotted and caused a lot of mosquitoes and pests. Besides, spores dispersed out over the surrounding areas of the greenhouse, where, on account of moisture the spores also rotted and attracted mosquitoes and pests. He found a solution to keep the pests away as well as keep the mushroom greenhouse clean. But, this too did not solve the problem fundamentally. Gao then decided to invent a proper mosquito and pest repellant/killer.

One day, Gao found large mosquitoes and pests stuck around an old rapeseed oil jar under the window of his trash room. He remembered his conversation with a fruit farmer sitting next to him in a technology demonstration meeting, held a few years back. Insects continuously plagued this fruit grower's 30 Mu plantation of fruit trees. The farmer had surveyed various mosquito pesticides but found all them to be highly toxic. This fruit farmer had invented a pest control lamp, which comprised of a tough transparent cylindrical plastic around a lamp put on a basin. Mosquitoes and pests would be attracted to the lamp-light, hit the hard plastic and fall into the basin. This simple device worked well against small mosquitoes and pests but was not useful for insects with hard shells.

Photo Credit: Gao Dedian

Photo 6.6: Gao's Pest Killer

Gao improvised on the fruit farmer's device: (i) In order to increase the service life of the device, he purchased a transparent plastic bucket from a waste recycling station to replace the hard plastic; (ii) In order to enhance the brightness of the light to attract more mosquitoes, he fixed two mirrors with iron shelf on the upper and lower parts of the plastic buckets; (iii) He then coated the outside of the plastic bucket with a layer of rapeseed oil. Its sweet smell could attract mosquitoes and pest, which stuck to the bucket wall due to the oil. Since hard-shelled insects did not stick to the plastic bucket, Gao increased the viscosity of the oil by adding a sugary paste to the oil.

Gao's device was simple and practical. People could just wipe away the mosquitoes and pests stuck on to the bucket and coat another layer of the sticky mixture for the next use. About 50 grams of oil was needed for one time. Each device could save about RMB 50. It could kill mosquitoes and pests not only for mushrooms but also for vegetables, fruits and others produce[39]. The device was placed outside the mushroom greenhouse so that the attracted mosquitoes and pests remained out, while also benefiting the two nearby greenhouses as well. If the diameter of the plastic bucket was one meter, 80-100 watt bulb could be used. If the diameter was 50 cm, a 60 watt bulb was enough. Gao disseminated this invention by distributing free drawings of the device to his apprentices. They went back to their respective villages and set up small workshops for producing them.

Bag-free Needle Mushroom (Enokitake) Growing Technology[40] With Cold Frame Bean-sprout Type Fruiting Method for Mushrooms

Gao's bag-free needle mushroom (enokitake) growing technology and cold frame bean sprout type fruiting method got the national invention patent in 2012. One day in 2005, Gao went to the local wholesale market to sell his mushrooms. Usually, his wife went to the market to sell mushrooms and he remained in charge of production at home. He found that although the price of needle mushroom was one RMB higher per kg than that of oyster mushroom, they sold well. Known as Enokitake, this mushroom could not only be used for preparing delicatessen but also for hot pot. Gao thus, began to try growing Enokitake. But his output was not very good. He observed a local mushroom producer named Mr. Wang, using some kind of growing material that could grow six batches of mushroom. Gao used traditional method to grow needle mushroom. He used cottonseed hull as main raw material and did not add fertilizer. But, Gao could only grow two batches. Neither the quality nor quantity of his second batch of needle mushroom was as good as the sixth batch of Mr. Wang's. For obvious reasons Mr. Wang was reluctant to teach Gao his production technology. So Gao started looking for new ways.

Gao did some research and found information about the special fertilizer for needle mushroom. This fertilizer was not available locally. He went to the nearby Taoyuan County to buy this fertilizer on a trial basis. Also, although it could produce six batches of needle mushroom, the output quality was not the same as that of Wang's. Gao realized the poor quality of output could be on account of the problem with the ingredients of the fertilizer, but, he left the problem there.

There was also another problem: that of preserving moisture in the growing material/substrate. Gao added sawdust. Sawdust has high moisture retention capacity and contains rich lignin, which is needed for the growth of mushrooms. In order to improve the taste and nutrition, Gao added salt and corn flour. After repeated tests and trials, he also arrived at an appropriate ratio.

Needle mushrooms need a good amount of cellulose for proper growth. Gao added cotton waste/residue, which he found in abundance in cotton mills, to the substrate, since cotton is rich in cellulose.

Traditionally, special plastic bags are used for growing needle mushroom. But these bags are too small. Besides, only half of each bag is filled with growing material and is then folded. As the needle mushroom grows, the plastic bag's fold is gradually opened and pulled up. This prevented the growing material from falling out and the moisture level in the bag was also maintained. However, this method was time consuming and required effort, since the plastic bags had to be unfolded as and when the mushrooms grew. Gao developed a technique that did not require plastic bags. He replaced plastic bags with a wooden box. Growing needle mushrooms in the wooden box thereby reduced time and efforts. Gao developed this new technique in 2007, which not only saved labor cost, but also saved material cost.

Previously, Gao had developed a block-type mushroom growing technique. He applied this technology to needle mushroom production. He put plastic film in a 48cm long, 38cm wide and 15cm wooden frame. After spreading three layers of spawns and two layers of growing material, the film was tied up.

For a long time, seeding of needle mushroom had been carried in sterile rooms. Everything had to be sterilized by potassium permanganate in advance. But these sterile rooms were not affordable for all mushroom growers. A bottle of potassium permanganate costed more than RMB 30. In 1993, Gao had created a sterile area for mushroom inoculation by using steam, imitating the sterile room environment. He applied this technique to needle mushroom inoculation. He wrapped a plastic tube around the wooden frame and made holes on the tube. When steam went through the tube, it would come out from the holes and blow off bacteria in the air to form a sterile surrounding area. After the growing materials had been covered with hyphae, he put them on a concave seedling bed held in place by bamboo sticks. He wrapped the growing material block with sponge so as to keep moisture and prevent mushroom from dislodging. The growing material block would then be turned upside down after harvesting three batches of mushrooms after which, another three batches of mushrooms could be produced.

This bag-free technique allowed the hyphae to be grown in agricultural beds instead of bags, where they could not only absorb nutrients from growing material but could also absorb various microelements and moisture directly from the soil. Mushrooms grown through this technology were strong and tasted delicious. Table 6.8 is a comparison of production costs and benefits before innovation and after.

Developing Organic Pesticides

Gao replaced carbendazim[41] and dimethoate[42] with biological insecticide solution whose main components were salt, plant ash and tea seed cake. This new pesticide was not only environmentally friendly and low cost, but also promoted the growth of mushrooms and killed insects. Gao also invented a kind of nutrient solution (formula: pound spinach into juice and then add 30 per cent water and 30 per cent MSG)[43].

Table 6.8: Comparison between before and after needle mushroom growing method innovation

	Traditional method	*After improvement*	*Notes*
Working efficiency	— One bag could only fill 0.3 kg growing materials. — One worker could fill 60 kg growing materials per day.	— One mould could fill 25 kg growing materials. — One worker could fill 1,000 kg per day.	
Labor cost	150 RMB for every 60 kg growing material	10 RMB for every 60 kg growing material	In 2014, the income of each person per day is 150 RMB
Cost of raw material used to wrap growing materials	— Each needle mushroom bag cost 0.15 RMB. — Every 60 kg materials needed 200 bags. — The total cost was 30 RMB.	— Every 25 kg materials need a piece of plastic film, which costs 0.5 RMB. — Every 60 kg plastic film only cost one RMB.	The price of 2014
Yield	Every 60 kg material could produce 60 kg mushroom	Every 60 kg material could produce 100-120 kg mushroom	
Earnings[44]	Gross income for every 60 kg material is 720 RMB	Gross income for every 60 kg material is 1,200 to 1,440 RMB	In 2014, the local price for needle mushroom per kilogram is 12 RMB

Source: Provided by Gao Dedian.

Adding salt: The application of salt in substrate was due to Gao's observation. One day, in the early 1990s, two bags of salt accidentally fell into the water vat. One of it melted in the water. Gao used the salty water for trials and tests. He noticed that when this water was used, the produce were large sized mushrooms and there were fewer pests. Gao believed that the explanation for this could be that microorganisms needed for growing mushroom had to eat food for survival. Since salty water tasted good it must have made the food delicious, which the microorganisms preferred. Thus, microorganisms grew fast, healthy and strong so that they could win the 'war' of fighting pests in the substrates. The pests could not get enough food and hence could not survive. Gao tried various proportions of salt in the substrate so as to increase mushroom output as much as possible.

Adding plant ash: Gao's keen observation led to the use of fly ash for mushroom production. There was a vegetable field near the north side of Gao's mushroom greenhouse. In autumn, one villager planned to grow cabbage in this field. So he piled dried vines of hyacinth bean, peppers and other vegetables and burnt them. At that time, Gao had two mushroom greenhouses. One was open and the other was covered. Gao was watering mushroom in the open greenhouse when the plant ash blew into his greenhouse and settled on his mushroom caps. This did not attract his attention. But later he found that the outputs of the two greenhouses were different. The growth and yield of mushrooms with plant ash were significantly better than one without.

Local farmers had always used plant ash for sprinkling over the leek plants after they had been cut. This prevented the newly sprouted leeks from turning yellow and also kept the pests at bay. Realizing this, Gao began to test with different ratios of water, plant ash and salt. He also experimented with different combinations of plant ashes, such as straw ash, peanut shell ash, rice husk ash, sawdust ash, and rape straw ash. In addition, Gao also found that the impurities in plant ash had to be filtered out before use.

Adding tea-cake: The idea of adding tea seed cake to the new formula came from Gao's mother's daily practice. Gao grew mushrooms on the hillside to imitate the natural conditions. Usually the production of first batch of mushrooms was quite good. But the second batch of mushroom could not grow because the termites under couch grasses ate the hyphas of mushrooms. Gao used different proportions of salt and plant ash to solve this problem but failed. One day, he suddenly remembered his mother used tea seed cake to wash clothes. The cakes being alkaline, he thought, it might have an insecticidal effect. So, Gao added tea seed cake to the original formula of salt and plant ash. After repeated trials, he finally succeeded. Gao also found out that tea seed cakes should be soaked overnight to bring out all the active ingredients.

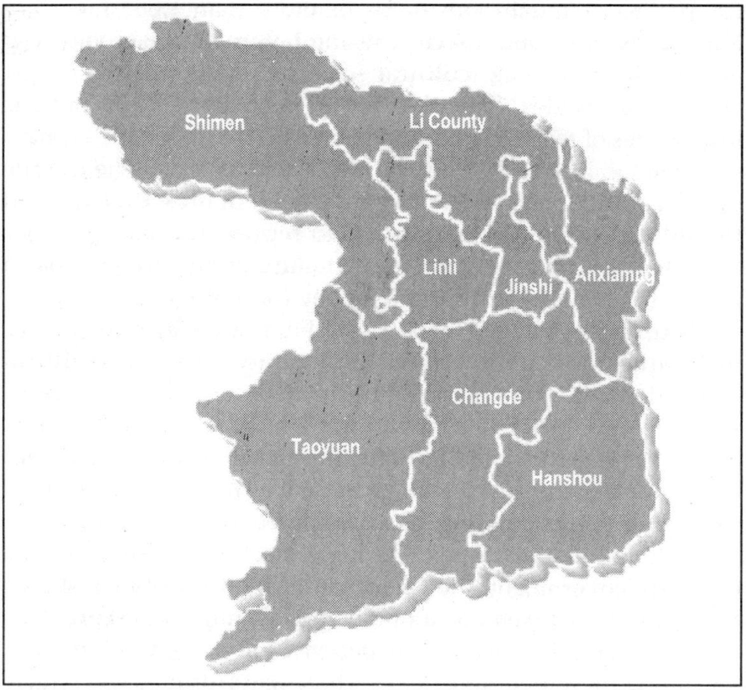

Map 6.2: Changde City and Counties

One of Gao's apprentices also ran into a similar problem. He grew mushrooms directly in rotten trees on the hills. He could not grow the second batch of mushrooms but he had no idea why. He was unaware that there were termites under the rotten trees. He consulted Gao. As per Gao's instruction, he used the formula. The apprentice was able to grow six batches of mushrooms, and there was no problem of termites until the culture was totally used up. It proved that this formula was effective. Moreover, this formula also killed cutworms.

Gao's apprentices came from over 20 provinces. They often contacted each other and formed a network to share their problems and solutions. Gao collected information from them and carried out experiments to find solutions. He disseminated his achievements to apprentices for free trials. If they succeeded, Gao then trained more people.

In 2012, the Dingcheng S&T Bureau appointed Gao as a special S&T Commissioner to Huayanxi Vegetable Cooperative. The

Cooperative's mushroom fields of more than 1,000 mu were infested by pests and insects, causing failure of mushroom crop on hill slope. The agricultural scientist's solution was use of chemical pesticides. Gao asked his apprentices to try his organic insecticides of tea seed cake and plant ash. He shared his formula with the local farmers. Once, he was asked as to why he did not produce and market the organic insecticides that he had formulated to the Cooperative. Gao replied that being a S&T Commissioner, he could not allow failure of mushroom crop in thousands of fields, just to earn money for himself!

Interestingly, the farmers of Huayanxi applied Gao's techniques and innovations to vegetable and agricultural cultivation too. Gao's organic insecticide was used in powdered form on mushrooms cultivation. The agricultural farmers converted this into liquid form to kill vegetable pests and insects. For example, if the rape seedlings are soaked in the pesticide liquid for a while before planting, there would be no insects/pest, as the latter do not like that smell. During a meeting organized by the Changde government, the Chairman of the Cooperative shared this story and thanked Gao for his help in solving the pest problem. He also shared his villagers' experiences of using Gao's organic formula in the agricultural fields. Thus, Gao's formula was widely diffused among local farmers both in mushroom and agricultural industries.

The Development of New Materials for Mushroom Production

Changde is the largest cotton producing area of Hunan Province. There are lots of crop straws and stalks, including rape straw, wheat straw, corn stalks etc. Using cotton-stalks as raw material for mushroom cultivation is quite promising. In recent years, Gao has used and experimented with various straws and stalks to replace cotton seed hull in mushroom production in order to reduce cost. He also experiments and carries out various researches on mushroom growing technology.

Wherever Gao went, he would carry back some straws and stalks to carry out experiments. Gao's research not only helped people recycle waste, reduce mushroom production cost and protect environment, but also increased their income. Initially, farmer households or factories were quite happy to have their crop waste picked up or cleaned for free, by others. However, after seeing that these wastes could also be used for mushroom production, they began to charge.

Gao travelled throughout Changde to study soil conditions of different areas, such as its *p*H, temperature and humidity, and understand the types of mushrooms that could be grown in different areas. Different wastes have different formulas, different processing method, and are suitable for particular types of mushrooms. Some may be suitable for the production of enokitake while some are suitable for oyster mushrooms. Gao compared their yields, taste and cost and accordingly formulated the substrate to be used for the production. For example, straws contain rich fibers. No cotton seed hull was needed while using straws to grow mushrooms. But, if other materials are used, cotton seed hulls need to be added. The following are some of the options he found for growing mushrooms.

Case I – Using cottonseed hull: Since Changde is the largest cotton producing area of Hunan Province, cotton fields are spread over 1.5 million mu, of which approximately 20 Mu are in Dingcheng. Gao's cooperative set up a cotton stalk smashing and processing unit in the production base of Hunan Provincial Cotton Science Research Institute, which could process over 6,000 tons of cotton stalks annually.

In 2010, the price of mushrooms went down, requiring a need to reduce production costs. As a result, Gao began to develop a new technique of using cotton stalks to grow mushrooms. "Cotton growers could earn RMB 70 or more per Mu of field, if they could smash and recycle cotton stalks. Mushroom cultivators could save 50 per cent production cost, if they used cotton stalks rather than cotton seed hull. If all of Changde's cotton stalks could be made good use of, the city's income would increase by millions of RMB. For example, 450,000 tons of processed cotton stalks could produce about 400,000 tons of mushrooms and increase RMB 240 million in profits."[45]

Since cotton stalks contain various types of bacteria in large numbers, if used as substrate, only one batch of mushroom could be produced. Later, the bacteria would eat up the hyphae. Gao processed cotton stalks by a three-time fermentation technique and used steam to further sterilize them. The effect was quite good[46]. This innovation happened by accident. Once, Gao had gone for a meeting. So, he covered the cotton stalks with plastic film to keep the moisture intact. Next day, when he came back and opened the plastic film, he found that there were black and red bacteria on some crushed cotton stalks. The temperature at that time was about 40°C. Gao was disappointed. He thought these crushed cotton stalks could no longer be used. But, he could not bear to throw them away. So, he just turned over the stalks several times and covered them again with the plastic film. The next day, when he opened the film, he found that those black and red bacteria disappeared. Instead, now there were some gray and green bacteria. At this point, the temperature of the stalk pile had reached about 60°C. Gao turned them over again a few times and then covered them again. On the fourth day, after the film was opened, only the black bacteria were left. And the temperature at this time was 80°C. Gao noted that lifespan of different bacteria at different temperatures were different. The higher the temperature was, longer the life span of bacteria was.

Gao now understood that different bacteria germinated at different temperatures. Bacteria that germinated at 40°C would die when the temperature reached 60°C. By the same process, if the temperature reached 80°C, the bacteria that germinated at 60°C, would die. If stalks were subjected to the conventional one time fermentation instead of three times, and if the temperature was increased to 100 directly with steam sterilization, the bacteria that germinate at lower temperature would remain dormant. Thus, bacteria would not be eradicated completely.[47] In order to make the stockpile free of the various types of bacteria, after the three-time fermentation, Gao heated cotton stalk pile with steam for two hours to kill those bacteria that geminate under 80°C.

Case II – Using bamboo scraps: Huayanxi Mushroom Cooperative is located in an old forest. There are three chopsticks production plants nearby. Chopsticks are made from bamboo. This process produces bamboo dust. There are also a lot of waste chopsticks. These wastes were earlier burnt. But, after a ban on their burning, these wastes were dumped along the rivers and in forests, some on the mountains, polluting the environment and water in these rivers. In 2012, Gao developed the technique of growing mushrooms by using chopstick scraps. Gao's innovation not only solved the problem of environmental pollution, but also reduced cost and brought economic benefits.

Case III – Using lotus seed shell and sawdust: Lotus is grown on a large scale in Changde. The lotus seed shells were of little use and also caused environment pollution. Disposal of the lotus seed shells troubled lotus cultivators a lot. Gao invented the technology to produce mushrooms by using lotus seed shell. Initially, those lotus cultivators did not know the purpose for his collecting lotus seed shell. They did not charge Gao for the same, but were in fact very happy that Gao helped them deal with the wastes. Later, when they learnt that the lotus seed shell could be used for mushroom cultivation, they began to charge money, about several hundreds of RMB per ton!

Case IV – Other Materials: Gao also tried to use sawdust, rice hull, peanut shell as raw materials for mushroom production. In 2012, price of 1-ton cotton seed hull in Changde market was RMB 2,000, rice hull was RMB 600, and lotus seed hull was RMB 800. Sawdust was free. In 2014, cottonseed hull price increased to RMB 3,200 and lotus seed hull was over RMB 2,000 per ton. Sawdust also begun to be sold for a price! In 2015, cotton stalks were still available for free. Only freight charges had to be paid. Expecting the price of raw materials to go up, Gao has started to using other materials like mountain weeds to grow mushrooms.

Marketing Innovation

As part of his fitness routine, Gao cycled early every morning. He often saw a florist. He wondered whether he could learn marketing method from him to increase the diffusion of his technique. Instead of waiting for the mushroom producers to come to him for purchasing the substrate briquettes that he prepared, he directly went to the market to sell the same from 2013 onwards. The market price of oyster mushroom was RMB 6 per kg. Gao sold his mushroom at RMB 10 per kg. He sold 1,000 kg oyster mushroom in this way from September to December that year and increased his income by RMB 4,000. From 2014, he began to sell substrate briquettes to consumers directly and let them enjoy the fun of fruiting mushrooms.

Technology Diffusion

Gao diffused his new techniques and technology through training. Gao states that more than 6,000 apprentices across the country from 20 provinces and cities have been trained on his 'Grass becomes Mushroom' or 'Straw becomes Oyster Mushroom' technology. Interestingly, Some apprentices then further trained others in this technology. For example, someone from Jiangxi province cooperated with Know-all Magazine, which has an annual circulation of over one million, through correspondence course and then himself earned over one million every year[48]. Some of his trainings have been free, altruistic, to help people in distress. Some have been the source of his income.

Gao's altruistic efforts are narrated below:

- One success story of his training is in Wenchuan County, Sichuan. This county suffered a huge earthquake in 2008, and the farmers of the county lost everything. After earthquake, farmer Du from Wenchuan came to Gao to learn mushroom cultivation techniques. Gao patiently trained him in all skills for free; from stock culture, to spawn to scale production. Du then regained his wealth by cultivating mushrooms.
- Another success story is that of a young man in Gao's own village, who did not do any work and hence the villagers did not respect him. Gao trained him in mushroom production, which then led to increase in wealth of this young man.
- The third example is that of a very poor farmer, Lin Changhong, from Muzhai cillage, Huitong county, Hunan, who made money by selling his blood. He came to Gao to learn mushroom cultivation technology. Gao taught him for free and also arranged free accommodations and food for him and before he left, gave him spawns, free of charge!

Gao has adopted four broad approaches for training to earn a income:

(i) Cooperate with the government – After the success of 'straw become oyster mushroom' technology, the county S&T Bureau approached him to help him apply for the patents as well as for research projects. Rural technology management office of Agriculture Bureau helped him diffuse innovation and cooperated with him to enroll and train students. Gao and S&T Bureau conducted the training program for five to six years. They trained dozens of students every month. Generally, a trainee could master the technology within one week. Gao charged them for training[49] but provided them free accommodation and food. He charged less from the disabled people. Since Gao's training program was backed and guaranteed by the government, it gained legitimacy among the students. Rural technology management office took 20 per cent of the training fees, while Gao got 80 per cent. The income of rural technology management office was mainly used for paying advertisement expenses.

The Government often organizes specialized technical training for farmers. It is usually an expert team that carries out these trainings. Gao is often invited as an expert to train in the mushroom cultivation technology. For example, in 2012, Gao was invited as an expert for the training of disabled persons in the 'Sunshine Project'[50] of Dingcheng District. There are more than 30 towns in Dingcheng and Gao went to each town to train the people. Roughly about 30 disabled people were trained in each town. Another example is the organizing of mushroom cultivation technology training three times a year by Dingcheng S&T Bureau, which trained about 1,000 people every year.

Most of the participants of the trainings organized by the government are large cultivators, party members and village group leaders. Deputy Town Chiefs in charge of the town's industrial economy and heads of agricultural management stations also participated in the trainings. After getting permission, Gao's training video was used for distant education by Organization Department[51] of Dingcheng.

In 2012, the Dingcheng S&T Bureau appointed Gao as a special S&T commissioner to Huayanxi Vegetable Cooperative[52]. He used his innovation and solved the pesticide problem of the mushroom production base[53].

(ii) Collaborate with research and other institutions – The Mushroom factory of Hunan Cotton Research Institute was located near Hongyun Village. The Institute also came forward to support Gao in technology promotion. The arrangement was that the mushroom factory was responsible for enrollment and Gao was responsible for training. The income was divided equally amongst them. Their cooperation lasted for two years. Together, they trained 10 to 20 students per month. The training program was later terminated due to institute's bankruptcy.

In 2012, Selenium-rich Products Research Institute of Taoyuan county, Changde cultivated a type of mushroom rich in selenium. In collaboration with the Institute, Gao introduced this technology to Huayanxi Cooperative. In 2013, Gao was appointed as a Special S&T Commissioner of Changde City (totally there were only two Farmer Special Commissioners in Changde). He collaborated with Xiang Li Ren Company. He then introduced his various mushroom production technologies to this company.

Gao has also imparted trainings at the Changde Mushroom Association from which he earns some income. The Association's executive council in its meetings held every six months decide on the training objectives, content, methods and number of people to be trained. Changde Agriculture Commission funds all trainings organized by Changde Mushroom Association. Annual training funds available are RMB 50,000. For example, in 2011, the Executive Council decided to focus on the promotion of *lentinus edodes* (Shiitake) and black fungus. The association is responsible for the communication with the government. Vice President of the association is responsible for implementing works.

(iii) Self-Advertizing – Enrollment through advertisement has been the main form of Gao's technology diffusion. He has seen this as his income generating activity. But, the advertising costs are quite high whereas the fee received per student is in the range of RMB 1,000 to RMB 2,000. Thus, the revenue model is not viable. In addition, imparting the training is hard work. Gao has to incorporate the latest research and improvements to the training course every time. Graduated students would always come to Gao for help whenever they faced a problem for which he never charged them.

(iv) Other Approaches for Diffusion – Gao has promoted his efforts through media. The program 'Golden Land' of CCTV2 reported Gao's innovation of 'straw becomes oyster mushroom' after it got the national invention patent in 2002. After that, dozens of news media reported it, such as China Patent Newspaper, China Technology Market News, China Daily Market, Hunan Daily, Hunan Broadcast Station, Hunan TV's Program Countryside Exploring[54], Hunan S&T Newspaper, Hebei Farmer's Newspaper, Heihe Daily, Rural Know-all, etc.

Gao receives many mails and letters from all over China and he answers them all![55]. He is the president of Xin Yuan Cooperative and trains the cooperative members regularly. Gao has written many articles for reference purposes and gives lectures to college students. He also has new research achievements every year. Whenever mushroom cultivators face any problem, Gao always shares all his research results and knowledge, regardless of payment he receives and time-spent. Sometimes, he even spends his own money doing training.

Organizational Innovation for Technical Innovation Diffusion

Gao's innovation is accompanied by entrepreneurship. Organizational evolution happens during the diffusion of his innovation. His mushroom cultivating organizations went from being a small mushroom cultivation unit, to an officially registered production base, and then to a cooperative with functions of production and management, and finally to a mushroom research institute, which was set up under the suggestion and guidance of the government. Both, the research institute and the cooperative promoted the research and diffusion of Gao's innovations. The Changede Mushroom Association expanded the scale of innovation diffusion. The various institutions that have come up to promote Gao's production method are discussed below.

Hong Yun Mushroom Plant (1996)

After the success of 'straws becoming oyster mushrooms', Gao built several greenhouses to grow mushrooms by the roadside. One day in 1996, a group of people led by the then Governor of Changde, came cross these greenhouses on their way to a factory. They were surprised to see that straws were being used for mushroom cultivation. Soon, the local TV and news channel covered Gao's story. After watching the TV program, the Dingcheng S&T Bureau helped Gao apply for patent. In 1996, Gao set up Hong Yun Mushroom Factory. In the beginning, Gao did not apply for a business license for the factory, but only registered it as a production base in the Technology Management Office of Agricultural Bureau, Dingcheng. With Hong Yun Mushroom Plant as a base, Gao trained students throughout China. With his help the local village residents were able to generate large incomes and raise their standards of living. On noticing this, the Party branch secretary of Hongyun Village, suggested that he teach mushroom cultivation to some poor households.

Hongfa Mushroom Base (2000)

Hongfa Mushroom Base was set up on the likes of Hong Yun Mushroom Plant. In 2000, Gao rented 35 Mu of wasteland to develop a mushroom cultivation and production base and registered it as Hongfa Mushroom Base to replace the Hong Yun Mushroom Plant. At the start, 10,000 households became members of the base through a system of shareholding. The shareholders contributed either through their skills, raw materials, and/or any other form of contribution.

Rural Technical Trading Market/Dingcheng Mushroom Research Institute (2002)

In 2002, Hunan Agriculture Department directed all districts, counties and cities to set their own rural technical trading markets as requested by Ministry of Agriculture. Science and technology Office mandated that all companies, which carried out technology research and production should obtain the 'science and technology trade license' before selling technical products and that all the technical products should be traded on the market. This is the background for the emergence of 'rural technology market' as a concept. Technology Management Office of Dingcheng Agriculture Bureau, after several investigations, found that Gao not only carried out technical research but also did technology trading. This met with the requirements of setting up technology trading market. So they suggested that Gao set up Dingcheng Mushroom Research Institute, Changde, which had as its part Dingcheng Rural Technology Trading Market[56]. The exchange market mainly sold mushroom production technology through training. Its income per day was only RMB 100 to RMB 200.

Thereafter, Gao applied for and obtained research grants through this institute from Changde City government (S&T Bureau), Dingcheng District government and Hunan Science and Technology Department, among which funds from the S&T Bureau accounted for the most. The annual average funds he received were RMB 130,000. In order to make his research achievement more effective, Gao trained and guided mushroom cultivators during the annual training organized by the government.

Although the institute is not very large, its research content is practical and covers the whole chain of mushroom production. Its research achievements have won the second prize of Scientific and Technological Progress Award for two years. Dingcheng S&T Bureau supported Gao with RMB 50,000 every year in the name of management fee of the technology exchange market.

Technology trading market is mainly trading technology (paid training programs for mushroom cultivation, technology) and technical products (selling mushrooms). Dingcheng government supports the market with several thousand RMB or provides production materials of equal value every year. In addition, it is also supports enrollment for the training programs. Hongfa Mushroom base (it is also the cultivation and production base of the research institute) and technology market of the government have combined together for mushroom cultivation technology diffusion.

Xinyuan Mushroom Cooperative (2010)

In 2008, Gao set up Xinyuan Mushroom Cooperative with Hongfa Mushroom Production Base, as its base. This was the first mushroom cooperative in Dingcheng since the implementation of the 'Law on Farmer Professional Cooperative'. Gao's cooperative had 128 members (households). It combined together the functions of research, growing, processing and marketing of mushroom. Besides, more than 300 larger mushroom cultivators have connections with Gao's cooperative[57]. The cost of production was reduced by standardization of raw materials' supply, production formula, and mushroom production/cultivation by the members. As the volume of production increased, they gave their products a uniform brand. The cooperative trained its members about the technology. Members were responsible for production and the cooperative for selling the products. The cooperative developed good management practices such as holding regular meetings to discuss successes and failures and learning from them.

Relationships among The Base, Research Institute and Cooperative

The Research Institute focused on research and the cooperative and base, concentrated on making economic profits. Gao's research institute carried out the research, which were implemented in real time by the cooperative. Thus, the research achievements were directly transformed into economic benefits. The base implements the institute's research experiments and through the cooperative, the successful researches are translated into large-scale production. Members of the Hongfa Mushroom Production Base form the core members of the cooperative. Hongfa Mushroom Base is the experimental production base for the cooperative. All the learning's from the cooperative members' production activities are the learning for the Base, which then takes input from the research institute to find answers to the problems in production. The production base is set up on an area of about 50 to 60 Mu land. The cooperative members have their own production areas. Thus, the research achievements of the research institute after being tested in the market are then transformed into economic benefit through the cooperative. Thus, the Research gets converted into production by the farmer-members of the cooperative.

Changde Mushroom Association

The most important of all institutional set-ups, was the Changde Mushroom Association. Although Gao did not set up this institution, his innovations were greatly promoted through it. He also got many opportunities to communicate with and learn from others, through this association. Ma Yongchun, Chairman of the Association, always consulted Gao regarding management issues and sought his advice. This is how Gao's links with the Association started and has continued till date.

Background

In 2008, the Association of Changde Mushroom Producers started its operation as per the directive of the Hunan Agricultural Bureau. Leaders of the city agricultural bureau learnt about Gao's innovations from Hunan TV and CCTV2. So they asked Gao to be Chairman of Changde Mushroom Association. Considering that he was only good at technology research and lacked management expertise, experience and communication skill, and was already committed to many training programs, Gao suggested Ma Yongchun's name as Chairman and himself as the Vice-Chairman of the Association.

Ma Yongchun was an innovator as well as a successful entrepreneur[58]. He spent one month surveying the cooperatives in all the counties of Changde City and selected one from each county as member of the Association. Chairman of the Cooperative was also the President of Branch Association of Changde Mushroom Association and Vice President of the Changde Mushroom Association. Changde Mushroom Association is a district level association and the branch associations of Changde Mushroom Association are county level associations. These branch associations are under the leadership of Changde Mushroom Association. There are totally nine branch associations. The presidents of branch associations were familiar with each other and were prestigious local people. Their cooperatives were influential. So, it was quite easy for their cooperation. Gao was selected as the Vice President of the Changde Mushroom Association. Changde Agricultural Bureau (later renamed as Changde Rural-work Department) gave them guidance. Each year, the Association was supported with funds for training the members[59].

Main Responsibility

The Association is an important tool for the government to manage and support the development of mushroom industry. The main duty of the association is to promote new technology among members and propose policy suggestions to government. This Association holds three meetings every year, of which two are executive council meetings and one for feedback on trainings. The executive council meeting is held every six months, in which, the half yearly working plan is decided. The working plan is with regard to approach and methods of training, number of people to be trained on the whole and in each training, objectives and content of training and other relevant issues. The chairmen of the various branches of the cooperative formed the board of directors. They discuss the main agenda and work that needs to be done throughout the year at the beginning of the year and execute these plans after reporting to the government. The association's main responsibilities are:

(a) *Promote new technology:* In 2010, the price of cotton seed hulls increased to RMB 2,800 per ton. Increased production cost, greatly affected the mushroom cultivators' profits. The association thus reached a consensus; to promote mushroom cultivation technology that uses cotton stalks. The Association organized trainings and branch chairmen were responsible for implementing the technology. Since the smashed cotton stalks were fluffy and had more volume as compared to the cottonseed hulls, the quantity that could be filled in one bag was 30 per cent less than that of the latter. This reduced the mushroom outputs. Although Gao tried different ways to solve the problem, he failed. Later on, Ma's research institute developed a microbial starter cultures[60], that processed the cotton stalks and reduced its volume so that one bag could be filled with 20 per cent more substrate. This greatly improved output and increased the farmers' income.

There is one potential risk for government to organize training for mushroom growers. That is, if the technology failed, the government would be considered responsible. The Association did not want the blame to be apportioned to the government and hence were careful in selecting technology that it promoted. The Association had put in place a process to select the technology that would be promoted. The Association would present to the local government, for approval, the technology and scheme through which it wanted to promote a particular technology. For the selected technology, a standard operational procedure was put in place. For example, when the association was set up in 2008, Ma proposed to promote Gao's briquettes mushroom cultivation technology. But Gao thought that this technology was not mature. There was no accurate experiment data of increased output, benefit and reduced cost. Gao did not promote it until 2009.

(b) *Improve the function of cooperative to achieve scale effect*: The main purpose of setting up of the Association was that the members could take advantage of uniform production and management systems. An association can reduce production costs (if inputs are purchased in bulk) and achieve benefits of large-scale production. For example, in the past, each cooperative had to go to Wuhan and Changsha to buy raw materials by themselves. The association set up a mushroom production material shop, to buy raw materials in bulk for the cooperatives. A member of the association set up a chaff factory to recycle associate members' waste mushroom sticks. After simple process, he sold it to the feed factory. This member benefited and it also helped solve the problem of waste mushroom sticks. The bulk production of a standardized quality can also help in marketing the products.

(c) *Increase influence while partnering with government*: The association often carried out surveys on local mushroom production and proposed suggestions to the government. Under the suggestion of Changde Mushroom Association, Changde government decided to ask every county to set up mushroom production bases of thousands of Mu. In 2013, the government invested RMB 3 billion in the Changde Mushroom Association Base.

The success of the Association's production base was on account of the following reasons as summed up by Ma and others:

- The government only supported mass production. Raw materials for Changde mushroom production are mainly cotton stalks and straw, including some corn stalks and corncob. According to Ma Yongchun, the consumption of stalks in Changde mushroom production in 2011 reached over 10 million tons. But because the total mushroom production was not mass-produced, it could not get the benefits of the national sustainable economy policy subsidies (which required that if ten thousand stalks could be used, the government would provide subsidy of RMB 150 per ton on purchase of the raw material).
- To attract companies to invest in mushroom processing, mass production was required. The mushrooms processed by the investors were mainly exported abroad. The investors required mushroom production in bulk for which the mushroom production bases had to be in thousands of Mu of land, which could produce standardized mushrooms. Although the annual total yield of mushroom in Changde was over 90,000 tons, its mushroom production was scattered. There were many varieties of mushrooms. The output of each variety was small. There was not a single variety that had mass production.
- To attract mushroom cultivators back to their hometown, mass production base is useful. In absence of that, the mushroom growers go to the North, where the big markets

are there, to cultivate mushrooms. Mushrooms are sold when they are fresh. Because of this limitation of marketing, the mushroom cultivators prefer to cultivate closer to the markets. The Association arranges for about 2,000 mushroom cultivators to take all their equipment and inputs for mushroom cultivation, to places near big markets throughout the country, where they rent huge greenhouses. They grow mushrooms there and sell these in big cities. But the North has very cold winters. They live in the poor greenhouses and carry out their work. From being from South, the mushroom growers are not acclimatized to the harsh Northern winters and find it hard to survive. Mushroom growers tend to wake up early in the morning at 3 am to 4 am, pick mushrooms and reach the wholesale market by 6 am. This way of living is very difficult. Young farmers would not like to live the same toilsome lives as their parents and hence only older ones go, who find it even harder to withstand the northern winters and poor living conditions. Mushroom produced in this way accounts for 40 per cent to 50 per cent of the total output of Changde City. By developing large mushroom cultivation base in Changde City, this seasonal out migration of the mushroom growers can be reduced, and youth will then have work available near their native village.

Conclusion

Gao's journey of innovations has been that of passionate determination, learning from reading, observing and experimenting and then diffusing the knowledge and technique developed, amongst the larger masses. He innovated different types of mushroom cultivation, using locally available biomass wastes such as agricultural waste, sawdust, bamboo dust etc., or whatever he could lay his hands on. He innovated with regards to all processes of mushroom production. The idea was to simplify mushroom production so that common people could participate in the same. Use of locally available materials would help in reducing the cost of production, which was also beneficial to the local people. But, his innovations had little formal scientific training. The methods were simple and crude so as to say. The equipments were not sophisticated. To a scientist's eye, this would appear very naïve. There is, however, a need to translate these learnings into scientific literature, which would help new mushroom cultivators' to find answers to various problems that they may encounter. This is where a formal link between academic and research institutes would have helped Gao. The redeeming feature of Gao's work was that the local government officials appreciated his work and invited him to train others and advise them, when needed.

Technological innovations alone are not adequate. Institutional innovations to diffuse technology are also necessary. This case study also shows that Gao's enthusiasm of promoting mushroom cultivation throughout the city, in all its counties and villages, resulted in setting up institutions to support and then promote these cultivators. The primary need was to help the cultivators set up greenhouses for mushroom cultivation. Gao supported that. Together, these greenhouses became the base for mushroom production. Gao himself set-up a research institute to experiment with technological improvements at the suggestion of the local government. This research institute assisted the mushroom bases where production was happening. The widespread diffusion of production occurred when the cooperative that was set up, assisted the farmers to cheaply procure raw materials, help them in mushroom production and then in marketing of the mushrooms. The farmer-producers became members of the cooperative. Hence, there has been even institutional innovation to meet the challenges of a market economy.

Gao begun to experiment from 1998 onwards and has continued to be active, as we see in Table 6.9. He was active till 2011, the latest data we have. He has registered six patents (Table 6.10). He has received eight awards, one at the national level, a few at the provincial level, a few at the city level and then at the village level (Table 6.11). Thus, hard work and perseverance has paid off.

The journey has been also replete with government support at many points in time (Table 6.12), from 1986 all the way up to 2013. There are two areas where the local and provincial governments have assisted him; one in diffusing his innovation and other in considering him as an expert trainer in mushroom production. Imparting training provided him income. Besides, he has received funds from the local government for undertaking research. He has been funded to undertake demonstration projects

Table 6.9: Chronology of Innovations by Gao Dedian

Year	*Innovation Description*	*Impact*
1988	Producing oyster mushroom with straw	Reduced cost; common mushroom cultivators could use this technique: mushrooms produced with straws taste like wild mushrooms
1995	Fully-open mushroom inoculators	Improve inoculation efficiency and reduce inoculation cost
1996	Improvement in breeding materials. It contained rice (or millet, or grain, or corn, or sorghum), glucose, gypsum, plant-ash, dried worm-cast power, rice-rinsing water, cottonseed hull, lime and dried soil in the vegetable field.	Materials are readily available and inexpensive
1999	Creating an artificial wild mushroom growth condition	Reduced cost; mushrooms grow better; mushrooms taste like wild ones
2011	Developing biological pesticides	Not only environmentally friendly and low cost, but also promoted the growth of mushrooms and killed insects
1990-2011	The development of new materials for mushroom production [e.g. lotus seed hull (2008), sawdust (1990), rice hulls (1995), chopsticks scraps (2011), smashed cotton stalks (2010), corn cobs£ 2008)]	Reduced production costs; materials are easy to get.

Source: Interview with Mr. Gao.

with regard to mushroom cultivation. His work being recognized, he was appointed as S&T Commissioner in a local vegetable cooperative. Lastly, he also received help in applying for patents for his innovations. A good local government—innovator partnership can be seen here in the promotion of new techniques of mushroom cultivation, so as to enhance productivity and hence income on one hand and reduce the cost of production through utilization of locally available biomass waste as main base of production, on the other hand. This case is as much of an individual's grit and determination as of the facilitative role played by the State in promoting such individuals.

Table 6.10: Patents received by Gao Dedian Mushroom Technology

No.	*Year*	*Patent*	*Brief Description of Patent Content*
1.	1995	Fully-open mushroom inoculators	It used liquid fuel, charcoal, and briquettes as fuel. The fuel burned in the stove and created a sterile area over the stove. Inoculation in this sterile area could greatly improve the efficiency, which was more than10 times faster than traditional method.
2.	1999	Steam Generator	Compared with other steam generators, this steam generator only needs one equipment. It adds a straight tube and four bent tubes to enlarge the heating area. It could generate more steam. Water left could be measured by a pole through the inlet tube. There is a basin with water over the bucket. Water in the basin could be added to the bucket through inlet tube.[1]
3.	2001	Seed production and bionic wild production technology of mushroom	The novel breeding materials contain rice (or millet, or grain, or corn, or sorghum), glucose, gypsum, plant ash, dried worm cast power, rice-rinsing water, cottonseed hull, lime and dried soil in the vegetable field. Mushroom production materials include rice straw (or wheat straw, corn stalks, weeds), dried garden soil powder, lime, gypsum, salt, plant ash, potash, wood chips, and rice water.
4.	2008	Bagging machine for mushroom substrate (Innovator name written on the patent certificate is Gao Honghua, Mr. Gao's son)	Realized the mechanization of bagging; it could replace human labor and saved cost. In the past, three persons were needed. One person could only fill 150 bags of mushroom fruiting substrate per day. With this new machine, only one person is needed. He/she could bag 100 bags per hour. Common mushroom grower could make this machine by himself. The cost for one is only RMB 500 to 600.
5.	2011	Mosquito and fly killer for edible mushrooms, vegetables and crops	An electric bulb is covered with a lampshade, which is made of glass, or plastic film, or stainless steel sheet. A layer of special substance (mixture of rapeseed oil, white or brown sugar and adhesive) is coated on the lampshade. Several holes are drilled on the upper and lower part of the lampshade to ventilate and dissipate heat. Two round mirrors are arranged on the upper and lower part of the lampshade to enhance the illumination intensity to attract more mosquitoes, flies and other insects. Compared with traditional mosquito and fly killers[2], this device is green and non-polluting. Materials are easily available. It could also kill beetles.

(*Contd.*)

Table 6.10 (*Contd.*)

No.	*Year*	*Patent*	*Brief Description of Patent Content*
6.	2012	Needle mushroom bag-free cultivation and cold frame bean sprout type fruiting method	Replace plastic bags with a movable mould and plastic film to produce needle mushroom mycelium; simplify the cultivation procedure; save labor and production cost; mushroom mycelium block could be turned over and used again and again for six times, which increased the conversion rate by 100%. The method is used for artificial needle mushroom cultivation, can simplify the working procedure of needle mushroom cultivation so as to improve the yield and quality of the needle mushroom, and is more beneficial to large-scale industrial production of needle mushroom so that the investment is saved and the economical benefit of needle mushroom farmers are obviously improved.[3]

Sources: Interview with Mr. Gao and below mentioned websties.

1. http://www.google.com.hk/patents/CN2280408Y?cl=en&hl=zh-CN&dq =高德典&ei=g46FU77fDsH38QWa2oGQAg (accessed on May 30, 2014)
2. http://www.google.com.hk/patents/CN102210293A?cl=en&hl=zh-CN&dq =高德典&ei=iI-FU5ikMIrq8AWohoG4Bg (accessed on May 30, 2014)
3. http://www.google.com.hk/patents/CN102084781B?cl=en&hl=zh-CN&dq =高德典&ei=zY-FU7eJDNH08QWIqIHABw (accessed on May 30, 2014)

Table 6.11: Chronology of Awards of Gao Dedian

Year	*Awards*	*Issuing authority*
December 1997	Excellent Inventor of Changde	Changde Patent Management Bureau, Changde Innovation Association
October 2000	First Prize of Changde Science and Technology Progress Prize	Science and Technology Progress Prize Review Committee of Dingcheng District, Changde City
2001	Hunan Province Technology Market Golden Bridge Prize (RMB 10,000)	Hunan Province Technology Market Golden Bridge Prize Review Committee (Under Hunan Technology Market Management Office)
March 2007	Advanced Scientific and Technical Worker	People's Government of Dingcheng District

(*Contd.*)

Table 6.11 (*Contd.*)

Year	*Awards*	*Issuing authority*
October 2010	Advance worker of National Mushroom Industry	China Edible Fungi Association
March 2011	Mushroom Expert of Huayanxi, Dingcheng District	National Forest Park Management Office of Huayanxi, Changde, Hunan Province
January 2013	Advanced Worker	Hunan Province Edible Fungi Association
April 2013	Ecological Agriculture Science Popularization Guidance Experts	Changde Aged S & T Worker Association

Source: Interview with Mr. Gao.

Table 6.12: Provincial/County Government Policies for supporting grassroots innovations

Year	*Policy*	*Brief Description of Policy*
1986	Personal help	The village leader of the time believed Gao's innovative capabilities and often encouraged him. He even helped him rent 3,000kg of straw from the neighboring village to continue his experiments.
1990, 2002£ ¬ 2010	Set up factory, production base and cooperative	Suggested by the government officials, Gao set up the Hongyun Mushroom Factory (suggested by Dingcheng Agricultural Bureau), Hongfa Mushroom Production Base (2002, change from "factory" to "base"), and Dingcheng Xinyuan Mushroom Cooperative (2010, suggested by Agricultural Bureau of Dingcheng) successively.
1996	Dingcheng S&T Bureau helps in Gao's innovation diffusion	The Dingcheng S&T Bureau took the responsibility of widely diffusing Gao's innovation through media; contributing to Gao's to enroll more students. Many times the Dingcheng S&T Bureau received calls to get assurance about genuineness of Gao's innovations. The bureau verified Gao's achievements as well as explained his story. The technology exchange market linked Gao and local government, who then jointly diffused the mushroom production technology.
1997	Help apply patent	The people at the Dingcheng S&T Bureau helped Gao apply for patent. In 2002, after five years' waiting, Gao received the first invention patent of Dingcheng.

(*Contd.*)

Table 6.12 (*Contd.*)

Year	*Policy*	*Brief Description of Policy*
1998	On-the-spot training	Changde Agricultural Bureau organized an on-the-spot training for the technicians. Gao shared the technique of dwarfing too a sinensis trees without reservation.
2002	Establishment of rural technology exchange market and the exchange market should have a carrier	The Dingcheng S&T Bureau suggested Gao's mushroom research institute become the carrier of the Dingcheng Rural Agricultural Technology Exchange Market. The local government gave Gao's mushroom research institute a small amount for research each year. Sometimes, the local government gave Gao production materials as well, such as plastic film, bamboo poles etc. Each year, the local government also gave Gao several thousand RMB to run the technology exchange market.
2004	Sunshine Project of Training for the Transfer of Rural Labor	The government gave Gao RMB 200 RMB for one hour training.
2008	Set up of Association of Mushroom Production	Guided by the government, mushroom growers in Changde also set up an Association of Mushroom Production and Gao was elected as its vice president. Each year, the association received support of RMB 50,000 to train its members. Gao's innovations were easily diffused widely through this institutional arrangement.
2008	Distance training (organized by District party committee organization department)	Gao's training video was used for distance education by the local government.
2010	Local government officials' help	They informed Gao about the project application and helped Gao modify the proposals. They also lobbied to the higher government organizations to give Gao various supports. For example, before his retirement, the formal director of S&T Bureau personally asked the Governor of Dingcheng to give Gao support of RMB 5,000.

(*Contd.*)

Table 6.12 (*Contd.*)

Year	*Policy*	*Brief Description of Policy*
2011	The training of disabled persons in the "Sunshine Project" of Dingcheng District (organized by Changde City Disabled Persons' Federation and Agriculture Bureau)	There are more than 30 towns in Dingcheng and Gao went to each town to train the people. Roughly about 30 disabled people were trained in each town.
2012	Appointment from Dingcheng S&T Bureau	Gao was appointed as a special S&T Commissioner to Huayanxi Vegetable Cooperative by the Dingcheng S&T Bureau.
2012	Demonstration and Promotion of Mushroom Cultivation Technology	Project of Changde City S&T Bureau.
2012	National Subsidy Project of Thousand Mu of Mushroom Base	Ministry of Finance Project. The research was related to development of in forest economic activities, such as mushroom production in forests. Central government financial support was RMB 300,000; provincial financial support was RMB 100,000; city level support was RMB 20,000 thousand; and self-raised funds were RMB 791,300.
2012	Application and demonstration of bionic wild production of *Lactarius deliciosus* strains	Hunan S&T Planning Project, provincial finance support of RMB100,000; city level support of RMB 50,000, and district level support of RMB 20,000.
2013		Ministry of S&T Project given to Chinese Academy of Forestry, Project fund is RMB 300,000. Gao Dedian is a member of this project.

(*Contd.*)

Table 6.12 (*Contd.*)

Year	*Policy*	*Brief Description of Policy*
2013	*Lactarius delicious* Artificial Wild Cultivation Techniques	Project of Dingcheng S&T Bureau, project funding of RMB 20,000.
2013	People's government of Changzhi County — Subsidy Measures of strengthening agriculture and benefiting farmers 2013[61]	Farmers' Professional cooperative subsidy: New farmer professional cooperatives could receive subsidy of RMB 3000 to 5000. Exemplary cooperatives at provincial level to receive subsidy of RMB 100,000. City level exemplary cooperatives to receive subsidy of RMB 50,000 thousand from the county finance bureau and county level exemplary ones to receive RMB 30,000. New energy construction subsidy: Construction projects of new rural large renewable energy and peasant household renewable energy to be fully supported and subsidized to the greatest extent.

Source: Interview with Mr. Gao.

NOTES

1. Mushroom cultivation requires humid climate and moderate temperatures, between 50 and 70 degrees Fahrenheit.
2. On February 25, 2013, one of the authors interviewed Ma Yongchun, the Director of Changde Mushroom Association, at Technology Management Office of Changde Administration of agricultural management.
3. On February 25, 2013, one of the authors interviewed Ma Yongchun, the Director of Changde Mushroom Association, at Technology Management Office of Changde Administration of agricultural management.
4. On February 25, 2013, one of the authors interviewed Ma Yongchun, the Director of Changde Mushroom Association, at Technology Management Office of Changde Administration of agricultural management.
5. On February 25, 2013, one of the authors interviewed Ma Yongchun, the Director of Changde Mushroom Association, at Technology Management Office of Changde Administration of agricultural management.
6. http://www.emushroom.net/news/201209/18/12185.html

7. *Suggestion on the 12th Five-Year Development Plan of National Edible Fungi Industry,* Document for The 5th Member (Representative) Congress of China Edible Fungi Association, 2010.10.27, provided by Gao Dedian.
8. Material for The 5th Member (Representative) Congress of China Edible Fungi Association, provided by Gao Dedian.
9. *Suggestion on the 12th Five-Year Development Plan of National Edible Fungi Industry (review draft),* Document for The 5th Member (Representative) Congress of China Edible Fungi Association, 2010.10.27, provided by Gao Dedian.
10. http://news.xinhuanet.com/fortune/2012-09/18/c_113120210.htm (accessed on May 30, 2014).
11. http://zixun.mushroommarket.net/201401/22/160104.html (accessed on May 30, 2014).
12. http://hn.rednet.cn/c/2012/09/17/2753070.htm (accessed on May 30, 2014).
13. "To Strengthen the effect, To Speed up the development of edible fungi industry of our province", Work report of General Council of Hunan Edible Fungi Association, 2012.
14. *Changde Mushroom Industry,* 2012, published by Rural Work Office of Changde People's Government.
15. Income of the local people at that time was less than one thousand RMB.
16. If cottonseed hull was used, cost would be over 10,000 RMB per 10,000 kg mushroom (the price of late 1980s).
17. In late 1980s.
18. Spawn is Mycelia of mushrooms or other fungi grown in specially prepared organic matter for planting in beds (*Source*: http://www.thefreedictionary.com/spawn, accessed on September 22, 2014). Mycelia is the vegetative part of a fungus, consisting of a mass of branching, thread like hyphae (*Source*: http://www.thefreedictionary.com/mycelium, accessed on September 22, 2014).
19. The method got the national invention patent in 2001. It was the first invention patent of Dingcheng District since its foundation 18 years before.
20. Hypha is a long, branching filamentous structure of a fungus. In most fungi, hyphae are the main mode of vegetative growth, and are collectively called a mycelium. Source: http://en.wikipedia.org/wiki/Hypha, accessed on September 22, 2014.
21. Hongyun Village was quite near from Changde urban. He spent ten RMB buying a reading card every month from the city library. He often went there to read books and magazines.
22. Monopotassium sulphate.
23. Seeding is through inoculation in mushroom production.

24. Many people who had grown mushrooms for dozens of years also came to learn seed production technology from Gao.
25. Dipotassium sulphate.
26. Magnesium sulphate.
27. It is very troublesome to clean the tube walls if stained and then it would remain stuck on the inside of tube-walls reducing its possibility of reuse.
28. Mushroom spawn is simply any substance that has been inoculated with mycelium, the vegetative growth of a fungus. Mushroom spawn is used to transfer mycelium onto substrate from which mushrooms grow. Mycelium is the vegetative part of a fungus, consisting of a mass of branching, thread-like hyphae.
29. Spore is a minute, typically one-celled, reproductive unit capable of giving rise to a new individual without sexual fusion, characteristic of lower plants, fungi, and protozoans.
30. Currently, a lot of mushroom research institutes and mushroom production companies still use this traditional method.
31. Author of the article was a retired university professor who had done research on mushroom for a long time.
32. Steam inoculation method applied for patent two months earlier than Gao's full-open inoculation method, but was not approved.
33. This method is still used a lot.
34. If 50 kg growing materials are provided, 4.5 kg spawns are needed for bagging-type growing method. But 7.5 kg spawns are needed if using block-type and agricultural bed-type growing methods.
35. "Scientific mushroom growing, way to get rich", *Farmer Counselor*, Gao Dedian, 1997.05.
36. In recent years, mushroom growing scale becomes larger and larger. Bacterial infection caused by improper manual operation and lack of labor become the two most important problems. Wu Jinyang, a farmer from she Autonomous County of Jingning, invented a mushroom inoculation handgun. It improved the efficiency by three times and solved the problem of bacterial infection.
37. This bagging method was still used in a program of mushroom production technology held in June 2014 by "Nong Guang Tian Di" of CCTV7.
38. The drawing was drawn by professionals invited by Gao and city S&T Bureau. Gao paid 5,7000 RMB patent application fee. From the next year, he had to pay 100 to 200 RMB as patent maintenance fee every year.
39. Shi Jinchi, a farmer form Wugen Town, Wenling City, Zhejiang Province, invented a kind of "spectrum mosquito killer", which costs about 100 RMB. Its effect is quite good. One spectrum mosquito killer could kill 50,000 mosquitoes per night if put in a livestock farm. Mr. Shi could sell over 10,000 mosquito killers one year.

40. This means that the needle-mushrooms are grown without a bag.
41. According to Gao's estimation, a mushroom grower could earn 4 RMB net profit per kg growing material if adopts his innovation method to grow needle mushroom.
42. This is a fungicide.
43. This is an insecticide.
44. In 1990s, Gao was sick, the doctor told him to eat more spinach because it was rich in trace elements, such as amino acid, which was easily absorbed by the body. Therefore, Gao thought that mushroom might also like spinach juice. Adding MSG was that Gao thought MSG could make food delicious. People like MSG, mushroom might also like to eat MSG.
45. Quoted from Gao's speech "Brilliant future of mushroom growing with crop straw and stalks" given on Working Conference of Changde Mushroom Association, February 27th, 2013.
46. Because corncob contains a lot of sugar, which could produce other bacteria, it should also be fermented for three times.
47. A local mushroom production base sterilized by steam for 48 hours, but failed.
48. This was not fair, argued one Ma Yongchun. He suggested to Gao to imitate the practice of the periodical's few offices in Jiangxi to impart training through correspondence courses. This could increase Gao's earnings as well as diffuse the technology faster. He also suggested Goa to produce the products for training by himself and get economic benefits. Ma then took this responsibility upon himself and suggested that Gao focus on technology research. The former has business sense and the latter has technical talents.
49. In 2015, the training fee is RMB 2,000. Accommodation and food are free. Training generally lasts for two weeks.
50. The government paid Gao RMB 200 for training each household. But this was even not enough for him to pay his petrol costs. Because Gao could not drive, he had to ask his son to drive him to the training spots. Gao treats it as a kind of honor and contribution to the society. He is happy about this.
51. Organization Department is an important organ of Communist Party of China (CPC). The national level organization department is called "Organization Department of the Communist Party of China" (*see* https://en.wikipedia.org/wiki/Organization_Department_of_the_Communist_Party_of_China). It has branches at every level of government. It is responsible for the party personnel assignments and the construction of the CPC.
52. Special S&T Commissioner refers to technicians who are appointed by S & T Department of the government. They do not have salary. But they can be shareholders with technology. Generally, they could

get several thousand RMB at the end of the year according to their contribution.

53. Gao spread not only the pesticide formula but also many other innovations for free. In the past, this mushroom was grown in greehouses using soilless cultivation technique. But, it tasted bitter. Gao successfully dwarfed this plant and enabled the grower to pick up the product like picking tea leaves. This method increased its production and also solved the problem of bitter taste. The Changde Agriculture Bureau organized an on-the-spot training on this technique for the technicians. Gao shared his innovation with them without reservation.
54. It is the name of a TV program of Hunan TV. Its Chinese name is "Xiang Cun Fa Xian", which means searching typical events in the rural to show the changing rural China.
55. Gao requests them to send a stamp together with their letter so as to reduce his reply cost.
56. Research institute is under the leadership of Dingcheng Rural Technology Market Management Office. This office is separated from S&T Bureau. Vice District Mayor who is in charge of S&T affairs is its district level leader. There used to be a state-owned mushroom research institute. It went bankrupt due to bad management. So did another mushroom research institute of Li County.
57. There were over 20 mushroom cooperatives in Changde. Each of them had about 100 members (households).
58. The reasons for Ma to be chairman of the association are firstly his son was old enough to inherit his company; secondly, he wanted to do something for local mushroom growers.
59. There are also Hunan Mushroom Association at provincial level and China Mushroom Association at the National level.
60. Culture that performs fermentation. The starters usually consist of a cultivation medium such as grains, seeds or nutrient liquid that have been well colonized by the micro-organisms used for fermentation.
61. http://www.czsnlw.com/xz/html/01010109/news_201392216358.html (accessed on May 30, 2014)

7

Conclusions and Way Forward

Macro Policy Environment—The Context

This book has presented the innovations related to energy-saving devices and reuse of biomass resources as a way forward towards a sustainable and equitable future. The chapters have discussed the overall innovation situation in the country with regards to use of biomass and also the efforts put in by the individual innovators to improve local production methods. But, these innovation efforts have to be viewed against the strong national level macro policy and legislative background that has contributed to the overall environment for innovation. At the macro or national level, the laws related to energy and environment on one hand and the ecosystem of policies, policy implementation rules, programs and projects on the other, have created conditions forcing grassroots innovations.

The important laws are framed at the national level. These laws identify the targets for actions in specific areas and state clearly the actions that will receive the national government support and actions that will be regulated through standards. These laws also specify the extent of support, mainly financial support from the government, limits put on activities and penalties for the violation of these laws. To help achieve the proposed targets in the action areas, the laws usually clearly specify the government's monitoring systems. Sometimes, the laws also specify projects for the implementation of the law.

For example, the "Law on the Prevention and Control of Air Pollution" requires that all government entities above the county level establish pollution monitoring systems and levy heavier fines for illegal activities that cause pollution. According to the Law, the government specifies the consumption limits of coal in the efforts to reduce the amount of air pollution caused by coal. It also imposes a permit system on factories for the emission of major air pollutants. This then, has led to farmers innovating devices that reduces coal consumption and hence, the idea of innovating the gasifiers that have been discussed in this book. This law has also prohibited burning of biomass and hence the farmers have been forced to find ways of recycling the biomass. Hence, there have been innovations to use biomass as raw materials in household energy generation through use of gasifiers or semi-gasifiers. Farmer like Gao Dedian is using the biomass waste entirely for different purpose; as strata for mushroom growing. Chapter 2 also discusses different innovations for reuse of biomass, but, the detailed case studies about them have not been presented in this book.

The "Environment Protection Law" imposes strict obligations on enterprises regarding pollution prevention and control, and provides for more severe penalties. The Law implements a control system for total emissions of key pollutants. In addition to implementing the national and local pollutant discharge standards, enterprises are also mandated to follow the emission standards of key pollutants allocated to the enterprises.

Following the laws, there are policies and the implementation rules to explain and specify the laws. The policies usually are issued in terms of notifications, plans, opinions etc. The policy implementation rules normallydeal with purpose for, extent and procedures for financial incentives. At the third level of programs and projects are the tools of policy implementation.

The policies, policy implementation rules, and programs and projects are proposed by different government agencies based on the national level legislation. Thus, different government programs and projects support promoting the biomass use in rural China. The grassroots innovators Liu Yongquan, Gao Dedian and others discussed in the book have benefited from different government programs. Hence, a holistic understanding of the situation is required in assessing the government support for innovations in the use of biomass in rural China.

The Overall Situation of GRIs

This book brings together innovations by the farmers, particularly in the use of biomass for productive as well as energy purposes, against the overall context of GRIs in China and the policies related to environmental resources. The farmers left to their own devices have innovated to find solutions to improve agricultural productivity, energy security and production of clean energy, disposal of agriculture waste on one hand and their sustainable deployment on the other, and through all means improve their living conditions. Although the GRIs pertain to technical innovations to a great extent, there were also institutional innovations for diffusing the new technologies. The GRIs will continue, as in a country as large as China, local adaptation of technologies would require both technical and institutional innovations.

The innovators' database shows that the innovators are spread across all the provinces of China. But, their concentration is more in the less developed regions than in the developed regions, as penetration of technology is easier and faster in the former as compared to the latter. The data also shows that the innovators are young in age, one third falls in the age-group of 30-40 years and another quarter in the age group of 40-50 years. Innovators do not belong to any younger age group because they require financial wherewithal to take up such work and also need sustenance during the period they are innovating. The innovators are largely males and in spite of improvement in women's education levels across rural areas, the gender gap in this area has not been bridged.

Most of the innovators have received formal education, up to junior high school, that is, up to class nine (level to be reached under the compulsory education policy). A limited number of them have taken vocational training. The grassroots innovators have also not benefited from the government training programs, in spite of the easy availability of these programs (*See* Zhang and Mahadevia, 2014). The innovators have learnt these skills on their own for their respective innovation activities. This is an important policy concern.

Each innovation in the overall statistics is just a number. But, behind each innovation there is a story of grit and struggle, against all odds, for all the innovators. The three case studies presented in-depth in Chapters 4, 5 and 6 respectively in this book, are such stories of individual perseverance in their beliefs and faith in their efforts. Individual innovators like Liu Yongquan and Gao Dedian, apart from financial resources, put even their family lives at stake. Frustrated with repeated non-productive efforts, dedication of time and family resources brought them to the brink of poverty, Liu Yongquan's wife left him. But he did not stop. Eventually, when Liu Yongquan received recognition and appreciation from the government, his wife rejoined him. Similarly, Gao sold his houses to set up a mushroom experimentation greenhouse.

Energy security and clean energy have emerged as the two most important concerns of rural households, for which they have undertaken innovations. Many innovations (62 in the database) have been related to domestic energy needs and out of these, 21 innovations were related to gasifiers. This explains the selection of the case of Liu Yongquan being discussed in this book (Chapter 4). Liu Yongquan wanted to develop a gasifier that used biomass as fuel without causing indoor/local air pollution. He was not successful in his endeavor and hence shifted to innovating semi-gasifiers. Due to the demand/need in the rural households, many innovators in the country attempted to develop a gasifier, but the technology did not succeed.

Motivations for Innovations

Many innovators undertook innovations for the sheer joy of the same, for example, Gao Dedian (Chapter 6), who constantly innovated in mushroom growing technology. In the larger database too, there have been innovators who have undertaken multiple innovations. The detailed case studies presented in the book are all selected from the larger database. Many other innovators, having no choice innovated to bring about a solution to the local problems! One solution to a problem led to another for which a new innovation was required and thus the cycle of innovation continued, as in case of Liu Yongquan (Chapter 4) and Suo Wenbin (Chapter 5). All the innovators in the database too, innovated for the joy of it or for finding solutions to local problems. Very few innovators began innovation with the purpose of commercializing the innovation. But, on innovating, they then commercialized the same. Three out of four innovators belonged to regions that did not have a tradition of innovation but they innovated to provide a solution to their immediate problems.

Another motivation for innovation has been altruistic feelings among these innovators. Gao Dedian wanted to repay the support he had received from the village in his early days by helping the village residents earn more income through mushroom farming. Liu Yongquan and Suo Wenbin wanted to reduce local pollution caused by the unused and scattered agriculture waste. Hence, they undertook an innovation that would deploy agricultural waste that would in addition reduce energy costs for the rural households.

Diffusion

Innovation diffusion is a complex process, even if a company promotes it. It is difficult even if the government back it, as was seen in the case of the semi-gasifier diffusion. For new technology diffusion, collateral technologies also have to be diffused. For example, if semi-gasifier has to be diffused, briquette-making technology has to be made available and diffused. In the villages where the government intended to diffuse semi-gasifiers, as discussed in Chapter 4, briquetting machines too had to be made available. The government had to find an entrepreneur, who took the responsibility of delivering the briquetting machine to the villages that had purchased the semi-gasifier.

Diffusion of the innovation happens if there is a demand for the diffusion. In one of the pilot village selected for diffusion of semi-gasifier of Liu Yongquan, part of the village did not have a demand for the product. A segment of the village had households with high income, who had transited to using electricity for cooking and heating. But, the decision about selection of pilot villages was taken at the prefectural city level, based on the principal of equity in terms of geographic location. Hence, pilot villages for diffusion of this innovation were selected based on different criteria and not based on expected demand of the innovation. Thus, even if the government decides to support innovation diffusion, the policy regarding the same has to be based on ground reality, which would require initial survey of the region to assess the demand.

Good innovations may fail at the diffusion stage, even though it has received significant government support, sometimes even more than what the innovators have received for the purpose of innovation. But, even then, commercial viability of these innovations has remained a big problem. For example, Suo Wenbin did innovate a small briquette machine that could be used in different types of biomass. Indeed, biomass quality and characteristics vary with the region and a machine has to be flexible enough to take any of these as feeds. But, he was not successful in marketing his machine, which found only limited application. Liu Yongquan was put in contact with local entrepreneurs to market his gasifiers, but, due to a defect in the device and a wrong marketing strategy, as we would discuss later, by the private company, resulted in lack of diffusion through commercial route. Similar is the story of most grassroots innovators.

The innovation has found diffusion only if the innovator has been altruistic to diffuse his innovation. Gao Dedian did just that for many years. Hence, he could build an association, a base for mushroom production innovations and then a cooperative for mass diffusion of the techniques. His altruism was motivated by his being a benefactor of altruism of the village residents in the past, when he was new to his adopted village where he shifted after his marriage.

Financing Mechanisms

Most grassroots innovators have taken up innovations using their own finances. They have received very little support from the government; both in terms of receiving training on S&T that would help them innovate and initial finance. This, in spite of the fact that the national and local governments do have enough dedicated funds for farmers' S&T training and education and for technology research (*See* Zhang and Mahadevia, 2014). Further, lack of financial support has also dissuaded women from taking up innovational research.

The data compiled for Chapter 2 show that majority of the innovators, with the exception of a few, faced financial problems while undertaking innovation. Those few who did not face financial problems were the ones who were able to garner support from the local government. For example, Gao Dedian (Chapter 6) and Liu Yongquan (Chapter 4) had received many grants from the government through research projects. Farmer Chen Guangxing of Tianjin City too, had benefited on account of multiple applications for research projects (Zhang and Mahadevia, 2014). But, that does not seem to be the overall trend as discussed in Chapter 2, wherein 84 per cent innovators stated that they did not have funds for innovation. Of those who did obtain initial funds, two out of five did so from informal sources and four out of five also tapped government funds.

Role of Private Sector

Small local companies have shown a keen interest in commercializing the innovations and marketing the products of the innovators. In fact, many of them have been in search of such innovations. There have also been cases of frauds, for example, the setting up of briefcase companies for selling the drawings and videos of gasifier manufacturing. In contrast, there have also been many genuine efforts at marketing the products of the innovators. For example, Liu Yongquan was put in contact with a local company by Hebei Agriculture Bureau, so that Liu's gasifier could be marketed. The gasifiers were subsidized by the local government, which also ensured business for the private company. The private companies, therefore, have been willing partners, if there is government support available to them. Local companies have also taken the innovator as a partner (shareholder) in their company to commercialize the innovator's product through an arrangement of offering the innovator technology-equity. This also has happened in case of Liu Yongquan.

The local companies, however, do not have the expertise to understand the viability of a technology and cannot even assess the future market for the same. Hence, some of them have ended up making losses. For example, something similar happened in the case of Liu Yongquan. Liu's gasifiers were faulty as he had not been able to solve the problem of tar formation in the gasifier. In due course, those who had purchased these gasifiers abandoned them and the company promoting the gasifiers incurred losses. Another company overestimated the demand of Liu's gasifier and ended purchasing expensive equipment for production and incurred heavy losses. Sometimes, the local entrepreneurs are not aware of the market situation at the national and global level. Their investment decisions are based on knowledge at the local level. They do not have guidance from any agency regarding the market potential of any innovation. Hence, eventually, Liu's gasifiers did not earn the entrepreneurs any profits!

Institutional Innovations

The multiple innovations by many of the innovators are generally minor engineering innovations. But, the feat has not ended here. The innovators have gone ahead and engaged in institutional innovations, particularly for diffusion. Cooperatives are special institutional structures, particularly in context of China, that have assisted the farmers in productive work. The Li Min Cooperative agreed to produce briquettes so that Suo Wenbin's small briquette machine could be marketed. This is a classic example of institutional innovation. This cooperative survived and could sustain itself because of the sweat equity put in by the members, while most others in the county and nearby areas failed. Suo Wenbin himself became a member of Changzhi Productivity Promotion Centre through which he promoted the small briquette machine device.

In Gao Dedian's case, there were a series of institutional innovations. He was first instrumental in setting up an association, which was followed by setting up a base where the experiments with different production technologies and methods were carried out and lastly a cooperative was set-up, where normal farmers became members and replicated the innovated technology, methods and products on a large scale. The task before Gao was to ensure that large volumes of the same quality in each type of mushroom could be produced so as to take advantage of large scale economy in marketing.

The marketing of Suo Wenbin's gasifier and then semi-gasifier too, was possible due to institutional innovation. For example, the company that marketed Suo's semi-gasifier to rural households in pilot villages required that the straw/biomass briquettes should be readily available as fuel. Since the villages did not have machines to produce briquettes and the same not being easily available in the market, an entrepreneur decided to provide briquette machines to these villages, so that the village residents who had purchased the semi-gasifiers could use them. The institutional innovations, therefore, have also been responsive to solving an immediate problem on hand.

The problem, however, is that most of these institutional innovations are linked to the individuals and are dependent on them. The cooperative—Li Min Cooperative—was successful because of the dedication and hard work of its members, who all happened to be family members or relatives. Had it been a commercial enterprise, the cooperative may not have survived!.

Zhang and Mahadevia (2012), in the case study of an innovator, Lü Shengzhan, of Hua County, Henan Province, found a different form of institutional innovation. The case portrays synergetic interactions among the three pillars or triads of governance: the government, the Chinese Communist Party based organization and the Chinese People's Political Consultative Committee, at the local level along with the local NGOs, to promote not just grassroots innovations, but also their diffusion for local economic growth. Lü Shengzhan himself has been an innovator and has had many of his innovations patented. But, he could promote his innovations, motivate others including school children to take up innovations and market his innovation through the institutional arrangements as mentioned above. He was appointed as a member of the People's Political Consultative Committee, which led to his and his innovations' acceptance.

Role of Government in Biomass Related Innovations

At all levels, the government has played an important role in the process of innovations and their diffusion in China. In particular, the local governments have played a very stellar role as discussed below.

While the innovators did not get enough support from the government for innovations, they did get strong support from the government for innovation diffusion. About 30 per cent stated that the government directly or through trade fairs, supported them in diffusing innovations. In Liu Yongquan's case (Chapter 4), we see that the local government helped him a number of times, by subsidizing a private company to market his innovations. The local government, that is, the Changzhou city government, purchased Liu's gasifier and installed the same in the houses in a township developed to house the Three Gorges dam rehabilitees. Liu Yongquan was put in contact with a local company by Hebei Agriculture Bureau, so that Liu's gasifier could be marketed. For that purpose, the company was given the rights to sell Liu's gasifier, against which, the local government provided a subsidy of RMB 200 per gasifier in the pilot villages selected under the program of New Village Construction. Suo Wenbin's innovation was also diffused through the pilot villages under New Village Construction program. Gao Dedian, received help from the government for diffusing his innovation, in the form of setting up training programs. He was hired by the government for imparting training in these programs, funded by the local government.

All innovators mentioned in this book, have obtained government support and have also benefited from various government programs. Zhang and Mahadevia (2012 and 2014), reported similar cases of Lü Shengzhan of Hua County, Henan Province and Chen Guangxing of Tianjin City, who benefited from such programs. These two innovators applied for funds under government projects that supplemented their own funds. Li Min Cooperative too, obtained grants under different schemes of the government, such as grants for environmental protection, improvement in briquetting machines, support to demonstrative cooperatives etc.

Most people dream/desire to do something new! But the desire to actually pursue their dreams and take up innovation as mentioned and presented in this book, were fuelled by these innovators' exposure to what was happening in other parts of the country. Liu Yongquan and Gao Dedian were inspired to innovate after reading about the relevant topic in journals and newspapers. Education has played a major role in innovation. Education in China is publicly funded and it is mandated that everyone should have a basic education upto class nine, i.e., junior high school. Hence, universalizing education up to class nine has created local capabilities to learn new ideas, which in turn have led to innovations. Thus, the government policy at the national level has indirectly played an important role in GRIs.

Another important facilitative condition with regard to GRIs, has been the presence of government research and development institutions at the provincial levels. For example, Gao Dedian took training at the Hunan Academy of Agricultural Sciences; Chen Guangxing (Zhang and Mahadevia, 2014), took help from local research institutes when he faced difficulties. All these are publicly funded institutions and their easy accessibility has helped the local innovators.

Energy security and clean energy have emerged as two important concerns of rural households, for which many innovations were undertaken. These aspects are in tandem with the national level agenda. Hence, such innovations have received government support at the time of their diffusion. The innovations related to energy security as well as sustainable and renewable energy sources, have received funds under the national policies and programs, as these fulfil the objectives of the national legislation (Air Act, Environmental Act, Renewable Energy Act) and also climate change commitments of the government.

However, there is a mismatch between the government policies. For example, the large briquetting machines are subsidized but the smaller ones are not. The economics of large briquetting machine requires large quantities of raw materials but these are not easily available. Collecting agricultural waste from each farmer's land is a difficult task unless the agriculture shifts to large farm-based. To produce briquettes using agricultural waste in the current situation requires that the production is decentralized, which in turn, requires small briquette machines to be subsidized. But, that is not the case. Hence, people requiring small briquette machines are buying large ones; wasting their money on one hand and under-utilizing the available capacity, on the other! Li Min Cooperative was forced to purchase large machines when they actually required smaller ones. Another mismatch is considering the biomass-based enterprises as commercial industries and levying commercial rates on electricity consumption, when, in fact, the electricity should be made available to such enterprises at subsidized rates, similar to what the agricultural industries gets!

Although there is encouragement and subsidy available for enterprises that would reuse biomass, these companies require large plots of land to keep their raw materials. Land prices in the rural areas are also high due to land scarcity. The enterprises are, therefore, facing a great difficulty in the upkeep of their business. It is necessary that land is easily available to these enterprises and for this the local government can step in and provide lands on rental basis as and when required.

For biomass energy to gain popularity, it needs to be marketed as a cheap and viable alternative to coal, especially in the rural areas. If cheap coal is easily available, rural households would not be interested in taking pains to use biomass fuel either through the gasifier or semi-gasifier. The innovations of two innovators, Suo Wenbin and Liu Yongquan, did not find successful commercialization as towards 2012, the coal prices declined and the rural households shifted back to using coal. There is a need for the government to intervene and control the prices of different energy sources to encourage or dissuade their use.

Ecosystem of Local Governance

There are many operational difficulties in sustainable use of local biomass. The first and foremost major problem is the collection of biomass from the fields for conversion into briquettes. The agriculture waste, which is a valuable biomass, lies scattered across the farms. Most farms are small due to their fragmentation over time. Each farmer may not have adequate biomass to convert the same into briquettes. Even if he had, the briquetting machine has to be small, like the one Suo Wenbin innovated. But, most farmers are unlikely to purchase these machines, since they would be used only twice a year, post harvesting in case there is double cropping. The solution to this can be that the farmers could rent such a machine; but, then again, the machine supplier/distributor would have to stock a large quantity of these machines, in order to make them available to all the farmers in a short span of time, between the harvest and the next sowing season. The logistics is difficult. The farmers, therefore, prefer to burn the agricultural biomass rather than reuse it. Moreover, 'sending back to the earth' is feasible only in alternate years. If the biomass is left around, it rots and attracts pests, thus creating further problems and pollution.

Then, what is the solution? The solution is to get a local entrepreneur or a cooperative [for example, ones like the Li Min Cooperative (Chapter 5)], to collect all the biomass of the village and deposit it at one place where it can be converted into briquettes. The local government could provide support by making the agricultural waste collection machinery available at low or no cost and by designating land where the biomass waste could be dumped. Thus, the reuse of biomass as a renewable energy source would work only if a proper system of local governance is in place. The reuse of biomass as fuel is also not as easy, due to a variety of biomass being available. Some biomass can be converted into briquettes, while some can only be converted into pellets. Both types of machines would have to be made available at the local level. The investor would need complete support from the local system of governance, in order to purchase the machinery and run the enterprise. Thus, there has to be a local governance ecosystem that functions for the decentralized biomass energy production and use. Can this ecosystem function without government support? Based on the case studies mentioned in this book, the answer is 'No'.

The biomass energy systems are labor intensive. They are viable only if cheap or free labor is available. Li Min Cooperative was successful mainly because all its members worked free of cost.. In the current situation of young, working-class populace migrating to the cities, there is a shortage of labor, which in turn has also increased the cost of labor in the rural areas. Thus, only the elderly or those no longer eligible for the labor market are available for such work. The labor charges have to be either paid through social security system or be subsidized by the local government if such enterprises/cooperatives have to function in the rural areas. In other words, the issue has to be supported through policy measures.

Policy Concerns Related to Innovators

The case studies presented in this book give details of the trials and tribulations of the innovators over a sustained period of time. The innovators, without formal training in the areas of their innovation, have worked as mechanical engineers (Liu Yongquan and Suo Wenbin) or chemical engineers (Gao Dedain). But, their efforts could have been easier if there were appropriate policies in place other than the macro level legislation, schemes and programs.

All the innovators have worked with their own funds. There has to be more financial support made available to the grassroots innovators for innovating. China's S&T investments have increased and the Ministry of Science and Technology (MOST) is flush with funds. Some of these funds could support programs to finance grassroot innovators. That does not seem to be the case as Zhang and Mahadevia (2014) have pointed out in the case of Chen Guangxing, the government programs, even if they do support and fund the grassroots innovators, the money provided is insignificant.

In China, many farmers undertake research for their own interest, and they may not necessarily be aligned with the local development priorities and therefore, may not qualify for government support. Grassroots innovators should be trained to identify relevant research projects and utilize government policies and programs. In Zhang and Mahadevia's (2014) opinion, this kind of training should be integrated into the farmers' S&T training programs mentioned in the loop of three pillars: "S&T education and training—research support—diffusion support".

Now-a-days, the internet has filled the gap on knowledge with regard to various technologies. Otherwise, earlier, the grassroots innovators depended on spurious information about the innovation, as was evident in the case of the gasifier. There is a need for the government to create a data depository to disseminate achievements with regard to new innovations, in order to guide the upcoming innovators. For commercialization of innovations, there should be a market research company/organization, supported by the government; to give advice to the local entrepreneurs about the latter's investment decisions. Otherwise, the start-ups would fail, as we see with regard to Suo Wenbin's innovations.

Lastly, innovation thrives in a local ecosystem that supports production of knowledge, financing of formal education, continuing knowledge creation outside the formal system, local level institutions of research and development, land policies and labor policies. The biomass-based local economy will require not just national level policies and schemes but also local level policies and scheme that deal with the entire ecosystem of support that are mentioned in this paragraph. China will have to continue to create such integrated local ecosystems in its ongoing phase of transformation.

Bibliography

Berdegué, J.A. (2005): *Pro-Poor Innovation Systems*, Background Paper, London: DFID.

Bi, Y.Y., D.L. Wang & C. Y. Gao (2008): *Straw Resources Evaluation and Utilization in China*, Beijing: China Agricultural Science and Technology Press.

Biggs, S.D. (1992): "A Multiple Source of Innovation Model of Agricultural Research and Technology Promotion", *World Development*, 18(11), 141-149.

Byerlee, D. & G.E. Alex (1998): *Strengthening National Agricultural Research Systems: Policy Issues and Good Practice*, Environmentally and Socially Sustainable Development Series, Washington DC: The World Bank.

Cao, G., X. Zang, Y. Wang, & F. Zheng (2008): "Estimation of Emissions from Field Burning of Crop Straw in China", *China Science Bulletin*, 5. pp. 784–90.

Chambers, R., A. Pacey, & L.A. Thrupp (1989): *Farmer First – Farmer Innovation and Agricultural Research*, London: Intermediate Technology Publications.

Chen, L., N. Heerink & M. VandenBerg (2006): "Energy Consumption in Rural China: A Household Model for Three Villages in Jiangxi Province", *Ecological Economics*, 58 (2), pp. 407–20.

Chen, L., L. Xing & L. Han (2009): "Renewable Energy from Agro-residues in China: Solid Biofuels and Biomass Briquetting Technology", *Renewable and Sustainable Energy Reviews*, 13, pp. 2689-95.

China, National Bureau of Statistics (NBS) (2011a): *China Statistical Yearbook, 2011*, China Statistics Press, Source: http://www.stats.gov.cn/tjsj/ndsj/2011/indexeh.htm, (accessed on May 7, 2016).

China, NBS (2009): *China Rural Statistical Yearbook, 2009*, China Statistics Press.

China, NBS (2010): *China Rural Statistical Yearbook, 2010*, China Statistics Press.

China, NBS (2011b): *China Rural Statistical Yearbook, 2011*, China Statistics Press.

China, NBS (2012): *China Rural Statistical Yearbook, 2012*, China Statistics Press.

China, NBS (2013): *China Rural Statistical Yearbook, 2013*, China Statistics Press.

China, NBS (2014): *China Rural Statistical Yearbook, 2014*, China Statistics Press.

China, NBS (2004): *China Statistical Yearbook 1996–2004*. Beijing: Chinese Statistics Press; 1996–2004 [In Chinese].

China, National Bureau of Statistics (2015a): *China Statistical Yearbook, 2015*, China Statistics Press, from http://www.stats.gov.cn/tjsj/ndsj/2015/indexeh.htm (accessed on May 7, 2016).

China, NBS (2015b): *China Rural Statistical Yearbook, 2015*, China Statistics Press.

Cui, M., L.X. Zhao, & Y.S. Tian (2008): "Analysis and Evaluation on Energy Utilization of Main Crop Straw Resources in China", *Trans CSAE*, 24, pp. 291–95.

Dai, L. and Z. Li (2001): "Methodology of Socio-economic Effectiveness and Extension of Integrated Rural Energy Development Project", *Transactions of The Chinese Society of Agricultural Engineering*, February.

Energy Research Institute, National Development and Reform Commission (2010): *Study on China Biomass Energy Technology Development Road Map*, Beijing: ERI. Accessed on May 27, 2015, http://csep.efchina.org/report/20111245453592.4263830135715.pdf/China%20Biomass%20Energy%20Technology%20Development%20Roadmap_by%20ERI.pdf

Fan, J., Y. Liang, A. Tao, K. Sheng, H. Ma, Y. Xu, C. Wang & W. Sun (2011): "Energy Policies for Sustainable Livelihoods and Sustainable Development of Poor Areas in China", *Energy Policy*, 39, pp. 1200–12.

Gan, Lin & Juan Yu (2008): "Bioenergy Transition in Rural China: Policy Options and Co-benefits", *Energy Policy*, 36, pp. 531-40.

Gao, L.W., L. Ma, & W.F. Zhang (2009): "Estimation of Nutrient Resource Quantity of Crop Straw and its Utilization Situation in China", *Trans CSAE*, 7, pp. 173-79.

Gonsalves, J., T. Becker, A. Braun, D. Campilan, H. D. Chavez, E. Fajber, M. Kapiriri, J. Rivaca-Caminade & R. Vernooy (2005): *Participatory Research and Development for Sustainable Agriculture and Natural Resource Management: A Sourcebook, (Volume 1: Understanding Participatory Research and Development)*, Laguna, Philippines: International Potato Center-Users' Perspectives with Agricultural Research and Development, Ottawa, Canada: International Development Research Centre.

Gosens, J., Y. Lu, G. He, B. Bluemling, & T.A.M. Beckers (2013): "Sustainability Effects of Household-scale Biogas in Rural China", *Energy Policy*, 54, pp. 273–87.

Gupta, A.K. (2003): "Learning from Green Grassroots Innovators: How Does a Tail Wag the Dog?", Keynote lecture presented at the *International Conference on Innovations in Technology and Governance*, organized by The Ash Institute of Democratic Governance and Innovation and The Science, Technology and Public Policy Programme at John F. Kennedy School of Government, Harvard University, Cambridge, 30-31 October.

Gupta, C.L. (2003): "Role of Renewable Energy Technologies in Generating Sustainable Livelihoods", *Renewable and Sustainable Energy Reviews*, 7, pp. 155–74.

Hellin, J., M.R. Bellon, L. Badstue, J. Dixon & R. La Rovere (2008): "Increasing the Impacts of Participatory Research", *Experimental Agriculture*, 44 (1), pp. 81-95.

Hippel, E.V. (1988): *The Sources of Innovation*, New York: Oxford University Press.

Hoffmann, V., K. Probst, & A. Christinck (2007): "Farmers and Researchers: How Can Collaborative Advantages be Created in Participatory Research and Technology Development?", *Agriculture and Human Values*, 24(3), pp. 355-68.

Huanghua Statistics Bureau (2009): *Huanghua Economic Statistic Year Book 2009*, Huanghua.

Jiang, Dong, Dafang Zhuang, Jinuing Fu, Yaohuan Huang, & Kege Wen (2012): "Bioenergy Potential from Crop Residues in China: Availability and Distribution, *Renewable and Sustainable Energy Reviews*, 16, pp. 1377-82.

Kowsari, R. & H. Zerriffi (2011): "Three Dimensional Energy Profile: A Conceptual Framework for Assessing Household Energy Use", *Energy Policy*, 39, pp. 7505–17.

Lin, G. & Y. Juan (2008): "Bioenergy Transition in Rural China: Policy Options and Co-benefits", *Energy Policy*, 36, pp. 531–40.

Liu, G. & L. Shen (2007): "Quantitative Appraisal of Biomass Energy and its Geographical Distribution in China", *Journal of Natural Resources*, 1, pp. 9–19.

Liu, Y.X., V. Langer, H.H. Jensen & H. Egelyng (2010): "Life Cycle Assessment of Fossil Energy Use and Greenhouse Gas in Chinese Pear Production", *Journal of Clean Production*, 18, pp. 1423-30.

Liu, W., G. Spaargaren, N. Heerink, A. P.J. Mol, & C. Wang (2013): "Energy Consumption Practices of Rural Households in North China: Basic Characteristics and Potential Low Carbon Development", *Energy Policy*, 55, pp. 128-38.

Liu, J., S. Wang, Q. Wei, & S. Yan (2014): "Present Situation, Problems and Solutions of China's Biomass Power Generation Industry", *Energy Policy*, 70, pp. 144-151.

Ma, H.Y., L. Oxley, J. Gibson & W. Li (2010): "A Survey of China's Renewable Energy Economy", *Renewable and Sustainable Energy Review*, 14, pp. 438-45.

Masera, O.R., B.D. Saatkamp & D.M. Kammen (2000): "From Linear Fuel Switching to Multiple Cooking Strategies: A Critique and Alternative to the Energy Ladder Model", *World Development*, 28, pp. 2083–2103.

Qiao, Q. (2011): *Application and Utilization of Caragana Microphylla of Shanxi Province*, NBS Survey Office in Shanxi, October 26.

Rajasekaran, B. (1993): "A Framework for Incorporating Indigenous Knowledge Systems into Agricultural Research, Extension, and NGOs for Sustainable Agricultural Development", *Studies in Technology and Social Change*, 21, accessed on February 20, 2011, http://www.ciesin.org/docs/004-201/004-201.html.

Reece, J.D. & J. Sumberg (2003): "More Clients, Less Resources: Towards a New Conceptual Framework for Agricultural Research in Marginal Areas", *Technovation* 23(5), pp. 409-21.

Reijnties, C., B. Haverkort, and A. Waters-Bayer (1992): *Farming For the Future – An Introduction to Low External-Input and Sustainable Agriculture*, London: The MacMillan Press Ltd.

Richards, P. (1985): *Indigenous Agricultural Revolution*, London: Hutchinson.

Shi, Y.C. (2008): *China Renewable Energy Development Strategic Research*, Beijing: China Electric Power Press.

Smith, K.R., G. Shuhua, H. Kun & Q. Daxiong (1993): "One Hundred Million Improved Cookstoves in China: How Was it Done?" *World Development*, 21 (6), pp. 941-61.

Thrupp, L.A. (1996): *New Partnerships for Sustainable Agriculture*, Washington DC: World Resources Institute.

Wang, G. (2001): "Technological Innovations of Rural Energy Comprehensive Construction", *Rural Energy*, May (In Chinese).

Waters-Bayer, A. & W. Bayer (2005): "The Social Dimensions in Agricultural R&D: How Civil Society Fosters Partnerships to Promote Local Innovation by Rural Communities", paper presented at EFARD 2005 Conference on *Agricultural Research for Development: European Responses to Changing Global Needs*, Zurich, April 27–29.

World Bank (2005): "Promoting Local Innovation: Enhancing IK Dynamics and Links with Scientific Knowledge, *IK Notes*, 76, accessed on February 20, 2011, http://www.worldbank.org/afr/ik/iknt76.htm.

Wu, B. and L. Zhang (2013): "Farmer Innovation Diffusion Via Network Building: A Case of Winter Greenhouse Diffusion in China", *Agriculture and Human Values*, published online, April. Accessed on May 15, 2013, http://link.springer.com/content/pdf/10.1007%2Fs10460-013-9438-6.

Xie, G., X. Wang & L. Ren (2010): "China's Crop Residues Resources Evaluation", *Chinese Journal of Biotechnology*, 7, pp. 855–63.

Zhang, L., Z. Yang, B. Chen & G. Chen (2009): "Rural Energy in China: Pattern and Policy", *Renewable Energy*, 34, pp. 2813-23.

Zhang, L.X., C.B. Wang, Z.F. Yang, & B. Chen (2010): "Carbon Emissions from Energy Combustion in Rural China", *Procedia Environmental Sciences*, 2, pp. 980-89.

Zhang, L.X., Y.Y. Feng & B. Chen, (2011a): "Alternative Scenarios for the Development of a Low-carbon City: A Case Study of Beijing, China, *Energies*, 4, pp. 2295-2310.

Zhang, L.X., Z.F. Yang, J. Liang, & Y.P. Cai (2011b): "Spatial Variation and Distribution of Urban Energy Consumptions from Cities in China," *Energies*, 4, pp. 26-38.

Zhang, L.X., C.B. Wang & A.S. Bahaj (2014): "Carbon Emissions by Rural Energy in China", *Renewable Energy*, 66, pp. 641-49.

Zhang, L. (2012): "The Stages of Political Innovation in Rural China's Local Democratisation: Four Cases of Villagers' Political Innovations", *China Report*, 48 (4), pp. 427-48.

Zhang, L. and D. Mahadevia (2012): "Institutional Architecture for Grassroots Innovations: A Case of Hua County, China", *Innovations and Development*, 2 (1), pp. 175-88.

Zhang, Q., D. Zhou, P. Zhou & H. Ding (2013): "Cost Analysis of Straw-based Power Generation in Jiangsu Province, China", *Applied Energy*, 102, pp. 785-93.

Zhang, Z.X. (2010): "China in the Transition to a Low-carbon Economy," *Energy Policy*, 38, pp. 6638-53.

Zhang, W., D. Song & Z. Wu (2012): "Status of Corn Production and Its Growth Strategy in Changzhi City", *Journal of Shanxi Agricultural Sciences*, 40 (1), pp. 4-10 (In Chinese).

Index